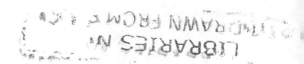

MATERIALS PRODUCTION
IN OPEN
AND DISTANCE LEARNING

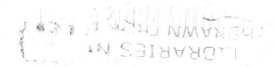

MATERIALS PRODUCTION IN OPEN AND DISTANCE LEARNING

Edited by
Fred Lockwood

P·C·P
Paul Chapman
Publishing Ltd

Paul Chapman Publishing Ltd
144 Liverpool Road
London
N1 1LA

British Library Cataloguing in Publication Data

Materials Production in Open and Distance
Learning
I. Lockwood, Fred
371.3078

ISBN 1 85396 236 8

Typeset by Dorwyn Ltd, Rowlands Castle, Hants
Printed and bound by Athenaeum Press Ltd., Newcastle-upon-Tyne

A B C D E F G H   9 8 7 6 5 4

Contents

Notes on contributors

Alison Ashby has worked as a project officer in the Institute of Educational Technology at the OU for the last six years. She is responsible for maintaining a student research database and supporting projects throughout the university. Previously she has held a number of posts in administration and computing in the former polytechnic sector.

Judith Calder is Deputy Director and Head of the Student Research Centre, Institute of Educational Technology, OU. She has undertaken numerous consultancies overseas on distance-taught course evaluation and programme evaluation systems. Her research interests include adult learning strategies, media use, change processes and evaluation for open learning systems.

Ellie Chambers has worked as Pedagogical Adviser to the OU Arts Faculty since 1974 and is Chair of the Humanities Higher Education Research Group. She has published widely, and has acted as consultant in distance teaching methods for the British Council in India and Poland.

Richard Freeman is a consultant in open and distance learning materials, training authors and other open learning staff.

David Hawkridge was a teacher and teacher trainer in Africa for 12 years. After doing educational research in the USA, he joined the British OU in 1970 and directed its Institute of Educational Technology until 1988. A past and present member of OU course teams, he prefers the alternatives.

Janet Jenkins has worked for over 25 years in open and distance learning. Now an independent consultant, she has worked for the National Extension College, the International Extension College, the Commonwealth of Learning and most recently the Open Learning Foundation. Much of her work has related to the development of distance education in an international context. She has published extensively in the field.

Adrian Kirkwood has experience of all phases of course and package development. He is currently undertaking research and evaluation studies on topics related to access and applications of media and information technologies, both within the OU and outside. He has published widely and co-authored *Personal Computers for Distance Education* (Paul Chapman, London, 1992).

After training secondary school teachers in Central Africa, **Clive Lawless** has worked in the Institute of Educational Technology, OU, since 1971, as a course designer in the Faculty of Arts, specializing in history and history of science. Research interests include concept analysis and concept learning.

Paul Lefrere is a lecturer in educational technology in the Centre for Information Technology Education at the OU and is a member of the Information Design Association. He uses DTP extensively, both at the OU and for laying out books, journals and, of late, material to go on to CD-ROM.

Roger Lewis is BP Professor of Learning Development at the University of Humberside. Previously he has worked in most major national UK open learning institutions, including the National Extension College, OU and The Open College. He has taken most of his own qualifications by open learning.

Fred Lockwood is heavily involved in developing open and distance learning materials both within the OU and as a national and international consultant. He has published extensively, is Series Editor of *The Open and Distance Learning Series* and has recently published *Activities in Self-Instructional Texts* (Kogan Page, London, 1992).

Alistair Morgan is a senior lecturer in educational technology and currently Deputy Head of the Student Research Centre in the OU's Institute of Educational Technology. He has published widely in research in student learning and curriculum design in open and distant learning. His recent book *Improving Your Students' Learning: Reflections on the Experience of Study* is published by Kogan Page.

Peter Raggatt is Director of the Centre for Youth and Adult Studies at the OU. He has published widely on vocational education and training policy and comparative education. His current research interests include workplace learning, assessment and accreditation and the evaluation of National Vocational Qualifications policy in the light of changes in the modes of production and the organization of work.

Bernadette Robinson is a psychologist who has worked in ODL for 18 years (16 of them with the OU). She has wide experience of consultancy work in developing countries and has run more than 200 workshops on ODL. Her research and publications are on teacher education at a distance, the use of telecommunications (including computers) and training.

Derek Rowntree is Professor of Educational Development in the OU. He has been developing self-instructional materials, and teaching other people to develop them, for more than 30 years. His chief interest nowadays is in applying distance learning approaches to vocational training and professional updating and his help is in demand both from OU colleagues and from many outside organizations.

After nearly 20 years teaching in further and higher education, **Hilary Temple** entered mainstream open learning through Open Tech and the Employment Department. Now with her own consultancy, Hilary Temple Associates, she specializes in helping people develop their own systems and materials (or doing it for them); project management and evaluation; and bringing together occupational standards and open learning.

Mary Thorpe has chaired and contributed to a range of undergraduate courses. She has extensive experience of the provision and evaluation of tuition and learner support generally. Her publications include *Evaluating Open and Distance Learning* (1993), *Open Learning for Adults* (1987) and *Culture and Processes of Adult Learning* (1993).

Alan Woodley is a senior research fellow in the Student Research Centre at the OU. He has written on adult students' progress in distance education, and on outcomes for mature graduates. He is currently carrying out research on equal opportunities and on problems of access to higher education for adults.

Hossein Zand received his Ph.D. from Indiana University, USA. He joined the OU in 1977. As a lecturer in the Institute of Educational Technology, he has worked with a wide variety of course teams across the university, particularly in mathematics. His research interests include the teaching and learning of mathematics at a distance.

Preface

The process of materials production in open and distance learning is seen as both a daunting prospect and as an exciting opportunity. This book attempts to dispel some of the apprehension and yet temper some of the enthusiasm. The chapters are grouped into three parts reflecting three accepted stages of materials production *planning*, *production* and *presentation*, with each chapter having an underlying theme – the desire to produce materials of the highest academic and technical quality that are also the most effective teaching material for the learners. Prior to each part is an overview prepared by a leading figure in open and distance education: Roger Lewis, Janet Jenkins and Bernadette Robinson respectively. They not only comment on the chapters within their part but also offer their personal view and opinions regarding this aspect of materials production.

I believe that the collection of chapters on planning will enable you to consider whether appropriate planning has been undertaken. Those on production will alert you to several key issues that can significantly influence the success or failure of the eventual product. The chapters on presentation will ensure consideration is given to strategic questions that effect course reception, support and operation.

The authors, many with national and international reputations, focus on those facets of open and distance learning which reflect current thinking, research and practice. However, we have tried to avoid a book that *talks to the initiated*, where chapters constantly refer to research, approaches and models assuming everyone is familiar with them. The chapters are based on research evidence and many years of experience. However, they are written in a relaxed and informal style which should provide you with insights into materials production and an essential foundation upon which to build your own work. It is my hope that both you and your learners will benefit from the content and style in which the chapters have been written.

Fred Lockwood

PART 1
PLANNING

Overview

Roger Lewis

Planning for open or distance learning (ODL) is clearly an important strategic activity. The kind of planning needed will depend on the particular context. I was fortunate, in the late 1980s, to lead a consultancy within a major British company. The company wanted to analyse all its training courses to identify which could be delivered by ODL, and the costs involved. To do this we had to design two planning tools: one through which we could 'sift' courses to identify candidates for conversion to ODL; another, a costing model that would enable us to compare the delivery costs of conventional training with the costs of ODL. Used together, these models produced a compelling case for a major investment in ODL.

The company was influenced by the kinds of cost saving described in Jane Henry's chapter (Chapter 1). Evidence from public and private sector training increasingly points to three significant benefits offered by ODL: employees reach defined objectives more quickly by this method, the training is more effective and trainees prefer it. Jane Henry concentrates on the best documented of these: the increased speed at which learning takes place. This means that employees can be away from productive work for shorter periods than with conventional training, cutting costs significantly.

But this experience is drawn from industrial training, where there is every incentive to reach defined training objectives as quickly as possible. What about the public education system? Traditionally, the speed with which students achieve objectives has been largely irrelevant – indeed many courses had no objectives at all, only a syllabus. Completion of assessment tests alone was not sufficient to pass – the student had also to attend the required number of teaching sessions.

This kind of system thus took little account of the differences between students, in terms, for example, of prior experience, competence and speed of learning. It was a truly teacher-centred system, and resources were allocated accordingly, basically dependent on the number of hours students were exposed to their teachers.

GENERAL/NATIONAL VOCATIONAL QUALIFICATIONS (G/NVQS)

Change is now in the wind, particularly in further education (it is still winging its way to higher education). The G/NVQ framework promises to open up mainstream educational institutions to a hitherto unprecendented degree. NVQs themselves are limited to occupational training; GNVQs, on the other hand, extend to mass school and college provision.

The two chapters by Freeman and Lewis outline the implications of the G/NVQ framework:

- Energy and resources are focused on assessment, not on teaching – how the learner performs is what matters.
- The focus is on outcomes, not processes; assessment and teaching are uncoupled and the route the learner takes to competence is irrelevant.
- Institutions will increasingly be rewarded by outputs rather than by the extent of lecturer inputs.
- The learner has to decide how to acquire, and prove, competence.

Richard Freeman points out that many ODL providers have operated only in cognitive areas, inculcating knowledge and understanding through tutor-marked assignments. They have not sought to develop capability. Thus the writer took an Open University course on Accounting and Finance for Non-Financial Managers, passed with distinction, but could still not handle financial data confidently at his workplace.

There are exceptions. Some ODL courses build in workplace activity, supervised and assessed by a mentor. The Zoo Animal Management course, planned in the late 1970s and described in *Open Learning in Action* (CET, 1984), explicitly attempted to relate theory to actual workplace practice, via a 'zoo tutor', whose responsibilities included assessment of the student's practical work.

The success of the zoo course shows that ODL is perfectly well able to handle competence development when necessary. The chapters by Freeman and Lewis indicate some necessary features:

- Explicit links to the workplace and arrangements for assessment there.
- The introduction of credit for prior learning.
- Help for learners to plan their routes to competence.
- Individualized delivery and assessment plans for learners.
- The availability of flexible learning materials.
- The provision of precise guidance on assessment for learners and tutors.
- Orchestration of a much wider range of 'learning supporters', with tutors sometimes playing a subsidiary role to others, such as line managers and mentors.
- Induction for learners into processes that may be unfamiliar to them, such as the use of competences and the preparation of evidence.

As I point out in my chapter (Chapter 3), ODL providers ought to be well placed to meet these requirements. They will have developed flexible delivery and assessment systems; their tutors will have evolved a learner-centred approach, with support delivered flexibly, by a variety of media; and their philosophy will be in tune with the values of the G/NVQ framework. ODL providers should thus welcome the stimulus of the framework, which will open up mainstream provision, for example through an enhanced use of learning workshops.

The other contributions in this part cover three key areas of course planning:

- profiling learners;
- choosing media;
- structuring the curriculum.

FINDING OUT ABOUT THE LEARNERS

In workshops to plan new schemes, presenters often begin by asking participants to think hard about the nature of the student body. Who are they? What are their main characteristics likely to be? In what context will they learn? How much time, realistically, will they have available for study?

Participants are asked to produce pen pictures of typical learners. These help later when other planning decisions are taken. They prove particularly useful in holding back academic colleagues from making unreasonable demands on their students, for example in setting far more work than could be achieved in the time they earlier agreed the learners had available.

Woodley and Ashby (Chapter 2) explore the difficulties of getting to know the student body in advance, and the value of drawing up a student profile. They discuss the practicality of how to create and access a database, giving an interesting example of the value of a profile, drawn from OU experience. As the authors point out, used sensibly the information can help designers meet student needs, with the spin-offs of 'improved institutional performance on any external teaching assessments and quality reviews', and information of considerable value for marketing.

CHOOSING MEDIA

Kirkwood's chapter on media selection (Chapter 6) is similarly based on substantial firsthand experience. Too often the media issue is singled out early on and the choice is made on technical potential rather than the likely circumstances of use. Unfortunately, funding, such as that provided by the Employment Department and the Funding Councils, usually encourages this tendency. The phenomenon of new media looking for a problem to solve is all too familiar: the past 20 or so years are strewn with the technological corpses of media applications designed carelessly of the needs of students and their tutors.

Anyone with experience of ODL planning knows that media selection has to begin with a consideration of the target learners. Learners must be able to gain easy access to the media and to any necessary equipment. The creation of a learning centre will not be the answer, unless this is physically close to the learners and matches their lifestyle. For example, when on campus open learning programmes are networked throughout the locations students already regularly frequent for other purposes, such as tutorial rooms, libraries, IT workshops and halls of residence.

Kirkwood also points out that, in open learning, learners need to exert control over the media. The quality of this interaction is also important. The newer media offer great potential here, but in practice interaction often seems to be tutor- rather than learner-driven.

Kirkwood ends with an interesting look into the educational application of recent developments in telecommunications and computer networking. These facilitate fluid interaction between a number of participants: they enable 'dispersed learners and tutors [to] communicate in ways that are more open-ended and less didactic than is usually the case in open and distance education'. As a result, teaching material might become less elaborate, prepared more locally to the learners.

STRUCTURING THE CURRICULUM

Another important planning dimension is the way the content of a course is structured. Clive Lawless's contribution (Chapter 5) warns against assuming that the content itself automatically dictates the structure of the learning material. Planners need to think about how learners actually learn. He quotes a telling study by Mager, which found that tutors and students approached electronics in quite different ways: 'whereas instructors specified moving from the part to the whole, students moved from simple whole to more complex wholes'. The crucial determinant seems to be the students' state of existing knowledge, something varying from individual to individual – along with learning style, level of learning ability and perception of the demands made by the learning task. These issues are particularly important in ODL, given the freedom learners often have in how they use the materials.

The chapters in this part cover a variety of planning backgrounds. The majority stem, however, from OU experience, in other words, from a context in which access is provided to new groups of students through distance learning. But perhaps the most interesting area to watch over the next few years will be more conventional further and higher education institutions who, forced by a variety of pressures, will make all their provision ever more flexible, not only to new students but also to their existing full-time clientele. I hope that colleagues faced with this challenge will find much to learn from the chapters in this part, interpreted as necessary to suit local circumstances.

1

Resources and constraints in open and distance learning

Jane Henry

Predictions about the increased need for training imply that the numbers involved and the expenditure on training will have to increase from current levels, hence any system of education that both saves money and increases effectiveness and access is good news. Open and distance education claims to do just this.

This chapter outlines the cost structure of open and distance learning (ODL), the potential savings it offers over more traditional approaches and the relative costs of different methods of course development, production and presentation.

COST STRUCTURE

In ODL initial expenditure is high but marginal costs – the costs of taking on extra students – are low. This means open learning is more cost efficient with high student numbers and offers increasing economies of scale, as shown in Figure 1.1.

ODL institutions with high student numbers are much cheaper per head than conventional teaching; cost savings in the order of 50 per cent over conventional education have been claimed. However if the comparison is with an institution producing quality multimedia material the break-even point requires a very large audience. For example, Athabasca needs thousands of students and The Open University tens of thousands before ODL compares favourably with conventional approaches (Rumble, 1989). A correspondence plus audio teaching service can produce courses at a fraction of this cost, but

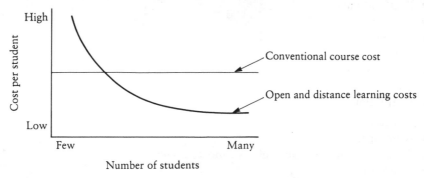

Figure 1.1 Comparison of ODL and conventional course cost per student

with a loss of quality in the service and the impossibility of doing justice to science and technology subjects.

You might like to calculate the cost per head of the conventional and ODL courses in your institution. The following list gives some of the costs you may wish to include in your calculations:

Development
- Market research
- Training course writers
- Library search fees
- Authoring
- Piloting

Production
- Wordprocessing
- Proofreading
- Editing
- Design
- Layout
- Illustrations
- Photographs
- Copyright
- Paper
- Printing
- Copying
- Audio production
- Video production
- Travel
- Software development
- Hardware
- Manuals and floppy discs

Presentation
- Storage
- Transmission
- Post and packing
- Tuition
- Travel
- Telephone
- Marking
- Exams
- Evaluation

Overheads
- Administration
- Share of building, heat, light, support services
- Marketing
- Records

The absolute sums involved in producing quality open learning material are substantial. For example, at The Open University a 400-hour foundation course costs between one and two million pounds to develop and produce, quite apart from any presentation costs. These seem to be enormous sums, but since these courses also attract large numbers of students – around 30,000 to 50,000 students over the eight-year course life – they remain economic despite the huge capital outlay, costing out at around £120 to £220 per student.

It is harder for quality open and distance learning to offer similar economies with small course populations. For example, a 200-hour quality multi-media course can easily cost half a million pounds to develop; with course populations of 500 a year this costs out at about £250 per student. However few open learning courses reach these kind of numbers. If the audience is only going to be a few hundred, more economic modes of development need to be considered, such as print and audio-based wraparound courses. If the audience is a few tens of students, off-the-shelf packages, if available, are likely to be the more economic way forward.

In short as numbers decline capital intensive distance learning becomes much less cost effective and the more individualized open learning comes into its own. For example, with small numbers, project-based courses (where about 85 per cent of the costs can be taken up in providing tuition and marking) become much more economic (Henry, 1990). So with small student numbers it can be more cost effective to negotiate the curriculum direct and base part of it round activities like projects which give the students a chance to study an area of particular interest to them, rather than taking the time to write substantial course material that few people will ever need.

COST SAVINGS

Substantial savings are reported by commercial users of ODL. For example, Coopers and Lybrand (1989) report savings of 50 per cent over conventional teaching in several comparative studies: in Abbey National's use of a computer-based training programme (CBT) to train 2,700 staff on terminals in their local branch office when time was available; Scottish and Universal newspapers use of print-based open learning materials with monthly tutorials to teach management to 600 staff at 25 sites; and British Gas's use of a mixed-media accredited open learning course to train would-be supervisors saved 40 per cent over the block release equivalent. The cost advantage with these kind of numbers is gained through cost avoidance, cost efficiency and cost benefit.

Cost avoidance

Coopers and Lybrand (1989) estimate that the major reason for ODL's preferential costings was the fact that staff spent less time away from work on ODL programmes. For example, Citizen Newspapers found that, though their off-the-shelf open learning package was nearly five times more expensive than the conventional equivalent, the extra expense was more than offset by avoiding lost sales though less time off work, and the package costed out at half the conventional alternative.

Since open and distance learning gives students the flexibility to learn at home or at work it can offer substantial cost avoidance savings – in accommodation, subsistence, travel and specialized buildings (classrooms, etc.) which would normally be incurred in conventional programmes. British Airways, for example, which maintains a network of 3,500 terminals worldwide and offers hundreds of computer-based courses through this network, report major savings in this area (Henry, 1991).

Cost efficiency

Cost efficiency has also been claimed through *reduced course length* with packages involving computer-based training and interactive video (Coopers and Lybrand, 1989). Savings of around 30 per cent have been reported. For example, the pharmaceutical company, Smith, Kline and French, found initial training was reduced from seven weeks to under five with computer-based training. They also report better understanding and retention (Zorkoczy *et al.*, 1984).

Cost benefit

Of course cost is not the only factor. ODL may well give *added value* for added cost, for instance reaching people who could not be reached before, such as trainees located around Europe, people on shift work, staff who cannot be released, parents at home with young children or those who live in isolated areas. Indeed Coopers and Lybrand (1989) concluded that such logistical factors were ODL's main attraction.

A number of trainers also report *improved performance*. For instance, Barclaycard found errors reduced from 1 in 2 to 1 in 1,200 partly as a result of some changes to the program that computer-based training had enabled them to recognize (Manpower Services Commission, 1981).

Specialized forms of ODL can also tackle things that could not be done any other way. For instance flight simulators offer pilots the chance to practise landing at a variety of airports around the world in a single afternoon. These are not cheap – an RAF part-task trainer can cost thousands of pounds and a flight simulator millions. Nevertheless they offer considerable economies because they avoid the need to train on even more expensive prime equipment.

What scope do you have for cost avoidance, cost efficiency and cost benefits in your courses?

COURSE COSTS

Open and distance learning is characterized by relatively high development and production costs, in contrast to the high presentation costs typical of traditional face-to-face education and training:

- Development costs include the staff time needed to *develop the materials*. Most of these are the *fixed costs* necessary to produce one of each text and audio-visual or other aid used in the course.
- Production costs include costs associated with *producing n* copies of the course *materials* for the students. Some of these are fixed but many are *variable* costs, for example, printing *x* thousand units, purchasing *x* cassettes, broadcasting *x* programmes and providing *x* floppy discs.
- Presentation costs include the costs of *distributing materials, teaching learners* and *marking* assignments. They *vary with student numbers*. There are also overheads associated with the cost of centres in which any practical sessions or tutorials take place.

The major ODL costs are the staff time taken to produce the material and payment for any tuition. The costs incurred in tutor-marked assignments, any relatively sophisticated experiment kits and printing are also non-trivial. In comparison the cost of graphics to brighten up the material, copyrights, course assessors and developmental testing of materials are often relatively minor costs.

Table 1.1 summarizes the cheap, moderate and expensive approaches to this form of education and an indicative audience size. However it should be borne

Table 1.1 Overview of cheap, moderate and expensive approaches to open and distance learning

Cost	Development	Production	Presentation	Assessment	Audience
Cheap	Buy in	Black and white print, audio	Correspondence, self-help	Exam (computer marked)[2]	Tens
Moderate	Wraparound	Graphics, colour, video	Conferencing	Essays	Hundreds
Expensive	Originate	Computer-based, interactive video	(Tutorial, residential school)[1]	(Projects, portfolios)[1]	Thousands

Notes
[1]Face-to-face tutorials, residential schools, projects and portfolios are all relatively labour intensive and expensive, hence they are in the 'expensive' row. However they are perfectly suitable approaches for small numbers. (Indeed with small numbers of students it can be cheaper to offer individualized projects and portfolios than distance learning courses, where the project of portfolio is offered instead of, rather than in addition to, originated material.)
[2]Conversely computer-marked assignments are in the cheap row, but are much more likely to be cost effective with large rather than small numbers of students.

in mind that costs vary markedly according to the quality of the product, the mix of media used and the particular form of development, production and presentation method employed.

COURSE DEVELOPMENT

Open and distance learning materials may be bought in, 'wrapped around' an existing book or video series or originated from scratch. Generally the bought-in and correspondence courses are cheapest, the wraparound courses incur moderate costs and the originated courses are more expensive.

Typically the more sophisticated the media the greater the development time needed. For example, Sparkes (1984) has suggested that whereas a one-hour lecture can take up to ten hours to prepare, a teaching text designed to occupy the student for the same period is more likely to take 50 to 100 hours, computer-assisted instruction 200 hours and interactive video 300 hours.

Existing material

Correspondence

Correspondence courses are often based on little more than a recommended reading list and a series of essay titles. This is a very cheap approach and offers students who are unable to attend conventional colleges an alternative route to accreditation. However drop-out rates are usually high.

Buy in

Increasingly ODL institutions are opting to buy in courses. The market for such courses is international (the annual Pergammon *Open Learning Directory* provides examples). Buying in saves development costs, can offer a quality product, releases more staff time for teaching and enables the organization to offer a topic they could not provide any other way. Coopers and Lybrand (1989) conclude that appropriate off-the-shelf packages can be cost effective with as small a number of learners as one.

Wraparound

One of the most common ODL approaches is to base the course round an existing set text. Here the distant educator then merely writes study guides to the existing set book(s), so development time is reduced.

Originated material

External consultants

If you are originating your own materials be sure to pick consultants who can write accessibly, limit the consultants' involvement to draft stage only (so you can amend their copy if their style proves to be inappropriate) and offer a staged contract where payment is conditional on satisfactory and timely delivery of material.

Internal consultants

The costs of materials developed by internal staff are generally more expensive than those produced by external consultants on short-term contracts; on the other hand they may produce better quality material. This approach is justified if the courses are aimed at large populations or a very high-quality product is required.

Quality material

Development costs of quality material can also be *offset* through sales, for example the OU and Henley Business Schools sell their courses all over the world. Courses may also be *customized* for different audiences, for example the OU's Efficient Health Manager is adapted from their Effective Manager course. An alternative strategy is to try for *sponsorship*, for example, the Health Education Council has funded some of the OU courses on Parenting and Health and Barclays Bank sponsored a marketing course.

PRODUCTION COSTS

Broadly speaking the cheapest courses restrict themselves to black-and-white print and perhaps some audio-cassettes. Moderately priced courses employ graphics, use some colour and may incorporate video. More sophisticated packages may employ computer-based media such as computer-assisted learning, CD-ROM and interactive video, all of which increase the cost considerably.

Print

The cheapest medium to use is print. Colour is still expensive to print and most packages restrict themselves to a colour cover or one extra colour in addition to black and white.

Desk-top publishing

The revolution in desk-top publishing means it is now much more practical for authors to produce extremely professional material using their own personal computer and wordprocessing package and avoiding the substantial typesetting costs incurred in paying the printer to design and layout each page. Institutions may find it well worth buying a few more tools. First, a graphics package so the authors can produce their own diagrams, then a scanner to enable authors to scan in graphics and text material. And perhaps, for a final flourish, some clip art packages to enable the author to illustrate material even more professionally. (Lefrere elaborates on these possibilities in Chapter 16.)

Co-production

Institutions with large audiences (thousands) and/or a famous author may be able to co-produce texts with well known publishers. This enables the publisher to make a larger print run, which offers considerable economies of scale, allowing both parties to purchase the books at a much cheaper price per head.

Audio and video

The use of audio and video to support print is widespread, because the technology is user friendly and, at least in the West, affordable and accessible.

Audio

Audio is particularly cheap. It is also has high access, even in quite remote parts of the world. Development costs are a fraction of those with video, and production costs are so low (about 50p to purchase and copy a 90-minute tape in the UK), that most providers treat audio-cassettes as consumables. In many cases the use of audio-vision, e.g. someone talking through a complicated circuit diagram or map, is an extremely effective way of teaching material that might otherwise be expensively produced on video.

Video

The cost of video productions vary considerably. In the UK £5,000 is sufficient to produce a half-hour programme of reasonable quality educational material (including graphics and some location shooting). 'Talking heads' can come much cheaper still, depending on what is required, but trainers would normally expect to produce a glossier product and might spend £25,000 upwards.

Tutored video instruction

Tutored video instruction (TVI) offers a cheap form of video-led open learning using simply produced videos and notes. For example, IBM bases their TVI on good presenters lecturing on state-of-the-art topics. The lecturer provides substantial notes by way of back-up. These videos and the accompanying notes are then distributed worldwide. Students watch these in a group tutored by someone who is only slightly more senior than they are. This means they have ready access to knowledge known by few people, have someone to ask questions when they do not follow; and that this tutor is relatively inexpensive.

Computer-based training

Computer-based training (CBT) is still relatively expensive to implement. Staff, software and hardware costs are usually substantial. Software development costs and the true costs of personnel needed to develop and maintain CBT are often underestimated. Running costs can also be high. Since CBT has particularly high development costs the ratio of capital costs to recurrent expenditure is much higher than in other forms of training, and student numbers are usually a particularly critical factor in its cost effectiveness.

Development costs

Software development can be very expensive. For example, the annual cost of software in the USA is many times the sum spent on hardware and, unlike hardware costs, software costs have not declined as good-quality software takes time to develop. For example, Jenkins (1982) has suggested that realistic development ratios for CBT range from 30:1 to 500:1 and in some cases more. He points out that though some claim 100:1 is the norm, 'many organizations revise their estimates upwards after genuine production experience'. Opinion varies, but many argue CBT is not worth doing unless you have substantial sums (thousands) to spend on research and development (O'Shea and Self, 1983).

What evidence there is suggests that on cost grounds alone the case for originated CBT is far from proven, for course populations of less than 500, unless the course adds value. With populations of 1,000 computer-led distance education compares very favourably with residential training. Jenkins (1982) claimed that with 100 students the cost of development is too great. Further, that even the cheapest approach – one author and a PC – is uneconomic with a few tens of students.

Delivery

Computer-based applications may be offered on networked systems or via PCs. Network delivery offers cost advantages when using spare capacity on an existing computer installation, purchased for a reason other than training – for example, British Airways using its ticketing terminals. In an organization with the relevant hardware this kind of 'embedded training' makes more efficient use of that equipment at negligible cost. On the other hand companies as big as Ford have found an open learning system based on PCs cheap, flexible and effective.

Computer-managed learning

In contrast, computer-managed learning (CML) is relatively cheap to develop and run. For example, the OU computer-marking system marks an assignment at a cost of about a tenth of the price of a tutor-marked assignment.

COURSE PRESENTATION

Many ODL courses offer contact through a variety of media. Those on a restricted budget may have to function with self-help groups or correspondence only. The next step up is the provision of telephone contact and audio and computer conferencing, approaches which incur moderate costs. The provision of face-to-face contact is usually considerably more expensive and any residential element much more so.

- *Correspondence.* The cheapest way of presenting ODL is via correspondence teaching; however, drop-out rates tend to be high. With sufficient density of population correspondence can be supplemented with self-help groups. Staff can facilitate their formation by circulating students' names.
- *Conferencing.* With dispersed populations audio conferencing via the telephone has been found to be cost effective. Computer conferencing is more expensive to set up as it requires learners to have access to a modem or terminal, and conference monitors need to be paid to manage conferences and delete unwanted material. Long-distance phone bills can also add up. However where learners are already using a conferencing system for other purposes, take-up is likely to be higher and the extra cost is marginal.
- *Tuition.* The majority of ODL students appreciate some face-to-face tuition. Institutions offering ODL locally can usually provide this fairly easily. Those with dispersed populations may opt to pay local staff from other institutions to provide some tuition. Meetings are generally held in existing educational or training facilities thus avoiding the expenditure of maintaining purpose-built accommodation.
- *Residential schools.* Certain subjects, for example laboratory science work and group skills, are likely to require or benefit from a residential component. This is relatively expensive because accommodation and subsistence costs are substantial, often accounting for two-thirds or more of the total residential costs.

CONCLUSION

This brief review of the costs of open and distance learning has suggested that it is expensive to develop, has low marginal costs and is most cost effective with large student numbers. With low student numbers it may offer added value for added cost, in certain circumstances. The chief savings are through cost avoidance, from a reduced absence from work, accommodation and travel expenses, and (some claim) personnel savings through course compression.

REFERENCES AND NOTES

(*Recommended reading starred*)

Coopers and Lybrand (1989) *A Report into the Relative Costs of Open Learning*, The Open University/Department of Employment.

Henry, J. (1990) *Low Cost Courses*, TCC Report no. 5, Institute of Educational Technology, The Open University, Milton Keynes.

Henry, J. (1991) *Cost Factors Affecting the Future of IT-Based Education*, TCC Report no. 53, Institute of Educational Technology, The Open University, Milton Keynes.

Jenkins, J. M. (1982) *Computer-Based Training*, Manpower Services Commission, Sheffield.

Manpower Services Commission (1981) *Looking at Computer-Based Training*, Manpower Services Commission, Sheffield.

O'Shea, T. and Self, J. (1983) *Learning and Teaching with Computers*, Harvester Press, Brighton.

*Rowntree, D. (1992) *Exploring Open and Distance Learning*, Kogan Page, London. Unit 6 gives an accessible review of the key costs incurred in developing an ODL package.

*Rumble, G. (1989) The economics of mass distance education, *Prospects*, Vol. XVIII, no. 1, pp. 91–102. A comparison of the costs incurred in ODL institutions aiming at large audiences.

Sparkes, J. (1984) Pedagogic differences between media, in A. W. Bates (ed.) *The Role of Technology in Distance Education*, Croom Helm, London.

Zorkoczcy, P. *et al.* (1984) Cost considerations, *Opportunities for IT-Based Advanced Educational Technologies*, Vol. 2, EC, Brussels.

2

Target audience: assembling a profile of your learners

Alan Woodley and Alison Ashby

In this chapter we look at the various reasons why you might want to know about your learners. This leads into a consideration of what information you might require and how you might collect, store and access it. A practical example is given for illustration.

INTRODUCTION

If you are teaching in a classroom situation and you notice that the students are smiling and attentive, you guess that you are on the right lines. If your students are looking bored or confused, you have the opportunity to review your teaching strategy, to discuss matters with your students and to make the necessary improvements. When you are running an open or distance learning course there are still possibilities for changes in mid-course, but they are likely to be much more expensive to make and more difficult to implement. The production of open and distance learning courses involves a large investment at the design stage. Therefore, by the time the course comes to be presented it should be stimulating and pedagogically sound. On the face of it, it would also seem to make good educational sense to say that you will design your course to suit your target audience, but this raises three basic questions.

First catch your student

What do you know of prospective students? If you are lucky your target audience may also be a captive audience. For example, you may be designing a course for a particular group of employees within your organization. You will know their characteristics from staff records and you know what skills they have to acquire. However, many course designers will not be able to gain a profile of the students until after the course has been designed because people don't sign up until there is a course to sign up for.

Coping with variety

Will a profile aid course design? Mature students on open and distance learning courses rarely form a homogeneous group. They vary in terms of their age, their motivation for study, their educational background, their personal study circumstances, etc. Therefore, while a profile of your would-be students will indicate the range of characteristics that need to be catered for, it will not necessarily solve all your design problems.

Knowing for other reasons

Can profiling help in other ways? We would argue that it helps in three important ways even if the information arrives too late to help in the design of your current course. First, it becomes a database that can be drawn on when designing future courses. Secondly, it allows you to monitor which types of student succeed on the course. Finally, it allows you to measure whether the course is attracting the types of student that it was intended to.

HOW DO YOU BUILD UP A PROFILE?

Given the problems of profiling your students at the course-design stage, what strategies are available to you? What procedures do you or your organization adopt? We would suggest four possibilities – but you may be able to think of others.

Pseudo-profiling

You may be able to identify groups of people who are engaged on similar courses to the one you are designing, or who are on courses which are likely to feed into your new course, or who for some other reason you believe will be very interested in enrolling.

Developmental testing

If you have the time and resources to test out an early version of your course on a group of students who have been recruited from the population of potential students, the testers themselves can be profiled to confirm or refute your assumptions. However, do not assume that volunteers are necessarily typical!

Administrative forms

A key time to gather information on students is when they come to apply or register for a place on a course. While only certain facts are needed for entry, e.g. name and address, course choice, most people are willing to answer a limited number of voluntary questions about themselves.

Student surveys

Additional information about students can be gained after they have registered by means of surveys. These can be censuses or sample surveys. They can be carried out by mail, by phone or at tutorials. It may even be possible to use computer conferencing.

WHAT GOES INTO THE PROFILE?

There is an infinite amount of information that you could collect and collate about your prospective students, but what will actually help you with your course design? This will depend to a large extent on the nature of the planned course and the target group, but we outline three basic types of information below.

Previous learning

A basic tenet of good teaching is that it should be pitched at the right level for the students – 'start where students are'. If you have a rigid admissions procedure this can be predetermined but in many situations you will need to discover this level. However you should be aware that measurement of previous learning involves the dimensions of time, level and relevance. For example, one of your students may have a degree while another has no formal qualifications. However, the first person may have taken their degree in an unrelated subject over twenty years ago, whereas the second person may have many years' work experience in the subject of your course.

Other study factors

There are a whole host of other factors apart from educational preparedness that will affect how students react to your course. Some of these will influence your course design, whereas others impact on the support you offer students.

Do the prospective students have access to equipment that you were thinking of using on the course – for example, phones, tape-recorders, video-recorders, computers, etc?

What is the students' motivation for taking the course? What are they aiming to get out of the course? Have they chosen to take the course or have they been told to by their boss? Are there penalties for failure?

What experiences do they have in work, community and family contexts that can be drawn upon to make the subject-matter more relevant and interesting?

What barriers may inhibit successful course completion – for example, unsupportive employer, difficulties with fees, highly mobile job, English as a second language, etc?

Target groups

What information you need will depend upon the purposes of your own course. If you want to ensure that the course is meeting the equal opportunities aims of your institution you may want to collect information on age, gender, disability and ethnicity. You may want to ensure that you are training your technical staff rather than your managers, or vice versa. Are you attracting students from across the country or only in certain locations?

SOME PRACTICALITIES

It is easy to get carried away and to say that of course we need to collect all of this information so that we know our students in minute detail. However, we must now come down to earth and decide what is actually feasible, given the nature of the course you are planning, the expected number of students and the likely impact of the information that you collect. There are always constraints of time and money, but there are also certain practical issues to face. Here are a few for you to consider. After reading them we suspect you will be able to add one or two more:

- While the new course may be of prime importance to you, it may be a minor concern for the students. They may not be willing to fill in long questionnaires or take part in in-depth interviews.
- Certain types of information, such as literacy skills, personality characteristics and learning styles, may be of great interest but they are extremely time consuming and expensive to collect on a systematic basis.
- If you are going to collect and store information on complex variables such as occupation and educational qualifications you need to know how you will transform it into numbers. Your basic choice is between getting the students to choose from a set of precoded answers or coding their open-ended answers at a later stage. The latter is more 'scientific' but can be very expensive if large numbers are involved.
- If you want to make comparisons with other courses, your data must be categorized in the same way.
- The application form is a good place to collect data but you will be fighting against pressures to keep it as simple and inviting as possible.
- Some topics, especially in the equal opportunities area, are extremely sensitive. It may be relevant to your course design to know about a person's religion or sexual orientation but the data might be impossible to collect.
- Some data go out of date. If you measure a person's occupation, their marital status, their educational qualifications, then their answers are only valid at a particular moment.
- If you collect information on prospective students and hold it on a computer, you are likely to be constrained by something equivalent to a Data Protection Act.

CREATING AND ACCESSING A DATABASE

Up to now we have considered the collection of data for a student profile. Questions concerning the storage and accessing of the data are of equal importance. If the numbers are small and the data are collected by you personally, you may be able to able to meet all your needs by manual or simple spreadsheet analysis. However, if it forms part of your company or institution records, access may have to be negotiated. It is in your interest to consider the following questions.

Who owns the data?

Data ownership is an important issue in all organizations and institutions. If you are planning a course for employees in a company the personnel department is likely to 'own' the data although not all companies have a separate personnel department. In these circumstances tracking down data ownership and indeed the records may be more difficult. In an academic institution the registry is likely to be the data owner although more comprehensive records may be held in individual departments. The first task is to try to establish who owns the data so that you can obtain permission to access the data.

How are the data held?

The next task is to establish how the records are held. Although it seems reasonable to assume that most organizations and institutions will have computerized records you may find that only part of the information you require is stored this way. For example, specific information concerning students or employees with disabilities may be on a manual system. In these circumstances you will have to weigh up the costs of retrieving the information against the benefits to be derived from having it.

How will you access the data?

The first consideration is the level of access. This will depend on whether you are personally allowed access to the data, either via the computer or manual records, or whether you have to specify the data you require for a third party to provide. The latter is far more limiting since initial profiling often throws up more questions which you may wish to pursue later.

Secondly, you will need to consider how you are going to access the data if you are given direct access to the data, especially if it is held on a computer system. If the data is held on a mainframe computer and you wish to transfer the information you are interested in to a PC you may need some technical support. Even if the data is held on a PC you will need to consider in what format or software package the data are held and ensure that you can transfer it to a suitable package on your own machine. You will also need to decide what is a suitable package for the analyses you intend to undertake. Spreadsheets are becoming more and more powerful but if you will need to recode a number of variables, create new variables and carry out more complex statistical analyses, a statistics package is likely to be more suitable.

If this starts to sound intimidating, don't worry. In most cases colleagues are only too happy to help and advise.

How will you hold and maintain the data?

At the course-planning stage, a research database that contains basic information on prospective students or employees and that provides simple frequencies and cross-tabulations, may be adequate for your purposes. However, once the course becomes 'live' you may wish to hold individual student records which include items such as demographic data from the application form, previous course histories if available, and details of progress through the course for monitoring and evaluation purposes. This will involve updating your database from administrative databases. You will need to ascertain at what points progress data such as assignment scores, attendance at residential schools, examination attendance and examination scores are available. In addition to the technical questions concerning how these data can be transferred, you will have to consider how often it is necessary to update your system.

As part of your monitoring and evaluation you may also wish to conduct surveys to collect student and employer feedback where relevant. If you hold your data in a statistics package you will be able to draw random samples for your surveys. In addition you may be able to cut down costs by omitting questions on data you already hold. Survey data combined with data from administrative records can provide a very rich research database.

Who should be doing it?

You might be asking why you as a course designer need to set up a profiling and monitoring system. Why can't the administration or personnel department provide the sort of analyses you require? It is possible that they can, but management information tends to deal in generalities whereas profiling and monitoring need to be tailored to the individual course. However, it still might not be worth your while to invest the time and energy in creating such a system. Certainly it might be worth 'buying in' expertise for *ad hoc* surveys. At the Open University we have a research department that provides an interface between the administration and the course designers.

AN EXAMPLE OF PROFILING IN USE – 'ETHNIC ORIGIN'

As part of an action plan on access and equal opportunities, The Open University began to monitor the ethnic origin of its students on a regular basis in

1990. The details of how this was carried out serve to illustrate a number of the points we have made above:

- The question was placed on the application form. This meant that we could compare the ethnic origin of those who did or did not become students. It also meant that, although the question was voluntary, most people provided the information.
- The actual format of the question was very similar to that used in the 1991 Census. We expanded and altered the options that people could choose, but we did it in such a way that they could be collapsed back into the broader categories of 'Asian', 'Black', 'White' and 'Other' that are used in other studies.
- The information became part of the student's computerized student record. Consequently we were able to look at topics such as representation, course choice and progress (see below); to merge this information with other characteristics in the profile such as age, gender and occupation; and to select samples for surveys or other special studies.

Initial results from the data suggest the following:

- OU students match the overall UK population fairly closely in terms of ethnic origin.
- The figures for part-time and full-time higher education courses elsewhere were broadly comparable.
- Black students tended to have lower previous educational qualifications on average and the Asian students held the highest qualifications.
- Black men were twice as likely as white men to be unemployed.
- Over one half of the black students and one quarter of the Asian students were in the London region. This appears to correspond to the geographic distribution of black and ethnic minority people.
- Compared to white students, black students entering the undergraduate programme were much more likely to choose the Social Science or Technology foundation course (see Table 2.1). They were relatively unlikely to choose Arts or Science. Asian students also tended not to choose Science or Arts and to prefer Technology, but not to such a marked extent. What stands out most is the relatively high numbers who chose the Maths foundation course.

Table 2.1 The foundation courses taken by new OU undergraduates (1990 and 1991) (%)

	Asian (n = 1,203)	Black (n = 1,099)	White (n = 36,042)
Arts	16.4	11.4	23.5
Social Science	23.8	36.3	23.8
Maths	23.4	15.8	15.0
Science	16.6	11.3	20.0
Technology	19.9	25.3	17.6

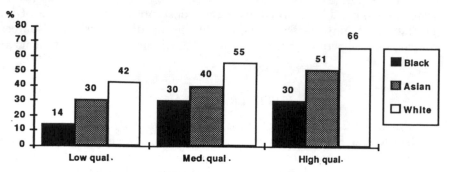

Figure 2.1   The percentage of new OU students who gained a course credit on the Technology foundation course in 1990 and 1991, analysed by ethnic origin and educational qualifications (course based)

- Black and Asian students were less likely to complete their first year of study with the OU than were white students. By combining information about ethnic origin, previous educational qualifications and course choice we were able to look for possible explanations for this finding. In Figure 2.1 we show the results for the Technology course as an example. We can see that white students fared better than Asian students, who in turn made better progress than black students, regardless of the level of previous qualifications. The progress made by black students with high qualifications was particularly disappointing on this course.

CONCLUSIONS

Student profile data can contribute to our understanding of adult learners, in terms of their characteristics, their goals, their expectations and factors affecting their motivation. Used effectively, and in combination with data on progress and student feedback, this information can help designers to create courses which will meet the needs of prospective students. This will lead to greater student satisfaction, which in turn will produce greater commitment to the organization providing the course and improved institutional performance on any external teaching assessments and quality reviews. It is also important for targeting. Increasingly we need to know whether our courses have attracted the types of student for which they were intended and, for marketing purposes, we need to know how to encourage more to enrol.

However, while it can be argued that it is a good thing to obtain a student profile, we hope that we have shown in this chapter that it is not a straightforward procedure that can be followed like a recipe book. There are a lot of areas that have to be negotiated concerning what data are needed, when and how they will be collected, in what form, by whom, etc. The answers to these questions will depend upon the nature of your organization and the types of courses that you are planning. Assembling and maintaining a student profile can be an expensive and time-consuming business. However, if it contains relevant and accessible information it can constitute the cornerstone of an organization's quality assessment policy. In this age of diminishing resources and increased competition, we ignore the needs of our prospective students at our peril!

FURTHER READING

Woodley, A. (1992) *The Ethnic Origin of Open University Students and Staff*, Student Research Centre Report no. 63, IET, The Open University. If you are interested in some actual results from the monitoring of ethnic origin, this report provides a detailed statistical analysis for the OU.

Woodley, A., Taylor, L. and Butcher, B. (1993) Developing an action plan for equal opportunities at The Open University of the UK: three perspectives on black and ethnic minority student issues, in D. Nation and T. Evans (eds.) *Reforming Open and Distance Education: Critical Reflections from Practice*, Kogan Page, London, pp. 150–68. This chapter contains a discussion of how one particular institution came to undertake ethnic monitoring and highlights the issues that affect how it is carried out in practice.

3

G/NVQs and open learning

Roger Lewis

A simple argument underlies this chapter: providers of education and training need open learning if they are to deliver the G/NVQ framework. The requirements of the framework are outlined, especially as they affect candidates (the candidates being the individuals interested in gaining a G/NVQ). The implications of these requirements are then considered under the headings of support, management and materials. Whilst the descriptions may make the process seem complex, in practice it is simple, once the necessary structures are in place.

The term G/NVQ is used throughout this chapter to refer both to National Vocational Qualifications (NVQs) and General National Vocational Qualifications (GNVQs). The main difference between the two qualifications is that GNVQs have been designed for delivery in full-time education with limited access to the workplace. GNVQs provide a foundation of general skills, knowledge and understanding. Possession of a GNVQ will not imply competence in an occupation immediately on qualifying. In all other respects the two qualifications are similar, sharing the qualities of openness described in this chapter. GNVQs are likely to affect schools and colleges profoundly. For more information, see the National Council for Vocational Qualifications Information Note 3, updated as of 15 March 1993.

REQUIREMENTS OF THE G/NVQ FRAMEWORK

G/NVQs are designed to be 'open':

- To people of all ages.
- To people with special needs (defined broadly, covering disability, equal opportunities, difficulty in gaining access to appropriate workplace experience).
- To inspection, via the published national standards.
- To credit accumulation, allowing individuals to collect credit from different awards and in any sequence.

Furthermore, individuals can take their own time in accumulating credit.

In his chapter on 'Competence-based training using open and distance learning materials' (Chapter 4), Richard Freeman emphasizes other ways in which the NVQ framework is open:

- Credit can be given for prior learning.
- Assessment is of outcomes, not of the processes through which individuals achieve these outcomes. This has the effect of freeing assessment from particular learning programmes.

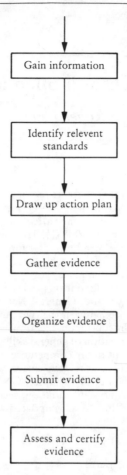

Figure 3.1   Stages of gaining a G/NVQ

These points are elaborated by Richard Freeman in his section on the implications for training.

What is the reality of this in its effect on the user? (The user covers three main groups: candidates, employers and providers of education and training.) The G/NVQ framework, whilst simple in concept, can in practice seem complex and hard to get catch hold of. There are several reasons for this. Unnecessary complexity is created by the use of jargon and bureaucratic language: awarding bodies and standards consultants are particularly guilty here. But some of the complexity is necessary. The standards themselves are, for example, expressed in general terms, because they have to cover a wide range of actual work situations. Furthermore, the arrangements made to create choice are often complex: people need help in using freedom wisely.

Let's have a look at the impact of the G/NVQ framework on the user by following the process through sequentially. Later we can look at the help candidates may need at each stage, and at the role of tutors (and others) and of materials, in giving this help.

STAGES OF GAINING A G/NVQ

What does an individual have to do to gain a G/NVQ? The main stages of the process are set out in Figure 3.1 and the notes that follow it. In reality the stages overlap, and an individual will go through parts of the cycle several times.

Gain information

Initially the individual needs clear and non-technical information on G/NVQs. Subsequently individuals who wish to become 'candidates' will then need more detailed information, for example about particular awards, timescales, costs. This may be provided via standard documents, supported by the opportunity to talk to an adviser. Figure 3.2 is an extract from a leaflet produced for staff in the Benefits Agency, explaining the Agency's Vocational Qualifications Programme.

Introduction

The purpose of this leaflet is to ensure that you are aware of the 'in-house' opportunity being presented, to gain a qualification which is directly relevant to the business needs of the Agency. The two areas in which National/Scottish Vocational Qualifications can be obtained through the Agency are Business Administration (for clerical and support grades) and management.

These developmental opportunities are available to all BA staff, at all levels.

. . .

What happens next?

Advisers and assessors the N/SVQ programme will be available in each Territory. In the scheme's first year, it is planned to have sufficient advisers/ assessors to cater for a maximum of 500 candidates in each Territory, plus up to 200 from BA Central Services. Additional advisers/assessors will be trained as the system develops, to cope with anticipated demand.

. . .

If you are interested in being a candidate, complete the back page of this leaflet and hand it to your line manager.

. . .

A note to line managers . . .

Undertaking an N/SVQ is not an easy option, although it is straightforward. Staff who are working towards a qualification are undergoing a developmental process which is of direct benefit to their area of work. You are asked to give as much support and encouragement as possible to any member of your staff who is accepted onto the programme. When a member of your staff is starting an N/SVQ programme, you will be advised about the specific standard they are trying to achieve.

Figure 3.2 Extract from a leaflet produced by The Benefits Agency for its staff (reproduced with permission)

Identify relevant standards

The candidate then needs to explore relevant standards. This is a circular process, moving into increasing detail as the candidate identifies first the units, then the elements relevant to their aspirations and experience. If in work, the candidate will be checking to see where their current job matches the standards and whether they are carrying out a particular activity in a way that will satisfy the performance criteria and range statements. Richard Freeman points out that candidates may need to 'rewrite' the competences, to make sense in terms of their own work. He gives an example of such 'contextualization' from the National Extension College's Essential Caring Skills course.

To work productively at this stage, candidates will need a good understanding of what constitutes 'evidence' and of how it can be collected. They will probably need support from an adviser/assessor who will help them to identify opportunities for the collection of the various types of evidence. Figure 3.3 exemplifies the main methods through which evidence can be collected.

Naturally occurring opportunities are best; for NVQs, this means collecting evidence during normal workplace activity. Candidates need to give thought to the selection of evidence: ideally one piece of evidence will satisfy a number of criteria simultaneously. Figure 3.4 is an extract from an assessor's report of an

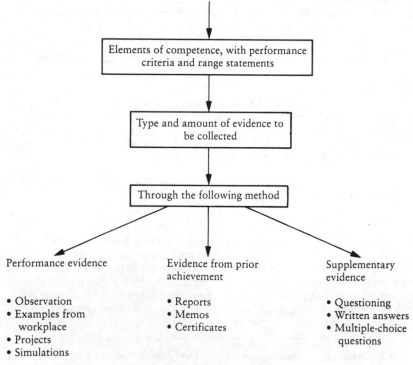

Figure 3.3   Evidence collection

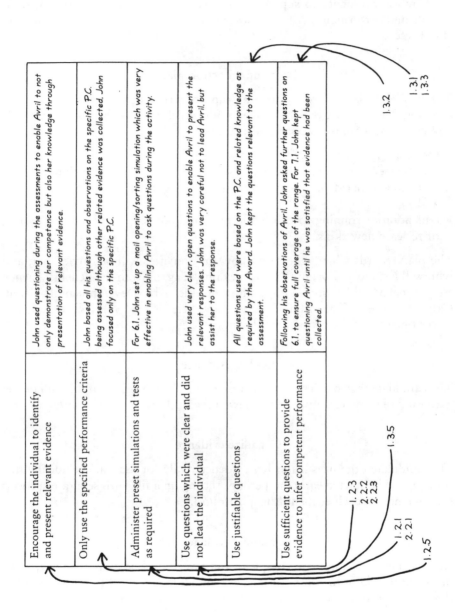

Figure 3.4 Evidence meeting a number of requirements (marginal annotations are in the sequence unit: element: performance criterion)

observation of a candidate for the Training and Development Lead Body assessor awards (two units). The arrows show how this piece of evidence is used by the candidate to support competence across a number of units, elements and performance criteria (these are indicated by the marginal numbers '1.2.1' etc.).

Draw up an action plan

The candidate is now ready to draw up an action plan with their adviser/ assessor. This will set out the elements for which they wish to gain credit. It will cover the actions necessary, which may include:

- the collection of evidence from the workplace;
- arrangements for the candidate to gain access to experience, such as secondment to another department or the opportunity to use different equipment; and
- education or training to gain underpinning knowledge and understanding, or to learn new skills.

The plan records when, where and how the activities will be carried out, and who will be involved. Figure 3.5 is an example, again from the Benefits Agency Vocational Qualifications Programme, produced by Development Division, Cabinet Office (Office of Public Service and Science, 1993a). Figure 3.5 comprises one half of the action plan document.

Gather evidence

The candidate then carries out the action plan. The main part of this will be the gathering of evidence, a process reviewed regularly with the adviser/assessor.

Organize evidence

The candidate organizes his or her evidence ready for assessment. Ideally this process will be started early on, perhaps setting up a file with separate sections for evidence on each element (the 'portfolio').

Submit evidence

At this stage the candidate completes the awarding body's paperwork, summarizing the claim to competence. The candidate will need to cross-reference the summary to the actual evidence contained in the portfolio.

Assess and certify evidence

This is carried out by the assessor, who scrutinizes the portfolio and questions the candidate as necessary, for example to check competence across the range.

VQ Programme Personal Action Planner

UNIT 10: CREATING AND MAINTAINING BUSINESS RELATIONSHIPS	B A INDICATOR	Name:	Element Assessed
Element: 10.2 Create and maintain professional relationships with customers and clients.	Using a professional and business-like approach to developing and improving customer relationships.	Line Manager:	Assessor: Date:

PERFORMANCE CRITERIA	Applies to my job	Does not apply to my job	I need training	I need practice	I should be able to produce evidence	I have the evidence and am ready to be assessed
(1) All customers/clients are greeted promptly and politely.			✓ (circled)			
(2) Known customers/clients are acknowledged by name in an appropriate and friendly manner.						
(3) Conversations with customers/clients are conducted in a manner which promotes goodwill and trust, and are timed to take account of work pressures and the needs of other customers/clients.				✓ (circled)	✓	
(4) In cases where knowledge or job responsibilities are exceeded, customers/clients are directed promptly and politely to an appropriate authority, in a manner which maintains the credibility of the jobholder and organisation.					✓	
(5) Policies, procedures and activities to promote customer/client trust, satisfaction and goodwill are actioned promptly, accurately and willingly.						
(6) Reasons for any delays/non-availability are explained politely.						

Provide examples here or on the form below

ACTION PLAN

What needs to be done	How it will be achieved	Who will action	When it will be reviewed
Learn what to do when dealing with the public.	Attend Customer Care Course	Training Manager to arrange and follow up	A date. Post-course date.
	Observe others at work	Line Manager to arrange and discuss observation and contacts	A date, within a month
	Accompany Visiting Officer	Adviser or line manager to arrange Visiting Officer discusses visit	A date, post visit
	Shadow Receptionist	Line manager to arrange Candidate asks questions	A date, During shadowing
Practise Customer Care Skills	Act as Receptionist	Adviser or line manager to arrange Adviser or line manager give feedback During practice Adviser or line manager relevant program Post practice	A date

Figure 3.5 An action planner

Development Division, Cabinet Office (OPSS) © Crown Copyright

The assessor then gives full and constructive feedback to the candidate. Only two judgements are possible: the candidate is competent, or not yet competent. Note the 'not yet': the candidate has not 'failed' but needs to collect further evidence. The assessor's judgement of 'competent' is then verified internally and by the awarding body's verifier, before certification.

OPEN LEARNING

This description of the G/NVQ process is necessarily formal and schematic. It cannot capture the fluidity of the process as it occurs in practice. But it does show the 'openness' of the G/NVQ framework. Strong emphasis throughout is placed upon the unique needs and circumstances of each individual. This is evident in:

- the negotiation of an individual action plan; and
- tailored arrangements to support the individual's collection of evidence.

The individual is thus expected to 'drive' the process; others – such as advisers, tutors and assessors – are there to support, not to pre-empt, the candidate's own decision-making.

The links between this and the thrust of 'open learning' are not difficult to make. A few years ago I defined openness as the provision of choices to individuals over such aspects of learning as:

- time, place and pace
- assessment
- content
- methods, route and media
- supporter(s).

Choice may be greater or lesser, and the extent of choice depends on the flexibility of the provider (Lewis, 1986).

But, as Richard Freeman points out in Chapter 4, in practice choice has usually been limited to that of time, place and pace. In particular, open learning programmes are often driven by printed linear texts with single start and end points, with little choice of route and with assessment limited to written assignments.

So what extensions of current open learning practice will be needed to realize the openness of the NVQ framework? In the next three sections I will consider this question under the headings of learner support, management and materials.

LEARNER SUPPORT

The kinds of support candidates need to gain G/NVQs can be deduced from Figure 3.1. Some of this support will be provided by printed material or access to a database, but a key role will be played by individuals close to the candidate. Informal support will be important, such as that from colleagues, other candidates, family and friends. What concerns us here, though, is the role of the professional, whatever their job title (for example 'lecturer', 'trainer', 'tutor').

Such professional supporters will need:

- information on the G/NVQ framework;
- information on specific G/NVQs;
- the ability to give information clearly and without jargon;
- the ability to negotiate plans with the candidate;
- a grasp of what constitutes 'evidence' and how this can be collected;
- knowledge of the different ways in which evidence can be organized; and
- knowledge of the requirements of awarding bodies.

Several people may carry out these activities. All concerned will, though, need to identify the candidate as the main decision-maker. The professional will use a range of strategies to support the candidate's increasingly confident exercise of choice.

The Training and Development Lead Body has defined competences for two key roles, those of the assessor and the adviser. These are set out in simplified terms in Table 3.1.

Staff operating successfully in open learning are well placed to carry out these roles. Open learning tutoring requires a focus on individual learners and their empowerment. The good tutor gives support flexibly, when needed, and by means that suit the circumstances (for example, by post or telephone when necessary). Tutors maintain flexible records of learners progressing at different rates. They give individual, rather than group, feedback. All this is congruent with the assessor and adviser roles.

Given the requirements of the framework, and the limitations of current assessment in most open learning courses, greater sophistication in assessment

Table 3.1 Roles and responsibilities for G/NVQ delivery

Role	Main responsibilities
Assessor	Identifies opportunities for the collection of evidence
	Judges performance evidence against criteria
	Makes the assessment decision
	Gives feedback
Advisor	Helps candidate identify appropriate standards
	Helps candidate match his or her experience to the standards
	Negotiates an action plan with the candidate
	Helps candidate collect and organize evidence for assessment

methods will almost certainly be necessary. (Richard Freeman (Chapter 4) and Peter Raggatt (Chapter 13) elaborate this point.) Staff also have to work to a framework devised by lead bodies rather than by educators.

MANAGEMENT

The manager is responsible for designing, running and monitoring systems that support candidates throughout the G/NVQ process. As manager, you may be a company trainer, either setting up your own internal provision or working with a local college. Or you may be directly providing assessment services to the public, as in a college of further education. Your system will need to deliver a wide range of support flexibly: information, guidance, assessment, feedback. Your colleagues will need accreditation to the national standards, summarized in Table 3.1. You will also need one or more 'internal verifiers' to:

- advise and support assessors;
- maintain the necessary records; and
- monitor quality.

Some candidates may need training before they can gather evidence. This is shown in Figure 3.6. Such training will often be on an individual basis, keyed into the action plan of a particular candidate.

The challenge to your colleagues will be similar to that encountered in moving from traditional teaching to open learning support. Staff unused to open learning may feel challenged by the emphasis on delivery to individuals rather than to groups and by the need to work in partnership with others, such as line managers. (Many other management issues exist, which I cannot discuss

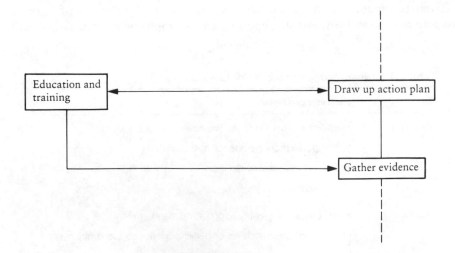

Figure 3.6 Figure 3.1 amended to show the place of education and training provision within the G/NVQ framework

in this chapter. Colleges will need, for example, to set up workshops both to simulate the workplace and to provide flexible learning opportunities. Again, colleges with experience of open learning often have, at least in embryo, the necessary accommodation and systems.)

LEARNING MATERIALS

The tendency is to think immediately of the kinds of 'open learning material' Richard Freeman describes in Chapter 4. But materials to support the G/NVQ framework need to be far more diverse. Each stage of the process can be supported by materials of various kinds. Table 3.2, building on Figure 3.1, shows this.

Sometimes the same piece of material will meet the needs of more than one role. Candidates, advisers and assessor, for example, will all need copies of relevant standards. At other times, the information will need customizing: the Benefits Agency scheme, for example, includes guides for both job holder and line manager. Both guides describe the way the Vocational Qualifications Programme works and its advantages. But, as the two extracts in Figures 3.7 and 3.8 show, the material is adapted to suit the differing perspectives of the two groups. Material may also need to be produced uniquely for one group – for example a guide for internal verifiers on record-keeping.

You may wonder what has happened to learning materials as these are usually understood. As Richard Freeman points out (Chapter 4), they will still be needed, but they will be orientated towards the collection of evidence for assessment purposes. They will be organized flexibly, not as long courses but

Table 3.2 Materials to support the candidate during the G/NVQ process

Candidate activity	Supporting material
Gain information	Presenters' notes, handouts, acetates
	Introductory leaflets
Identify relevant standards	Guides to standards
	Documents helping candidates link their experience to the standards
Draw up action plan	Planning documents
Gather evidence	Portfolio guide
	Examples of evidence
	The standards
Submit evidence	Awarding body documents
	Explanatory notes

WHY BOTHER?

N/SVQs bring a number of benefits to individuals. This section lists some of these benefits.

- You get a sense of achievement in carrying out tasks to a satisfactory standard.

- You get public recognition for the work you are doing, or have done in the past. You get credit by gaining a qualification.

- The recognition is national. It applies wherever you go, whoever you work for. It is not limited to your work with BA.

- N/SVQs are flexible. They are built up from units and you can get credit for a unit at a time. You can put your qualification together over a number of years, if you wish.

- N/SVQs are linked to the workplace. So you don't have to go away on a course or take an exam. You get credit by carrying out your normal job to the required standard.

Figure 3.7 Why bother? (From Development Division, Cabinet Office, 1993b)

as small modular components. They will be linked to the standards either directly at unit level (as in Figure 4.1 in Richard Freeman's chapter) or indirectly (for example, via the consideration of issues). They may play a role in developing the underpinning knowledge and understanding needed by candidates.

Responsibility for the development of the materials set out in Table 3.2 will vary. Generally, a publisher will produce the core learning material. The standards themselves, and any assessment guidelines, will be the responsibility of lead and awarding bodies. Materials more closely related to delivery, such as planning documents, will often be locally produced, or customized from existing models.

WHAT'S IN IT FOR YOU AS A LINE MANAGER?

N/SVQs offer a range of benefits to the organisation, to the candidate and to you – the line manager. Some of the benefits include the following.

- N/SVQs recognise the achievements of your staff. This should build their confidence and motivation.

- N/SVQs are flexible; credit can be built up over any period of time. This flexibility offers individuals and their managers room for planning.

- N/SVQs provide a framework for giving purpose and direction to staff training and development.

- N/SVQs help you, the manager, deal with staff as individuals, with their own flexible programmes for training, practice and assessment.

- N/SVQs rely on the support and expertise of local managers. They thus build your own role within the organisation.

- N/SVQs could give you yourself an opportunity to develop further your existing skills and to acquire new ones. You could collect evidence of this and gain credit, in the VQ Programme suited to your own job role, ie that of 'manager'.

- N/SVQs are useful in other ways, too. They can, for example, help you draw up job descriptions, select new staff, and carry out the appraisal process.

So N/SVQs should help your staff carry out their work more effectively and get credit for doing so. These qualifications are practical, observable, and rooted in the job to be done.

HOW DOES IT WORK?

This section gives you an overview of how the VQ Programme works. The diagram below shows the full sequence. More detail will be given at the introductory workshop.

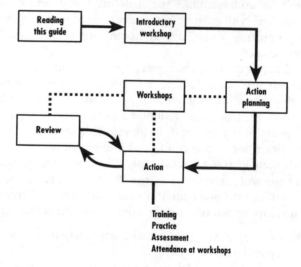

Training
Practice
Assessment
Attendance at workshops

We now go on to describe each step in turn, showing the people involved in each. You should pay particular attention to your own role.

Figure 3.8 What's in it for you as a line manager? (From Development Division, Cabinet Office, 1993c)

How suitable are existing materials?

Richard Freeman describes some of the requirements for core learning material, in his section on implications for open and distance learning. His main points are:

- in competence-based programmes clear boundaries exist for determining what content should and should not be included;
- radically different assessment methods have to be found to support assessors, precise guidance on assessment has to be produced; and
- the workplace (real and simulated) becomes an important learning environment.

Publishers of open learning materials are now getting to grips with the implications of G/NVQs. Even so, the points made by Rossetti in 1991 still largely apply. She points out that open learning packs often replace full courses and are designed to be worked through from start to finish. There may be an early statement inviting the learner to 'tackle it in any order that suits you', but nothing more is done to facilitate flexible use of the material. Learners need help in understanding the structure and relevance of the materials. Another problem with existing resources is the continuing assumption that the learner is acquiring knowledge at home rather than developing competence in the workplace.

More positively, however, open learning materials do usually contain certain features which, if extended, would support users wishing to gain G/NVQs. Objectives, for example, have for long been a staple feature of open learning texts. They perform a similar function to elements and performance criteria, especially if they are fully developed, including not only a statement of behaviour but of also conditions and standards.

Open learning packs, especially more recent ones, also feature activities. These were developed in the 1980s, as a response to the extension of open learning into practical and vocational areas. Activities are a good vehicle for developing competence. By completing them learners can:

- discover how generic tasks are carried out within their own particular organization;
- practise before tackling tasks in the workplace;
- collect evidence of performance; and
- acquire underpinning knowledge and understanding.

Activities can take a number of forms, including:

- diagnostic activities, to determine existing competence and identify areas for development;
- self-assessment questions, designed to promote underpinning understanding;
- simulations where 'real life' experience is not available; and
- projects, to cover several performance criteria and generate evidence.

Figure 3.9 shows typical activities. They are taken from the National Extension College ABACUS Business Administration series. (Fred Lockwood's chapter (Chapter 8) describes different models influencing the design of activities.)

Checklists are often linked to activities. Checklists help learners:

- consider all relevant aspects of performance;

PROJECT 2: Delivery services

1 Make a list of local and national delivery agencies (together with their phone numbers) that you may need to use, or already use.

2 Contact the agencies and find out the costs and security provided for:

- same day service
- next day delivery service
- Europe same day
- any special express international services provided
- how charges are calculated (e.g. by weight).

Set the information out as a chart or table for easy reference.

Date completed   Notes   File ref

Reporting accidents

All companies have (or should have) proper procedures for reporting accidents. Making a record of any accident is important. Suggest a couple of reasons why this is so.

Perhaps the most important reason is to provide a written account of the incident in case the injured person, whether an employee or visitor, wants to claim damages against the company. The record will also highlight any changes that need to be made to the company's safety policy and may highlight a particular hazard in the building.

Figure 3.9 Two examples of activities

Project	Yes	No	Target	Done
1 Presentation of documents Identifying examples of good and bad presentation	☐	☐	_____	_____
2 Reference file Establishing a reference file to help with: typing difficult text, spelling, punctuation and grammar, abbreviations, etc	☐	☐	_____	_____
3 Difficult photocopies Collecting examples of unusual or difficult photocopies	☐	☐	_____	_____
4 Binding Collecting examples of bound documents	☐	☐	_____	_____
5 Using photocopies to create an image Reducing and enlarging copies, cutting letterheads and pasting to create a master copy	☐	☐	_____	_____
6 Planning your work Making a weekly schedule of work and subsequently analysing it	☐	☐	_____	_____

Figure 3.10   A checklist

- carry out a job in the correct sequence; and
- check their own work.

Figure 3.10 shows a typical checklist, again from ABACUS.

Materials usually also contain feedback on activities. In-text feedback can be supplemented by comments from tutors, advisers or staff in the workplace. Materials for these other people can help ensure that feedback is full and well organized. (The Employment Department has commissioned work to match existing open learning material to NVQs. It has two objectives:

- To identify gaps in the coverage of standards and encourage action to fill these gaps.
- To enable learning providers to offer more open approaches to NVQs.

More information can be gained from the Learning Development Unit, TEED, Moorfoot, Sheffield S1 4PQ.)

CONCLUSION

To meet the requirements of the G/NVQ framework providers of education and training will have to ensure candidates can gain access to awards. They will also have to meet a wide range of individual needs. They will thus need the flexibility and learner-centredness now strongly associated with open learning.

I have argued that institutions delivering open learning successfully are likely to be well on the way to effective G/NVQ provision. Proponents of open learning can, indeed, welcome the G/NVQ framework as justifying their continuing investment in new systems, structures and materials.

REFERENCES AND NOTES

Development Division, Cabinet Office (Office of Public Service and Science) (1993a) Vocational Qualifications Programme, Business Administration Levels 1 and 2, London.

Development Division, Cabinet Office (Office of Public Service and Science) (1993b) *Job Holder's Guide*, Benefits Agency, London.

Development Division, Cabinet Office (Office of Public Service and Science) (1993c) *Line Manager's Guide*, Benefits Agency, London.

Lewis, R. (1986) What is open learning? *Open Learning*, Vol. 1, no. 2, pp. 5–10. This is a widely accepted definition of open learning.

National Extension College, ABACUS Business Administration Series, NEC, Cambridge.

Rossetti, A. (1991) National Vocational Qualifications: challenges and opportunities for open and flexible learning, unpublished paper.

4

Competence-based training using open and distance learning materials

Richard Freeman

An increasing proportion of UK vocational qualifications are becoming competence-based. This chapter explores the meaning of 'competence-based' and then looks at the implications of this for (a) training and (b) training using open and distance learning materials. Examples of a variety of competence-based open and distance learning materials are used to illustrate how the ideas discussed here are being applied in practice.

WHAT IS COMPETENCE-BASED TRAINING?

You have no doubt heard of competence-based training and its alter ego, National Vocational Qualifications (NVQs). You may be less confident about what exactly these terms mean and what their implications are for your work. If you are confused, then you are not alone because there would appear to be no agreed definition of what competence-based training is. Field and Drysdale (1991, p. 13) quote the National Council for Vocational Qualification's (NCVQ) definition of competence ('the ability to perform in work roles or jobs to the standard required in employment') but they take no further steps to define or explain the terms competence or competence-based training. This, despite the fact that the title of their book is *Training for Competence*. Nor can their meaning be inferred from a study of the book since, whilst it provides an extensive discussion of NCVQ policy statements, the book is more about good training *per se* than about some identifiably separate thing which might be called competence-based training. Similarly, three recent significant works on training and open learning (Buckley and Caple, 1990; Rowntree, 1992; Hodgson, 1993) do not even include the word competence in their indexes. Clearly, competence-based training is an elusive term.

Given this background I have felt it necessary to attempt a working definition at least for the purposes of this chapter. The definition which I offer is 'competence-based training is training which seeks to enable learners to acquire competences, using the NCVQ meaning of that term'.

Having conveniently offered a definition which refers to another definition, I must now turn to what the NCVQ means by competence.

WHAT IS A COMPETENCE?

The NCVQ describes a 'statement of competence' as an 'authoritative statement of the national standard of performance' (NCVQ, 1991, p. 2). A statement of competence can be subdivided into units of competence which 'have meaning and independent value in the area of employment to which the NVQ (National Vocational Qualification) statement of competence relates . . . In turn, a unit of competence can be sub-divided into elements of competence' (*ibid.*, p. 3). For example, the statement of competence for training and development at level 3 has 13 units. Unit 8 is 'Evaluate the achievements of outcomes against objectives.' This is subdivided into two elements:

1   Evaluate individual and group performance against objectives.
2   Evaluate learning programmes against the achievement of objectives.
(Institute of Training and Development, 1992, p. 43)

The relationship between the competence statement, its units and elements is shown in Figure 4.1. To gain the unit of competence 'Evaluate the achievements of outcomes against objectives', learners must be assessed on each element, two in this case. It is the characteristics of these elements which determines the nature of competence-based training. The NCVQ states that elements of competence should 'Relate to what actually happens in work and not, for example, activities or skills which are only demonstrated on training programmes' and should 'describe the result of what is done not the procedures which may be used' (NCVQ, 1991, p. 3).

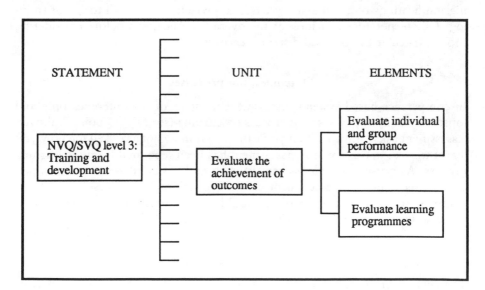

Figure 4.1   The level 3 training and development competence, showing unit 8 and its two elements of competence

WHAT'S NEW?

These two NCVQ criteria (there are five others) highlight the sharp move away from much traditional practice in education and training. Most importantly, the emphasis is on real work practice and its effective assessment. People who repair computers are expected to show that they can repair a real computer, not to describe how they might repair a hypothetical one. Managers learning interviewing skills are to be assessed through the observation of their actual interviewing skills, not through asking them to write essays about interviewing.

All this is sharpened even further in the NCVQ's criteria for an NVQ. The first three of these state that an NVQ must be:

- based on national standards required for performance in employment, and take proper account of future needs with particular regard to technology, markets and employment patterns;
- based on assessments of the outcomes of learning, arrived at independently of any particular mode, duration or location of learning;
- awarded on the basis of valid and reliable assessments made in such a way as to ensure that performance to the national standard can be achieved at work;

(NCVQ, 1991, p. 1)

IMPLICATIONS FOR TRAINING

Although this chapter is about open and distance learning, many of the training implications of a competency-based approach apply to all forms of training. I shall therefore first look at the overall implications before considering those particular to open and distance learning.

Outcomes, not processes

In competence-based systems, assessment must be of the outcomes only and must not in any way assess the process of learning (see NCVQ point 2 above). Assessment asks 'Show me that you can . . .'; it must not ask 'Tell me how you learnt to . . .'. In other words, assessment has been separated from the learning process. A course in which assessment is an end-of-course test is not competence based since the assessment is tied to taking the course. In a fully competence-based system, learners should be able to demonstrate their competence when they are ready, with or without taking the course.

Work-based assessment

The second big change involves the move to assessing actual work performance wherever possible (NCVQ points 1 and 3 above). Computer programming might be assessed through looking at real programs written at work; nursing might be assessed through looking at the actual care delivered on the wards; teaching skills might be demonstrated by the observation of classroom practice. Of course, there are situations where it is too expensive or too dangerous to assess real work. In these cases, the competence-based approach accepts simulation as a substitute.

Credit for prior learning

The third major change is in the introduction of the Accreditation of Prior Learning (APL). Whilst APL is not explicitly mentioned in the NCVQ criteria, it is implicit in the second criterion.

Once assessment is separated from the mode of learning, there is no need for learners to train for skills which they already possess. So any competence-based scheme must allow for each learner to require a different combination of units. Some will need all, some none, some a selection.

Taking these three major points (and many other implications which can be derived from the NCVQ criteria) we can see that the implications for training systems include the following:

- Learning and assessment have to be separated; the learner should be able to go straight to the assessment in order to demonstrate competence; 'going on a course' before having had a chance to demonstrate that the course is not needed should not occur in a competence-based system.
- Since a competence-based approach has recording credit for existing skills and knowledge as a central notion, it is hard to see how NVQs can be implemented without a parallel APL system.
- Courses must be accessible at the NCVQ unit level so that they match the APL credits; there would be no point in awarding an APL credit at unit level and then saying that the course was all or nothing.
- Wherever possible, assessment must be work based; that implies that the assessment undertaken by the learner will be based around the learner's work; it will no longer be possible to apply the same assessment items to all learners.

IMPLICATIONS FOR OPEN AND DISTANCE LEARNING

Open and distance learning courses tend to be characterized by (Hodgson, 1993, pp. 40, 88):

- separation of teacher (i.e. author) and learner;
- separation of tutor and learner; and
- the use of learning materials.

I could also add that open and distance learning courses tend to:

- be linear with a single start and end points and little choice of route through; and
- use written tests for assessment.

How does a competence-based approach affect these characteristics?

Given that an open or distance learning course is usually heavily determined by its learning materials, it is instructive to look at how those materials might have to change in a competence-based approach.

Implications for materials of APL

As soon as APL is available, learners cease to be (if they ever were) a homogeneous group. Courses which assume that every learner will study every unit in a predetermined order are just not compatible with APL. With APL, every learner might need a slightly different combination of units; this strikes a blow at the linear course. Competence-based courses are likely to be available in units with no prescribed, but perhaps a recommended, order of study. For example, The Open College course 'The carers' has five level-1 units, each printed as a separate booklet but none bearing a unit number. They can be studied in any combination and in any order. The units are titled:

- Promoting quality
- Health and safety
- Handling information
- Security
- Handling problems.

APL's impact on open and distance learning materials goes further than the need to unitize them. If it is the case that different learners need different combinations of units then (a) learners must be able to find which units they need before purchasing a course and (b) they must be able to purchase only the units which they need. At present, the tendency is to offer the learner help within the learning materials. Figure 4.2 shows an example of how this is done in the National Extension College ABACUS materials (NEC, 1990, p. 3). Helpful as the checklist is, the learner surely needs it before getting hold of the materials, not after. APL, then, produces a major challenge to the administrative systems of many open and distance learning providers. If you are involved in providing ODL how do you think your system may have to adapt in terms of content and assessment?

Content implications of work-based assessment

Planning course content has often been a relatively vague process. Many courses are developed by first describing a curriculum statement or a list of contents. Precise as such documents may appear on the surface, different authors have been legitimately able to interpret them very differently. Moreover, such course descriptions are susceptible to the gradual addition of new topics because of a feeling that the learners need them or that the topics might be useful. In open learning, this growth can continue as the learning materials are written with authors adding in new material that they personally feel needs to

Decide how good you think you are at each of the tasks and for each task listed give yourself a rating on the scale 1 to 5

1 = **I am not good at this at all**

2 = **I have some problems with this**

3 = **I am OK at this, but sometimes get it wrong**

4 = **I am fairly good at this**

5 = **I have no problems here at all**

Self-assessment : Processing payroll

22A Process documentation for wages and salaries   5 4 3 2 1

- calculating gross pay correctly from appropriate documentation
- calculating statutory and voluntary deductions
- correctly preparing pay slips
- keeping statutory and other records up to date, legible and accurate
- completing and despatching all returns accurately
- handling queries with tact and courtesy
- identifying and dealing with discrepancies in accordance with organization's procedures
- always maintaining confidentiality of information

22B Process direct payment of wages and salaries

- preparing wage packets correctly and issuing them
- following security procedures
- keeping records up to date, accurate and legible
- dealing with wage queries promptly and courteously
- maintaining confidentiality of information

22C Arrange credit transfers

- correctly preparing credit transfer slips
- completing bank schedules correctly
- passing schedules and transfer slips to bank
- dealing with queries about pay
- dealing with any discrepancies
- keeping all records up to date, legible and accurate
- following confidentiality and security procedures

If you have ticked 3 or less for any of the tasks listed, this workbook will help you to improve your skills in these areas. By the end of this workbook, you should be able to rate yourself higher.

Figure 4.2 A checklist to help learners decide whether they need to use a study unit on payroll processing

be there. All this occurs because, in the 'traditional' curricula, it is hard to fix clear boundaries. No easy rule can determine that X should be in the course and Y should not. (The difficulty of describing precisely materials in advance of writing them has previously been discussed in Freeman, 1991.)

This source of uncertainty is much reduced in a competence-based programme. There is now a much clearer boundary for determining what should and should not be included in a course. That boundary could perhaps be described by three rules:

- *Rule 1.* If the skill or knowledge is essential to satisfactory job performance, then include the skill or knowledge; if not, exclude it.
- *Rule 2.* If the skill or knowledge is to be included under Rule 1, it must be expressed in a form which can be demonstrated through work-based assessment.
- *Rule 3.* Learners should be given the opportunity to demonstrate their competence and need for training before being submitted to it.

For the open and distance learning-materials producer, these rules are a support and a challenge. A support because the designer has a clear means of making decisions on content. A challenge because many of the traditional ways of writing open and distance learning materials are just not suitable for work-based learning.

Assessment implications of work-based assessment

For open and distance learning, work-based assessment may represent the greatest of all the competency challenges. The nature of distance learning, in particular, has fostered the extensive use of written assignments for assessment. Other forms of assessment have tended to be overlooked because of their expense or because of practical problems. Competence-based training turns that situation on its head. Most of the assessment methods used in open and distance learning are simply not suitable to assess typical elements of competence. For example, consider the list below of performance criteria for the element 'Present information to learners':

- information is clear and accurate and presented in a tone, manner, pace and style appropriate to the needs and capabilities of learners
- visual support materials are legible, accurate and used in a manner which enhances the clarity of the information presented
- learners are encouraged to ask questions, seek clarification and make comments at identified and appropriate stages in the presentation
- clear and accurate supplementary and summary information is provided on request and where appropriate to reinforce key learning points
- visual aid equipment is maintained in full operating condition.

(Institute of Training and Development, 1992, p. 29)

It is hard to see how this element could be assessed without departing from most of the methods used to date in open and distance learning. We are pushed away from well tried methods such as multiple choice, short answer and essays and pushed towards asking the learner to produce evidence that the competency has been acquired. For example, the following shows just one part of the assessment for an Open College course on managing people:

1 Provide a training needs analysis on the skill requirements in your department to cover a period of six months. Make sure that this analysis is based on current work but also plans for anticipated changes to the work plan.
2 Carry out an appraisal interview and produce an appraisal form for one member of your staff which is countersigned by your manager and the staff member concerned.
3 As a result of the interview produce a plan of all the training and development needs for the same staff member for a period of six months.
4 Provide evidence of a follow-up interview for this member of staff in which you monitor, report back on progress and agree management and interviewee action. This evidence is likely to be an interview form which is countersigned by the staff member.

(The Open College, n.d.)

The emphasis in this example is on the learner producing evidence of performance. Although some guidance is given on the likely format, e.g. 'This evidence is likely to be an interview form', in general learners are challenged to find their own ways of showing that they have reached the required standard.

Just as the nature of the assessment items changes, so do the assessment skills needed by the tutor. However expert a tutor is at grading assignments, he or she may have little understanding of how to assess work-based evidence. Generally, as open and distance learning moves into competence-based training, substantial tutor training will be needed in the new assessment skills. Indeed, if a course is to lead to an NVQ, then the relevant awarding body will generally require the assessor to hold a relevant competence-based assessment qualification. In addition to the general training, tutors need much more precise guidance on assessment criteria than has generally been asked for on non-competence-based schemes. The following shows the extensive list of criteria used for just one work-based task on an Open College management programme.

Does the evidence:

1 Describe the hardware currently in use?
2 Describe the rationale for the selection and use of hardware?
3 Compare the key features/benefits of the hardware with at least one other suitable type of hardware?
4 Describe the software currently in use?
5 Describe the various applications of the software within the department?
6 Demonstrate correct use of technical terms?
7 Compare key features/benefits of the software with at least one other similar type of software?
8 Demonstrate that hardware will execute software identified?
9 Make valid recommendations for the alternatives to, or improvement of, the hardware and software?

10   Advise on potential benefits of alternative hard/software?
11   Give accurate and complete costs of alternative hard/software?
12   Present documents produced using software packages which meet the standards of presentation and accuracy set by [your employer]?
13   Demonstrate analysis of data using two software packages?
14   Show that data analysed is [sic] presented in appropriate pictorial and/or tabular formats?
15   Demonstrate that the participant has ensured that all procedures adopted and proposed conform to current legislation?
16   Describe valid procedures for ensuring data integrity and security?
                    (Reproduced by kind permission of The Open College)

Implications for course delivery and organization

Early distance learning schemes (such as The Open University undergraduate programme) and open learning schemes (such as FlexiStudy) were focused on the lone, individual, home-based learner. Much of the teaching technology (e.g. broadcasting) and the terminology (e.g. home experiment kit) emphasized the home as the place of learning.

In competence-based courses, the home usually remains a place of learning, but the workplace plays a significant and sometimes dominant role. It is at the workplace that the learner might collect data (e.g. company practice on disciplinary procedures), practise skills (e.g. meeting skills), use equipment (e.g. a computer) or gain support and advice.

Perhaps the biggest organizational shift is in terms of who is likely to be providing the support. In traditional open and distance learning, the key supporter is the tutor or tutor-counsellor. Frequently such tutors are part time and home based so, like the student, they are isolated. Tutors and students meet infrequently or, in many schemes, not at all. In a competence-based scheme, because the nature of the learning and the assessment pushes learning into the workplace, new opportunities for support are available. Tutors play a smaller role (or none at all in some schemes) but mentors and line managers appear. The following list shows the potentially wide-ranging role of a mentor in The Open College health care management programme:

- listen to problems
- provide encouragement
- give advice on how to study
- make suggestions about managerial skills
- discuss issues that come up at work
- provide information about the workplace
- give advice on the learner's personal objectives
- advise on career development.
                    (The Open College, 1992, p. 5)

Implications for learners

Most learners entering competence-based schemes have no previous experience of the approach. Its terminology (such as performance criteria and portfolios) will be new and confusing; the special skills it requires (such as preparing evidence) will not be there. If, at the same time, the learner chooses an open or distance learning approach, then that too may be new. All in all, competence-based open and distance learning presents plenty of challenges to learners. Unless programmes are designed consciously to induct learners into the new methods and skills, learners are not likely to succeed.

The two most important areas for consideration are interpreting the competences and preparing evidence. The competences and their performance criteria are necessarily written in formal, general language. It is not easy for learners to see how this relates to their jobs. One way of addressing this in open and distance learning is through helping the learners to rewrite the competences in terms of their own work. The following is an example of how to do this from the National Extension College Essential Caring Skills course. It is a translation of the competence 'The worker's dress, approach and own personal hygiene are consistent with recognized good health and safety practice':

General: Housecoat – clean everyday; changed during shift if badly soiled. Clean clothes underneath. Hair washed daily, worn tied back on shift. Hands washed before and after contact with sick clients; otherwise hands and nails kept clean at all times. Avoid anything but hypoallergenic handcreams. Hands always washed after toileting self or others, or after contact with urine, faeces, etc. Hands always washed before contact with food.
   Special: when dealing with urine, faeces and blood spillages: use disposable gloves.
   Special : when barrier-nursing: face masks and bonnets, housecoat to be changed on entering and leaving room.

(NEC, 1993, p. 3.2)

Helping learners to prepare evidence for assessment also needs careful attention in open and distance learning. The Essential Caring Skills package includes advice on:

- proving the value of your prior qualifications
- finding and creating workplace assessment opportunities
- understanding the assessment wording
- planning an assessment timetable.

(*ibid.*, pp. 2.1–2.13)

Although in the example just quoted the help is in the form of print-based activities, other methods of preparing learners for competence-based assessment are used, including induction programmes and assessment workshops.

CONCLUSIONS

Any training system which was not designed for competence-based training will require major changes to deliver this new form. Open and distance learning schemes are no different. It is clear though from the examples quoted that providers are finding that open and distance learning is fully capable of delivering competence-based training. In one sense, the task should be easier than in converting face-to-face courses: open and distance learning has always pushed a lot of responsibility on to the learner. Competence-based training just increases the learner's responsibilities still further. There are no signs that this is going to prove problematic.

REFERENCES AND NOTES

Buckley, R. and Caple, J. (1990) *The Theory and Practice of Training*, Kogan Page, London.

Field, L. and Drysdale, D. (1991) *Training for Competence*, Kogan Page, London.

Fletcher, S. (1991) *Designing Competence-Based Training*, Kogan Page, London. This is a clear account of the principles of competence-based training and explains how to design a training system around standards of performance. It does not, though, cover open learning so readers have to extend its ideas for themselves.

Fletcher, S. (1992) *Competence-Based Assessment Techniques*, Kogan Page, London. This work is a thorough explanation of the methods of assessment which can be used in competence-based training. Although it does not discuss open learning specifically, its principles are just as applicable in open learning as in any other form of training.

Freeman, R. (1991) Quality assurance in learning materials production, *Open Learning*, Vol. 6, no. 3, pp. 24–31.

Hodgson, B. (1993) *Key Terms and Issues in Open and Distance Learning*, Kogan Page, London.

Institute of Training and Development (1992) *Direct Trainers Award*, ITD, Marlow.

National Council for Vocational Qualifications (1991) *Criteria for National Vocational Qualifications*, NCVQ, London.

National Extension College (1990) *ABACUS Payroll Processing*, NEC, Cambridge.

National Extension College (1993) *Essential Caring Skills*, NEC, Cambridge.

The Open College (n.d.) *Managing People User Guide 3*, The Open College, Manchester.

The Open College (1992) *Mentor Guide Managing Resources*, The Open College, Manchester.

Rowntree, D. (1992) *Exploring Open and Distance Learning*, Kogan Page, London.

5

Course design: order and presentation

Clive Lawless

This chapter focuses on the order that subject-matter should and can be presented to students. It looks at the important influence of the subject-matter, the ways students study, the functions of the different elements and media and the way the course is made. Using models derived from case studies, different patterns of presenting teaching material are identified and analysed. The emphasis is on enabling students to develop sequences for their own courses.

INTRODUCTION

Imagine, for the purpose of this chapter, that you are involved in planning an introductory course in your subject area. The course is for students who will be studying part time and at a distance, and it has to introduce them to the major areas of the subject. The group's remit is to design and produce a course which will bring students with limited subject knowledge to a position where they can cope with study at a recognized level.

In what order should the disciplines (and the topics within them) be presented to students? What would be the factors which could or should influence your thinking? On what criteria would you make your decisions?

Keep this situation in mind as you read through the pages which follow. During the chapter you will be asked to relate your ideas for your subject-matter to the points being raised.

ORDER OF PRESENTATION AND SEQUENCE

In what order should the major topics, ideas and concepts in a course be presented to students? In particular how should the content of open and distance learning courses be sequenced? Course designers, evaluators and researchers have paid considerable attention to the teaching of specific topics, to particular teaching techniques and to general approaches to instruction. What has received much less attention is how the overall structure of a course can and should be organized, how the content, the subject-matter, of a course should be presented to students.

This issue is particularly important in open and distance learning where formal packaged courses have to be prepared for students to study away from immediate physical contact with teachers. Once produced such materials can be expensive to change and there is a danger that students, especially those with limited educational experience, may tend to follow rigidly what they perceive to be presented as the 'authority route' through the material. The issues the course teams face in the planning can be summarized as follows:

- To what extent is the course structure determined by the nature of the subject-matter?
- How (i.e. in what order) will students study the course?
- What will be the functions of the different elements and media?
- How will the structure and material of the course be affected by the way it is made?

BASIC MODEL

The most straightforward model for course structure in distance or open learning (or any other form, come to that) is illustrated in Figure 5.1. In this model students move in linear fashion from one teaching unit/text to the next.

The teaching texts/units are self-contained in that they contain all that the student needs to study the subject-matter. Except for very short sequences few courses would follow such a simple model. Although on occasion students,

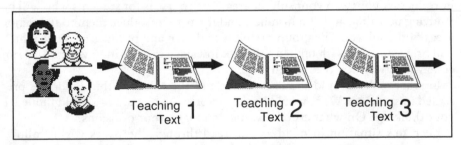

Figure 5.1   Basic model

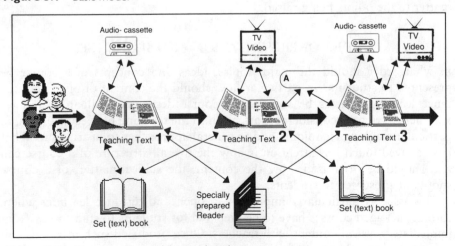

Figure 5.2   'Developed' open/distance learning course model

particularly those who study on commuter trains, express a desire for course structures like this it is scarcely practicable for long sequences. A range of elements and media are necessary to teach most subject-matters.

Figure 5.2 represents a more wide-ranging or 'developed' model for a distance learning course in which the 'teaching texts/units' are complemented by a range of other media: television, audio-cassettes, computers, set (text) books, specially prepared readers, home experiment kits and the tutorial support through assignments and tutorials and residential schools. However, the main teaching element remains the teaching text/unit. Students are guided in their study of the other media by the main teaching texts. But certain issues still remain: firstly, the exact function of the teaching units which often seem to be an uneasy compromise between 'teaching' and 'telling'; secondly, the ways students actually study the materials, which can differ quite markedly from that embodied in the structure by the course designers.

At this stage you will find it helpful to produce a model, possibly similar to Figure 5.2, indicating the potential route or routes for learners through you materials.

COURSE CONTENT AND COURSE STRUCTURE

It is easy to assume that the structure of a course will be determined by the nature of its content, that there is a 'natural' or obvious order in which topics should be presented. Some discipline areas, notably mathematics, science and technology, contain elements which are clearly hierarchical. One topic, concept or skill has to be mastered in order to understand the next, e.g. the meaning of 'velocity' needs to be learned in order to understand 'acceleration' (change in velocity) (Posner and Strike, 1976). Even in these areas where the range of subject-matter is as large as a full course, covering, say, a year's work, there will not necessarily be a hierarchical structure covering all or even most of the topics. The sequence, apparently obvious to experts or instructors, may reflect either the way they were themselves taught or a logical 'top-down' view of the discipline area that experience and expertise have given them. This may not reflect in any way the order which is required by actual students who may, for example, need help in relating new material to their existing experience.

In the humanities and social sciences, subject-matter is rarely linear or hierarchical except for very short sections. Nor is there any obvious order for an introductory course in science which aims to introduce the different disciplines of the subject. Course content is frequently chosen and assembled specifically for an individual course and its development and the clarification of the interrelationships is part of the process of constructing the course. This can be an intellectual adventure for the course designers – combining ideas and concepts in novel patterns and planning to present them in innovative ways. While this may be an interesting learning experience for the course designers, the danger is that the outcome in the way the course is structured can appear obvious and inevitable. The innovative, even tentative nature of the course structure may not be at all apparent to students who may find it more inaccessible to the extent that it was exciting for the course designers to make.

Case study 1

The main problem in planning the structure of a course on the history of technology, 1750–1914, was the need to reconcile four different strands in its subject-matter:

1. To tell the coherent and largely chronological story over the period 1750–1914 of each of the 14 technologies selected for the course.
2. To enable students to develop an understanding of how progress in the technologies was interrelated.
3. To introduce the main economic trends which influenced the ways these technologies developed or did not develop.
4. To provide a treatment of the social conditions which resulted in the technological changes and which in turn influenced them.

And also

5. To provide students with the opportunity to study the material in different ways and to follow their own particular individual interests.

The solution was to write essays on each of the 14 technologies and then guide students through them using three period-based Study Guides, which also provided treatment of the broader social and economic issues. Figure 5.3 illustrates this structure for a single Study Guide.

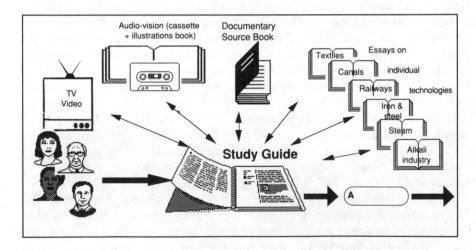

Figure 5.3   Study Guide structure: OU course A281 Technology and Change, 1750–1914

USING STUDENTS' STUDY PATTERNS: IN WHAT ORDER DO STUDENTS STUDY A COURSE?

It is easy for teachers at any level to assume that students study in the ways they set out for them. This is a suspect assumption in any educational situation but is particularly misleading in open and distance learning where students largely study on their own. When the first foundation courses were designed and what was for some years the 'traditional' Open University course format (see Figure 5.2) was being developed, there was an assumption that students would pace their studies by the content of the weekly 'unit' (defined as all the materials and activities for a week), and the influence of weekly television programmes was thought likely to be particularly helpful in this respect. What has actually happened is rather different. From surveys of students studying many different courses it is clear that most students are two to four weeks behind the notional weekly timetable. What determines the pacing of learners' studies are the assignments and their due dates. This should surprise no one who has studied the literature on student attitudes to assessment (see, for example, Miller and Parlett, 1974). Where a course or a package does not include assessment material, learners will need assistance to organize and pace their studies.

The basic point needs to be made that the sequence of the material presented to students and the order they study it in are by no means the same. This is particularly true in the context of open and distance learning where students can be flexible about how and where they study and free to choose in which order. This contrasts with face-to-face situations where lecture and seminar timetables exert considerable influence on how students study.

That students' perceptions of the order in which they can best study a subject differ from that laid down by 'experts' is well brought out in an important but strangely neglected study by Mager (1961). He faced the issue of whether learner-generated sequence would be similar to instructor-generated sequence. Using a sample of undergraduates, he gave them the freedom to start studying electronics by asking any question that interested them. He found that the subjects in the sample were: 'continuously looking for ways to tie new information to things they already knew.' Whereas instructors specified moving from the part to the whole, students moved from simple whole to more complex wholes. Learners' sequences for study were quite different from those set out by experts or instructors.

A similar approach, though from a different standpoint to Mager's empirical study, is that derived from cognitive psychology and information-processing models of memory. Under these models real or meaningful learning occurs when the individual learner links new knowledge with prior and existing knowledge (Ausubel, 1968; Ausubel, Novak and Hanesian, 1978; Novak and Gowin, 1984). Thus the crucial determinant of learning is the state of existing knowledge, the lack of it, or erroneous knowledge that the student already has. This calls for an order of study which may be quite different from that set out by the expert.

Case study 2

A comparative course on British and American history, 1760–1960, was designed around eight 'focus points'. Each focus point deals with a major course issue and carries an assignment. This recognizes the influence of assignments on students' patterns of work. Hence when students base their work around assignment dates they are also basing it around the main themes of the course. To some extent this is a question of 'if you can't beat them, join them'!

The structure of each focus point is illustrated in Figure 5.4. For each focus point there are six to eight interpretative essays, 6,000 words long, providing the 'telling' element. The 'teaching' is contained in a teaching unit which guides students through the essays and audio-cassette sequences and provides links to the television. The teaching units also refer students to relevant sections of the specially compiled 'reader', to items in the primary-source document collection and to the atlas/chronology book. These three items relate to the whole course but contain items specific to each focus point.

At this stage pause and consider the content of your course. Is the subject-matter likely to cause any problems when you decide the order of presentation?

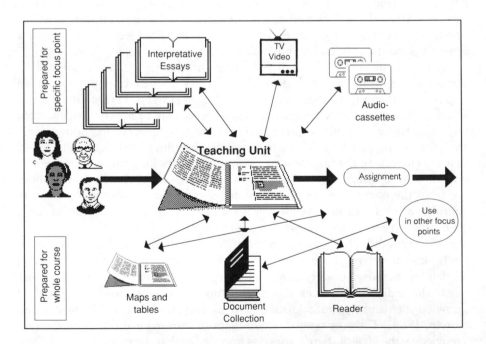

Figure 5.4 'Focus point' structure in the OU course A317 Themes in British and American History: A Comparative Approach, c. 1760–1970

COURSE STRUCTURE AND THE USE OF MATERIALS AND MEDIA

Consideration of different ways of ordering course content leads naturally to the issue of the nature and purpose of the teaching elements and media which present the subject-matter of the course. In the basic and 'developed' models (Figures. 5.1 and 5.2) described earlier, the key elements remain the printed word in the form of a 'teaching unit' or 'course unit', basically a self-instructional text. Such teaching texts are, typically, an uneasy compromise between *telling* and *teaching*. On the one hand these texts are concerned with *telling* in the sense of providing information, the basic subject-matter of the course and, on the other hand, they are concerned with *teaching*, with providing students with opportunities to develop deeper understanding of the subject-matter, to gain expertise in and to practise appropriate skills and to apply what they have learned in different ways. The attempt to combine these two functions can be an *uneasy* compromise because it is frequently unclear to students (and, indeed, to unit authors) what the purpose of a particular section or unit is. Often the overall impression is given that it is the conveying of information and its absorption by the student which is the predominant purpose. Development of understanding and learning skills appears to be largely left to chance. Even when teaching texts contain exercises and activities they tend to focus on comprehension of the information provided rather than the explicit development of skills.

INFLUENCE OF THE WAY IN WHICH A COURSE IS MADE

When students receive a course it often appears that one section follows the previous one in a carefully determined order. It frequently happens that, during the production process, draft teaching materials are produced in an erratic, not to say random, order with later units already in press before earlier draft units appear. This may be due to work commitments to other courses, to sickness or lack of resources. Whatever the reason it can have serious consequences if materials required for later in the course do not appear, or themes paraded as central to the course in early materials receive scant attention later on. These are extreme cases, but a more subtle lack of continuity is a real danger when materials are produced in random order.

In both the case studies the essays were all produced in draft form before work on the study guides/teaching units was started. The draft study guides/ teaching units were then produced in course order (i.e. the order in which they were presented to students). The aim is best described as 'cumulative coherence'. All materials were available for revision on an iterative basis before any were handed over for printing.

Do you have production problems which will affect the order in which the draft materials are produced? You will find it useful to list the steps you can take to minimize their effects.

THE WAY FORWARD – MODELS AND OPTIONS

In designing sequences to take account of these issues, we need to take account of the size of the segment of instruction: one type of sequence for an overall course structure may include other models of sequence for smaller segments within it. No approach offers a complete formula and different models must be taken as being complementary rather than exclusive.

Rowntree (1990) identifies a variety of sequence models: topic by topic, chronological order, place to place, concentric circles, causal, structural logic, problem centred, spiral sequence and backward chaining:

- *Topic-by-topic* sequencing provides students with instructional materials in a form that can be studied in any order. Even if provided with a guide there is a real danger that students will be confused about the relationship between topics and fail to develop their knowledge of the nature of the relationships. If the links are not important it raises the question of whether the topics form a coherent whole.
- *Chronological order* makes sense for the broad structure of, for example, courses in history, or stages in a scientific process. A rigid adherence to chronological order will make it difficult to explore underlying and explanatory themes and concepts. The two courses in the case studies had only very broad chronological structure before developing along thematic lines.
- *Place to place/concentric circles* are based on spatial or geographic relationships of subject-matter, for example anatomy, the chemical structure of a substance or roles in an organization.
- *Structural logic* or hierarchical structure, in which one stage has to be mastered before the next can be understood. Subject-matter experts tend to assume the existence of such hierarchies for learning, even where their existence is doubtful.
- *Causal structure* follows the sequence of explanation, branching out to enable students to understand its stages; it is a variety of structural logic.
- *Problem-centred* sequences start from a problem or series of problems which relate to students' experience or interest. A prime example of this is an OU course, Science Matters, which is based around problems such as pollution and global warming.
- In a *spiral sequence* concepts and their relationships are all (or nearly all) introduced at an early stage, then developed together so that students come to terms with them in increasing complexity over successive stages. From a psychological point of view such an approach is highly desirable but in practice it is difficult to sustain over large subject areas.
- *Backward chaining* involves going through a whole process and teaching the final step first. Rowntree provides the example of learning to interpret the results of a chemical test before acquiring the skill of carrying it out.

As an exercise, select three of these models which might be suitable for sections of your subject-matter and briefly outline how the sequence could be organized.

In evaluating the appropriateness of these models for particular learning situations and types of subject-matter, note how most of the models provide a link to the learner's experience and provide, in different ways, an overview of the subject-matter. This provides not only a way in for the learner but avoids the 'just learn this, you won't understand it until later . . .' syndrome!

FINALLY, YOUR COURSE

When all the models have been reviewed and analysed, the basic point remains that teaching, by whatever means, is a creative, human endeavour, as Van Patten, Chao and Reigeluth (1986, p. 466) point out: 'The role of macro-strategies in instruction is not well-understood.' This is as true for the creation of distance or open learning materials as it is for a teacher standing in front of a class. To set up really effective sequencing for learning it is likely to be the process of thinking through the issues and evaluating available models which will count, rather than following one particular pathway.

As a concluding exercise, list the issues you have to face in deciding the order of presentation of the materials for your course. Try sketching out a possible sequence or sequences.

REFERENCES

Ausubel, D. P. (1968) *Educational Psychology: A Cognitive View*, Holt, Rinehart & Winston, New York.

Ausubel, D. P., Novak, J. D. and Hanesian, H. H. (1978) *Educational Psychology: A Cognitive View* (2nd edn), Holt, Rinehart & Winston, New York.

Mager, R. F. (1961) On the sequencing of instructional content, *Psychological Reports*, no. 9, pp. 405–13.

Miller, C. M. L. and Parlett, M. (1974) *Up to the Mark: A Study of the Examination Game*, Society for Research into Higher Education, London.

Novak, J. D. and Gowin, D. B. (1984) *Learning How to Learn*, Cambridge University Press, New York.

Posner, G. J. and Strike, K. A. (1976) A categorization scheme for principles of sequencing content *Review of Educational Research*, Vol. 46, no. 4, pp. 665–90.

Rowntree, D. (1990) *Teaching through Self-Instruction: How to Develop Open Learning Materials* (revised edn), Kogan Page, London.

Van Patten, J., Chao, C. I. and Reigeluth, C. M. (1986) A review of strategies for sequencing and synthesizing instruction, *Review of Educational Research*, Vol. 56, no. 4, pp. 437–71.

HUMANITIES

6

Selection and use of media for open and distance learning

Adrian Kirkwood

Over the last decade the range of media available for teaching and training has increased considerably. New media (often 'hybrid' combinations of media or novel modes of delivery) have developed to such an extent that decisions about how best to use them in education and training must take account of many complex factors. This chapter will identify the main types of audio-visual media, computers and communication technologies that are currently available and will discuss a number of key issues relating to their selection and use for teaching and training.

THE RANGE OF EDUCATIONAL MEDIA

Rather than trying simply to characterize the strengths and weaknesses of individual media, I will attempt to provide a broad overview by considering a number of dimensions that relate to all media and which are important in establishing a strategy for choosing media. For many people developing open or distance learning materials the selection process involves trying to make best use of the limited range of media that are available to them; others may need to argue for additional media in order to achieve their desired learning outcomes. In open or distance learning, these 'electronic media' tend not to be used by themselves but are combined with text or with other media materials.

Audio

Can you think of any aspects of your teaching or training that might benefit from an audio component? If so, what form could it take?

Teachers and trainers often underestimate the contribution that sounds, music and the spoken word can make to open and distance learning. They can be used for direct teaching, tutoring or simply to provide some variety in the materials being studied: they can also be conveyed to learners by a variety of means. The telephone can be used for interacting with learners, either on a one-to-one basis or with a dispersed group linked into a telephone conference. Some teachers and trainers are able to make use of radio broadcasts, and these have the potential to reach a large, dispersed audience. However, the main disadvantage of radio is the fixed transmission times for programmes: learners may be unable to listen to programmes at the time they are broadcast or the material may have been intended to link in with aspects of their studies completed several weeks ago. Audio-cassettes offer much greater convenience, as they allow prerecorded materials to be used by learners at the time (and often the place) that suits them best. Learners are also able to control how the audio material is used; they can stop the tape and replay as required to interact with the material.

Video

Would your teaching or training benefit from the addition of moving images or the presentation of real events? Could you make effective use of animation or sequences that are speeded up or slowed down?

Television is a rich and flexible medium for education and training and there are a growing number of means by which television material can reach a viewer's screen. Unfortunately, terrestrial broadcasting and transmissions via satellite or cable are options available to only a limited number of educators and trainers. However, the video-recorder (VCR) allows prerecorded video-cassettes to be replayed and broadcast programmes to be recorded off-air for subsequent viewing. Like their audio equivalent, video-cassettes can offer learners convenience and control in terms of when and how they study the material. Video or television material can contribute to open or distance learning in many different ways: it can provide learners with 'vicarious experience' by demonstrating complex processes or making possible visits to locations that would be too costly or too dangerous to achieve in any other way; it can use animation or adjusted speed techniques to demonstrate changes over time; it can be used for the direct teaching of ideas, processes and procedures, or to present 'real life' case studies for analysis, or to act as a trigger to reflection and discussion among learners.

Computers

Would computer-based material contribute to your teaching? What computer materials could make a worthwhile contribution to your teaching?

Computers are increasingly being used for open and distance learning, either by themselves, networked to other computers or controlling sophisticated multimedia workstations. Computer-based training or computer-assisted learning is often made available to learners on stand-alone personal computers or terminals linked to a mainframe computer (which may be geographically remote). Computer networks (local, national or international) can give learners access to remote databases and enable them to communicate with other users by means of electronic mail (e-mail) or computer conferencing. Vast amounts of information in the form of words, sounds, pictures and animation are now available to individual learners by means of a CD-ROM drive connected to a personal computer (each CD-ROM disc can hold the equivalent of about 250,000 pages) or a domestic CD-I player connected to a television set. The cost of CD-ROM and CD-I players is coming down and there is a growing range of commercial software available. Interactive video (IV) is potentially very attractive in teaching and training, as it brings together the interactive potential of computer-assisted learning and the benefits of full-motion video sequences on a laservision video-disc. However, IV workstations are very expensive and the production of IV materials can be very costly due to the range of professional skills required.

ACCESS AND DISTRIBUTION

It is often claimed that one of the main advantages of open and distance learning is the flexibility it offers in terms of when and where study takes place. Media-based materials needn't reduce this flexibility too much. You should always begin the selection process by considering issues of access and distribution, because if learners cannot get access to your materials, it doesn't matter how good the teaching is or how much you've spent producing them. Whether they are studying at home, in the workplace or in some other location, learners must have access to suitable equipment to receive or interact with media-based materials.

While some media are capable of 'reaching' large numbers of learners in their own homes, others may be more suitable for use in a limited number of dedicated centres. Any decision about how media-based materials will be distributed to learners will depend upon the equipment required (e.g. readily available domestic technology, specialized workstations, etc.) and the location in which study will take place (e.g. at home, in local centres, etc.). However, any particular method of distribution has its own set of logistical and cost constraints: it can also have specific pedagogical characteristics (these will be discussed in later sections).

So, when you are considering which media to use for your open or distance learning the key questions are:

1.   *where* will the materials be studied; and
2.   to *what equipment* will learners have access?

Of course, an important factor determining the location of study will be *when* the learning is expected to take place: will it be ongoing, a one-off session (full or half-day) or a longer, concentrated course?

If learning is expected to take place mainly at home, the teaching materials should require only the use of 'domestic' equipment. Television material can reach a home TV set via terrestrial transmission, connection to a satellite/cable service or from a video-cassette. Currently in the UK nearly all homes have a television receiver and over three-quarters (77 per cent) of households have a video-recorder (Gunter and McLaughlin, 1993). However, only 10 per cent of homes can receive direct satellite transmissions and about 3 per cent are connected to a cable service. But access to these delivery mechanisms varies from country to country. For example, connections to cable services are much more widespread in Belgium and The Netherlands than in the UK, although home video-recorders are less numerous. Telephones have penetrated most households in industrialized countries, while audio-cassettes have an internationally standard format and can be played on equipment that is relatively cheap and easily transportable.

Sometimes more sophisticated media will be required if particular learning outcomes are to be achieved. In such cases it is necessary to provide learners with suitable equipment, either on loan for use in the home or (if appropriate) at their place of work. Some media equipment may be readily available to people working in their occupational settings (for example, video-recorders and computers in garages and factories, computer terminals in financial institutions), while elsewhere none may be readily accessible. If equipment is available at the workplace for other purposes, there are obviously advantages to be gained from using it for education or training as well (ensuring, of course, that this does not interfere with its primary use). However, a lack of standardization may create problems when trying to make secondary use of equipment in the workplace (or even in dedicated local centres). While audio- and video-players generally use standard format cassettes, there are greater variations when it comes to the use of computers and associated technologies (e.g. interactive video).

Many larger companies and educational institutions have created local centres to support open or distance learning and these generally allow a wide range of media to be used by learners. Usually, it is only in centres of this kind that learners can get access to media facilities like interactive video or teleconferencing equipment. However, access to such centres is not always convenient for learners as they may be located at some distance from home or the normal workplace and prebooking of the facilities may be required. Some open or distance learning courses include a short residential component at which groups of learners come together for group sessions. Such occasions allow learners to use media that would otherwise be inaccessible to them, as equipment can be set up specially for the event.

In whatever location you expect the learning to take place, you should consider what equipment is already available and what may need to be provided (and by whom). Is there any possibility that particular groups of learners will be disadvantaged by the use of certain media, for example video or computers at home? What contingency arrangements can you make for learners who, for one reason or another, are unable to get access to the media-based materials you are planning to use?

COSTS

Closely related to issues of access and distribution are the cost factors and these play a key role in many decisions that are made about the use of media for open or distance learning. Costs to the learners may include (if necessary) the expense of acquiring and operating equipment, travel to special centres, etc., while the cost of all teaching materials is normally included within a tuition fee (if applicable). When considering costs to the institution or organization providing open or distance education it is usually helpful to categorize them as *capital* or *recurrent*, or as being *fixed* or *variable*.

Capital and recurrent costs

Capital costs are the 'one-off' costs incurred in acquiring premises, equipment, etc. In terms of media for open or distance learning this might include the cost of setting up a sound studio, a video unit or a desk-top publishing suite. But in addition to these capital costs for production, there may also be 'local' capital costs for providing multiple workstations or equipping local study or training centres. If your learners are spread across a wide geographical area, you are likely to find that the total cost of equipment that is used by learners will be greater than the equipment costs for central production. So it makes sense to find out what facilities already exist and what equipment you already have, both for production and for use by learners. What additional provision is necessary or feasible?

Recurrent costs include the expenses that are incurred as long as the capital equipment is being utilized, i.e. staff and running costs, the production costs of learning materials, etc. If a central media unit is fully utilized, the recurrent (production) costs could well be greater than the capital (equipment) costs, particularly if video materials or computer software are being developed.

Fixed and variable costs

In media production, the fixed costs are those that are independent of the number of people for whom materials are developed. For example, the cost of producing and broadcasting a television programme remains more or less constant whether there are 20 or 20,000 learners who view the transmission. However, if the same programme were sent on video-cassettes to individual learners, the copying and distribution costs would vary according to the size of audience. So variable costs depend upon the number of copies required.

The fixed and variable cost components for different media vary. For example, you will find that both the fixed and variable costs of audio-cassettes are low, while both costs are high for interactive video. A computer-based learning programme designed to operate on a mainframe computer accessed from multiple terminals will have high fixed costs, but low variable costs compared with a similar CBL programme distributed on floppy disc to individual learners.

The number of potential learners is important in determining the cost effectiveness of any medium. So, for any particular teaching or training situation you will need to consider how many learners will receive the materials, because the presentation costs (copying, distribution, etc.) must be added to the production costs.

TEACHING FUNCTIONS

Both a video-cassette and a textbook can be very valuable in teaching and training, but they differ in terms of the type and the form of the information they carry. Because different media convey differing forms of symbol system (sound, written language, moving pictures, etc.), each has its own potential in terms of the teaching or learning that it can effectively promote. Table 6.1 (adapted from Bates, 1989) indicates the symbol systems for a range of media.

Table 6.1   Differences in symbol systems between media

	Lecture	Audio	Print	Computer	Video
Voice	✔	✔	✘	?	✔
Written language	✔	✘	✔	✔	✔
Colour	✔	✘	?	?	✔
Still picture	✔	✘	✔	✔	✔
Animation	✘	✘	✘	✔	✔
Events	?	✔	✔	?	✔
Full movement	✘	✘	✘	✘	✔

? = usually at higher cost, or only occasionally, or with difficulty.

Classroom-based teaching and training is still largely undertaken by means of the lecture or a similar form of presentation. It relies on the human voice to convey spoken language, although written words, diagrams and pictures can easily be provided to illustrate or reinforce the spoken word. If your teaching or training relies solely on printed materials, you can make full use of written language, symbols, diagrams, drawings, pictures and you can describe real events with words and illustrations. However, you cannot convey sounds or speech, animation or moving pictures. If you use computer-based materials, you can convey written language and symbols, still and animated pictures (possibly in colour) and, with some equipment, you may be able to include sounds or speech. Each medium you consider using can convey certain symbol systems, but not others.

An alternative approach is to consider your desired learning outcomes and then use this analysis to help in the selection of appropriate media. For example, any course seeking to develop skills in the use of a foreign language would need to include some means of conveying the sound of the spoken language; a demonstration of how a complex piece of equipment works would lose a great deal if moving pictures and sounds were not provided. Can you apply this sort of analysis to a teaching or training situation for which you must develop materials? Does it help to clarify what you can (and can't) achieve with the media you have available?

Most media are flexible, in that each can be used for a variety of teaching functions. However, while most media can present abstract knowledge and ideas, which are mainly conveyed through the use of spoken or written language, few media are able to present concrete examples of objects, processes, events, etc. Video material is a very rich and flexible medium capable of conveying both abstract knowledge and concrete examples, so it is particularly valuable for demonstrating procedures or events.

However, you shouldn't only consider the content or form of the teaching when trying to select which medium to use; the kind of learning skills to be developed must also be considered, e.g. motor skills, comprehension, problem-solving, interpersonal skills, etc. Certain media are better than others in terms of how they represent objects, facts, ideas, processes, etc., and their potential to develop learning skills. Text is particularly good for comprehension, abstract ideas, developing arguments, etc. Computers are good for rule-based knowledge, for which there are correct answers or procedures. Video material is particularly good for procedural and interpersonal skills and for conveying concrete examples. It is also good for presenting complex, real-life situations that require interpretation, where ambiguity may be advantageous and a variety of learner responses acceptable.

LEARNER CONTROL

Open or distance learning is more likely to be effective if individual learners can exert control over the media being used in order to interact with the educational content of the material. However, the extent to which learners can control and interact with media technologies varies in a number of ways: the ease and flexibility of use, the level of interactivity and the extent to which dialogue is made possible. Factors such as these may have a bearing on the selection of media suitable for a particular purpose or group of learners.

Some media technologies are easier to use than others, i.e. they are easily portable, require only familiar skills to operate, etc. Text materials and audio-cassettes can be used in many more locations than interactive video. They also tend to be more 'user-friendly' than most computer-based media.

Media-based materials also vary in the extent to which they allow learners to interact intellectually with the content. For example, the audience for radio programmes have no control over when the transmissions take place and cannot stop and review any sections they find unclear or wish to consider further. Learning is likely to be more effective if there are permanent materials with which learners can interact (books, cassettes, CBL on disc, etc.) rather than just ephemeral events like lectures and broadcasts. This can have implications for the design of learning materials. For example, video or audio material that learners will use from cassette need not resemble a broadcast programme; it can be structured in a format that encourages interaction and flexibility of use.

It is often claimed that computers offer greater potential for learner control and interaction than other media. In principle this may be true, but much depends upon the nature of the interaction that is facilitated. Most computer programs invite learners to respond to questions or to undertake activities and, on the basis of the responses made, the program can provide feedback and diagnose problems or misconceptions. However, the *quality* of the interactivity can be very limited because the questions posed and the forms of response that can be made are often teacher centred rather than being adaptable and learner centred (Laurillard, 1987).

Most media are restricted in the extent to which they allow learners to engage in some form of dialogue. Printed text materials, broadcasts, audio- and video-cassettes all provide one-way communication, although open or distance teaching or training materials using these media often attempt to simulate dialogue and engage learners directly (see, for example, Chapter 8 by Fred Lockwood).

Until quite recently only the telephone enabled dialogue to take place in distance learning. However, recent developments in telecommunications and computer networking have enabled communication between learners and teachers to take place by a variety of means, for example audio- and tele-conferencing, electronic mail and computer conferencing. In particular, computer-mediated communication not only facilitates two-way correspondence, but it can also support group and many-to-many communications; dispersed learners and teachers can communicate in ways that are more open-ended and less didactic than is usually the case in open and distance education. This can have implications for the design of teaching materials, which may no longer need to be centrally prepared and controlled.

REFERENCES

Bates, A. W. (1989) *Towards a European Electronic University: Technology and Course Design for European-Wide Distance Education Courses*, European Association of Distance Teaching Universities, Heerlen, The Netherlands.

Gunter, B. and McLaughlin, C. (1993) *Television: The Public's View 1992*, John Libbey, London.

Laurillard, D. (1987) Computers and the emancipation of students: giving control to the learner, *Instructional Science*, Vol. 16, no. 1, pp. 3–18.

PART 2
PRODUCTION

Overview

Bernadette Robinson

The production of ODL materials can be a creative and hazardous endeavour, as you may already have discovered at first hand. Most people new to it underestimate the time, thought and effort it takes, even for experienced writers and producers. Producing good-quality materials is not a mechanical process, depending only on technical 'know-how'. It raises fundamental questions about curriculum design, values in the teaching–learning process and relationships between teacher and learner. For these reasons, it is a demanding activity. Good-quality materials are not produced by chance. The six authors in this part show, in different ways, how to replace some of the chance elements with deliberate strategy. Some of them also question existing assumptions about producing ODL materials and suggest alternatives to be tried. For all of them, the underlying theme is the pursuit of quality.

GETTING STARTED: OPTIONS AND CHOICES

Faced with the task of producing materials, where do you begin? What's the best way? What are the options open to you? These are the questions explored in the chapters by Derek Rowntree and David Hawkridge. An underused (and commonly undervalued) option in the provision of ODL materials is the use of existing ones. One consequence of ignoring this option can be unnecessary duplication of effort (which might be better directed to adding value to what already exists). Rowntree's informative chapter (Chapter 7) will dispel readers' reluctance to consider this as a serious alternative. He provides a practical guide to the process of deciding whether and how to make use of of existing materials. He examines the pros and cons of either adopting or adapting materials and provides a checklist of criteria for evaluating a package, a useful aid for informed decision-making. Before taking the plunge into the production of materials from scratch, materials producers would do well to spend time checking the feasibility of this option as a first step.

If, for good reasons, you decide to create your own materials, their construction and production require a variety of expertise and roles. What is the best way to deploy this expertise? What kinds of groups or teams are needed? David Hawkridge (Chapter 9) takes a fresh look at several models for ODL teams, from the highly resourced course teams at The Open University to a minimalist model (of one). He assesses their various strengths and weaknesses. As well as questioning assumptions about the best way to produce courses, his chapter is also an invitation to experiment. You may wish to create your own kind of course team to suit your circumstances after considering the options he describes.

CONTENT QUALITY AND TEACHING EFFECTIVENESS

Having embarked on the business of creating materials, how can you ensure that the final product will be relevant to learners and will meet planned objectives? What can you do to ensure their quality during the production process? One important way of building quality assurance into materials production is developmental testing (a kind of formative evaluation). Hossein Zand's chapter (Chapter 12) provides a valuable guide to this. He shows how to tap different sources of feedback (subject specialists, colleagues as critical readers and learners) and how to make use of this to improve the quality of the materials. In my experience developmental testing is given too low a priority in many new ODL ventures and is sometimes neglected altogether, especially when resources are scarce and deadlines are pressing. To avoid this, developmental testing activities need to be included in project planning schedules and in initial resource allocation (of staff time and money). It is surprising how often this is omitted. Yet even small amounts of systematic developmental testing can produce significant improvements in the materials, provided there is opportunity and time allowed for revision in response to the findings.

Fitting the design of materials to the learner is also the underlying theme of Ellie Chambers' practical chapter on assessing learner workload (Chapter 10). As she says, this is a neglected aspect of materials development. It is often difficult for materials producers, especially those new to the job, to judge the workload they demand of learners. Even experienced writers get it wrong, as many learners can testify. Often writers and producers have an unrealistic view of the demands their materials make on learners' time. They probably use only guesswork or previous experience to base their judgement on. Here Chambers describes some rules of thumb for assessing learner workload in a systematic way. You will be able to test this out for yourself, to see if it is valid in your circumstances and for your groups of learners (for example, you may have a group who are learning in their second language, or learning a highly technical subject, or very young learners). One unexpected consequence of the assessment of workload in this way may be to improve the quality of course design in another. In reappraising the content, writers may be forced to distinguish more sharply between what learners 'must know', 'should know' and 'could know' (or know 'how to do') in order to become capable in some area or domain.

DESIGNING MATERIALS FOR INDEPENDENT LEARNING

Quality of learning outcomes is the focus of the chapters by Alastair Morgan and Fred Lockwood. Morgan (Chapter 11) examines the relationship between assessment design and the development of learner autonomy. Do some learning tasks militate against the development of autonomy and independence in learners? Do others facilitate? Morgan argues that the relationship is a crucial one because the design of assessment is a direct influence on the quality of learning outcomes. He is critical of the restrictive nature of 'orthodox' approaches to text construction and learning tasks, examining the underlying model of teaching and learning (that of 'banking' knowledge). He argues a strong and persuasive case for project-based learning as a vehicle for independent learners, and for allowing greater responsibility and control to learners. He gives an example of a project design (from an Open University course on 'Environment') which is unusual in basing it explicitly of an experiential learning cycle.

What are the implications of project-based learning for the presentation of such courses? Will the tutor's role be the same as on other courses or different? Morgan only briefly touches on these, though there are a number of changes which result. In my experience of organizing learner and tutor support for such courses:

- tutors play a more influential role;
- the tutor's role needs to be defined carefully and communicated or negotiated (some tutors are more anxious tutoring project-based courses);
- the distribution of resources and contact pattern for support shifts to different crucial points in the course. The initial choice-making phase is one crucial point for support and interaction (as Morgan suggests) since bad choices and plans can have disastrous consequences later on. The phases of data analysis and writing up are others;
- the tutoring load is likely to be heavier than more conventional courses because of higher levels of interaction between student and tutor (this may have cost implications);
- 'weak' students need more monitoring and support than on conventional courses; most students need more assistance with time management;
- tutors need more support and more opportunities for peer contact, consultation and exchange of learners' project work-in-progress; and
- the moderation of marking is more time consuming and needs more use of second (or third) markers (possibly incurring extra cost).

One item of material that is essential to produce for project-based learning is an informative and reassuring tutor's guide All of this is an argument for the production and presentation of materials to be planned as a whole.

Assessment, although very important, is not the only means of enabling learners to develop independence and autonomy in the course of studying ODL materials. After all, some courses or materials do not have assessment components. Another way is through the inclusion of activities in the materials. As Fred Lockwood shows (Chapter 8), the purpose of activities is not simply to get the learner to do something (*anything*) at points in the text. The activities reflect different intentions and models of learning and teaching held by the writer. Lockwood describes three approaches to designing activities. He shows how they can stimulate the learner to engage in a personal way with the content of a text or to go beyond it by applying it to their own world. The third kind ('dialogue') is a rather different form of 'activity' from the first two; it is a way of presenting the text to include other voices in order to avoid the basis of a single perspective and to stimulate reflective thinking. Quotations or 'other voices' can enliven a text powerfully, but need to be used discerningly (I find large amounts become tedious to read). There may be a point at which such dialogue would be better presented on audio-cassette, to bring some *real* voices into it. You might wish to experiment with this, to find the crossover point at which the audio medium becomes more appropriate. In my experience of working on ODL projects, the design of activities in texts is often one of the weakest elements. This chapter should prompt writers to rethink their approach to writing activities.

WHAT NEXT?

The chapters in this part provide a rich source of sound practical guidance. They also offer ideas for experiment in producing ODL materials. The next step is to try out some of them.

7

Existing material: how to find it, evaluate it and customize it

Derek Rowntree *

Most open learning depends on prepackaged learning materials. Do you have to develop your own or can you buy them off the shelf? How might you find out what packages are available ready-made? How can you evaluate their quality and value for money? Perhaps you can adapt an existing package to suit your learners' needs. Or perhaps you can write a study guide that will enable your learners to use materials that were never meant for open learning at all. And what might be the relative cost of all such options? This chapter should help you consider these crucial questions.

WHAT KIND OF MATERIALS DO YOUR LEARNERS NEED?

It is not usually thought adequate to direct open learners towards the nearest library and encourage them to browse at will. We normally provide them with specially written materials – or with existing materials that we have organized (and perhaps added to) specifically to meet their peculiar needs.

So what do your learners need? To answer this question, you probably need to talk with learners and with colleagues, clients and other interested parties. Through interviews, group discussions, telephone conversations, question-naires and brainstorming, you may be able to draft a specification for the kind of package your learners need.

What might your specification cover? Look at the sections in the evaluation checklist below. Try to agree and write down what you and your learners and colleagues would desire, or at least find acceptable, under each heading.

Evaluating an open learning package

Audience	For whom is it intended – e.g. what prior knowledge, interest, experience, attitudes and learning skills does it require? Is its target audience sufficiently like ours?
Objectives	Are the learning objectives sufficiently similar to those of our learners?
Assessment	How is assessment catered for (if at all) within the package? Is this consistent with what we might want for our learners?

*The author has adapted the material in this chapter from his book *Exploring Open and Distance Learning*, Kogan Page, London, 1992.

Coverage	Is the subject-matter appropriate to our learners and the objectives? Is it accurate and up to date? Broad enough? Balanced? Any serious omissions?
Time	How much time might the package (including any assessment) demand of learners? Is this realistic for our learners?
Teaching	Is the teaching method (e.g. didactic *v.* experiential) acceptable? Are media used appropriately? What kind of demands might be made on support staff – e.g. advisers, tutors, line managers, mentors, etc? Can we provide the necessary individual support?
Style	Is the style of the material suitable for our learners – e.g. tone, vocabulary, sentence length, examples, use of pictorial material? Is it lively and interesting?
Physical format	Is it attractive in appearance? Legible? Durable? Portable? Suited to how it will be used?
Reputation	Does the material (and/or the producers) have a 'track record'? Who has used it before? How well has it been received by other users?
Costs	How much to hire or buy? What additional costs are there – e.g. video players, support system, staff development, adaptations to package? Is this within our budget and/or that of our learners?
Availability	How easily/quickly can we obtain sufficient copies? Will it continue to be available?
Likely benefits	Are learners likely to get what they would expect from using the package? Is the organization?
Alternatives	How does this material compare with other existing material and with what we might produce ourselves?

WAYS OF OBTAINING A SUITABLE PACKAGE

Once you've got some sort of specification in mind (or preferably on paper) you can make a realistic decision about how best to meet it. Here you have three main options:

- Use an existing 'off-the-shelf' open learning package – with or without existing material of your own.
- Build on existing *non*-open learning material – e.g. textbooks or videos or from government departments.
- Plan and develop a custom-made package from scratch.

Make or buy?

The first of the above options is the cheap and easy way to get an open learning programme up and running – provided someone else has already developed a suitable package you can use. The second option – where you build your programme around materials that were not developed with open learning in mind – is rather less cheap and easy, but may still be much more so than the ultimate option of developing all your open learning materials from scratch.

Shall we make or buy? That is one of the first decisions to face an organization setting up an open learning system. By now there are hundreds of thousands of open learning hours available in packaged form – many of them of excellent quality.

Unless you are in business to develop open learning packages, it is wise to check what else is already available before you consider producing from scratch. Producing your own material can be costly in time, money and interpersonal stress. One can pay a big price for scorning other people's material merely because it's 'not invented here'.

There is no shame in using other people's packages where they are appropriate. Some institutions – like FlexiStudy colleges and the Open Learning Institute of Hong Kong which use chiefly materials from the UK Open University and other providers – have realized that their resources are better focused on providing learners with a support system. Nor do major organizations (often with their own open learning development teams) – like British Gas, ICI and the NHS – have qualms about using management education packages from The Open University, Henley Distance Learning, The Open College or whoever best meets their needs.

OFF-THE-SHELF PACKAGES

There is no shortage of existing material. But will any of it be suitable for your learners? How do you find out just what is available, decide what might be suitable and then get your hands on inspection copies? In what follows, I will suggest a number of ways of tracking down materials that may be suitable – starting off close to home and gradually widening your search. (I give addresses for all the organizations named at end of this chapter.)

Your organization

Have appropriate materials already been bought or made within your organization? Colleagues may know if anything is available in-house. If your organization has a librarian or resources person, he or she might be a good one to start with.

Local sources

Next you might turn to other local sources for information about who is using what in your area, e.g:

• local colleges or other delivery centres;

- local education authority (contact the organizer for adult education);
- public libraries (reference section);
- Training Access Point (TAP) terminals or offices; or
- your nearest Training and Enterprise Council (TEC) or (in Scotland) your Local Enterprise Company (LEC).

Other organizations like yours

Pay particular attention to other organizations (or sections within them) that are in the same line of work as yours. Some may not let you use their packages (or even see them) for reasons of commercial security. But others may be happy to let you use them (at a price) – especially perhaps if they will be able to use some that you are producing.

The Open Learning Directory

If your concern is with professional or vocational training, consult *The Open Learning Directory*. This is a catalogue of more than 2,000 open learning packages updated every year. Many large public libraries will have a copy for reference. If they haven't, they should be able to obtain one or tell you where you'll find one – perhaps in a local FE college. You may want to ensure it is ordered for your own organization's open learning library.

The directory is divided into 18 subject areas – from agriculture through engineering to social welfare. For every package in each subject area it gives a variety of information that should help you decide whether the material might suit you and your learners.

Producers' catalogues

You may want to gather catalogues from all the major producers of open learning packages – The Open University, National Extension College, The Open College, Open Learning Foundation and so on. Between them, they produce a vast range of academic, vocational, personal development and community education material.

There are many other producers catering for learners in specific occupational groups – glass, knitting, electrical engineering and so on. *The Open Learning Directory* has a section listing most of the producers and the main subject categories their packages cover.

International Centre for Distance Learning (ICDL)

If you want to spread your wings yet further and are interested in academic packages, contact ICDL. This is a documentation centre on distance education worldwide, based at The Open University but funded internationally. Its database carries details about more than 14,000 courses and programmes, more than 300 institutions and more than 3,000 items from the literature of distance education. The database can be accessed either by on-line computer or via compact disc.

Other sources

Perhaps you know of numerous other sources. You may be able to pick up news of packages in your field by scanning the journals regularly and attending the occasional training exhibition or conference. If you are concerned with National (or Scottish) Vocational Qualifications you may want to consult some of the databases produced by the Employment Department in which available packages are matched against the published competences.

EVALUATING A PACKAGE

Suppose you do come to hear of a package that seems to suit your specification – relevant subject area, right level, appropriate media, acceptable price and so on. The next step is to get hold of a copy and see whether it really is what you need. You may want to evaluate it from the viewpoint of both subject coverage and likely teaching effectiveness. And even if it seems suitable on those criteria, how will it fit in with your organization's constraints of time, money, staffing and other scarce resources?

Such evaluation is not to be rushed, if you want to avoid making an expensive mistake. It may take some time, especially if you have only one copy of the material and you want to involve others in the evaluation. For instance, if your first impressions are favourable, you may well want to get comments from:

- subject experts
- open learning experts
- administration colleagues
- contacts elsewhere who've used the materials
- learners' line managers
- tutors who know the intended learners
- the learners themselves.

Evaluation checklists

You may find it useful to work with a checklist when you evaluate. The one at the beginning of this chapter shows some questions I might ask about a package. But you'll need to draft your own checklist, based on your own concerns.

In fact, you may want to give different checklists to different people. For example, you may want to ask

- tutors to focus on whether the package seems likely to teach effectively;
- subject experts to focus on whether it teaches what it ought to teach; and
- learners to tell you what they like or dislike about it and how they think it might be improved.

Adapting a package

Even the best package you come across is unlikely to be one hundred per cent right for your learners. You may decide you need to modify or adapt it in one of the following ways:

- '*Badging*'. The content and treatment is all right but you decide to present the material with your colours and logo (perhaps in a new box or ring binder) to reflect your organization's image.
- *Study guidance*. You provide a study guide advising learners how best to use the package in your context, e.g. which sections are not relevant, where to go for help, tutorial arrangements, etc.
- *Local examples*. Again, the content and treatment is acceptable but you decide to add examples or case studies that are more closely related to your learners' interests.
- *New content*. Some parts of your syllabus have not been included, or parts of the content are unbalanced or outdated; so you add new material.
- *New media*. You decide your learners would benefit from an additional medium – so you produce, say, an audiotape or videotape to introduce a text-based package or you provide a printed takeaway 'souvenir' of a CBT package.

In any such amendments, we must respect the original publisher's copyright. That is, you can give your learners new material as well as the package material. But you cannot freely print your own customized version of the package, interweaving your new material with the original. If, however, you do want a customized version of the package, you may be able to negotiate with the publisher – as Rover did in getting a computer-based version of the 30-hour BASIC course that had been produced as a text by National Extension College.

PRODUCING A 'WRAP-AROUND'

Despite your best searches, you may find that no suitable open learning package has yet been published. Must you then either embark on what may prove to be the long and costly task of developing all the necessary materials from scratch – or else give up the idea of package-based teaching? Perhaps neither. There may be a middle way.

Although you have not been able to find suitable open learning material, you may be able to find other usable material. That is, you may know of books, videos, audiotapes, etc., that – while not produced with open learning (or even perhaps with any learning) in mind – are nevertheless pretty helpful in getting your subject-matter across. For example, consider

- textbooks
- manuals
- pamphlets
- newspaper clippings

- journal articles
- commercial leaflets
- videos/photographs
- audiotapes/discs
- practical kits
- CBT packs.

If so, you may be able to save a whole lot of time – and give your learners what they need – by writing a study guide that wraps around the chosen item or items and makes up for whatever they lack in open learning terms. (In passing, we might note that many 'mainstream' textbooks are now building in objectives, activities, user-friendly layout and other features that were once peculiar to open learning.)

Your job is to take your chosen items – which may be quite well made teaching texts or, at the other extreme, simply a pile of reference materials – and enable your learners to get what they need from them. From the very earliest days, for example, Open University courses have incorporated existing texts ('set books') – which learners are expected to buy – as well as providing specially written materials in a variety of media.

So, depending on what you judge to be missing, your study guide might contain any of the following items:

- advice on how to use the material
- learning objectives
- introductions/overviews
- summaries
- glossaries
- clearer explanations
- contrasting viewpoints
- alternative examples
- illustrations
- local case studies
- activities (especially locally relevant ones)
- feedback on such activities
- instructions for practical work
- assignments for discussion with tutor, colleagues, etc.

Again, you must respect copyright law. You can't reprint freely newspaper cuttings and journal articles or make a scrapbook of bits and pieces from whichever textbooks and manuals you happen to like the look of. You have two options. One is for you or the learners to pay for complete copies of any texts or other items you use. The other is for you to negotiate with the owners of the copyright to let you adapt their material and reproduce it in a form suited to your needs.

Even if you have to buy copies or pay for copyright permissions, producing a wraparound may still be cheaper than producing a complete package from scratch. Whether it is, of course, depends largely on how much work you need to do on your study guide and any other media you want to add. For example, you might want to offer case-study material on video- or audio-cassette; or activities and feedback in the form of a computer-based training package.

In general, the most expensive element of package-based learning is not the cost of the materials themselves or even the cost of high-tech equipment (where that is needed). Rather it is the salary costs of the people involved in materials development. Any approach that cuts down on development time (while still providing learners with what they need) is always worth considering very seriously.

WHERE MIGHT YOU GO FROM HERE?

- Find out which staff in your organization have experience of producing open learning materials. Get their views about the pros and cons of developing new materials compared with using open learning materials (or *non*-open learning materials) that exist already. You might consider setting this up as a seminar to share experience.
- Find and evaluate some existing materials, i.e.:
  — draft a specification for the kind of package your learners and your organization need;
  — seek out some likely sounding materials; and
  — evaluate the materials against your specification, if possible as a team exercise with other people.
- If you can find more-or-less usable materials, draw up a detailed list of what you would need to do by way of adaptation. (Try, if you can, to consult with some of your likely learners.)
- If you can't find any suitable open learning materials, see if you can find some suitable non-open learning materials – and draw up a detailed contents list for a wraparound study guide.
- If all else fails, consider a made-to-measure package, e.g.:
  — develop it in your own organization; or
  — collaborate with similar organizations; or
  — commission a specialist producer of open learning materials.

However, unless you have special needs – and a good supply of money, time and skills – the best advice is probably still that offered by Roger Lewis and Nigel Paine (1986):

> The arguments for choosing one of the other options are thus compelling. Time, money and effort should be saved. The end product is more likely to be good. The energies of teachers and trainers can be deployed in areas where they are more likely to bear fruit, for example in devising flexible support and management systems.

SOURCES OF OPEN LEARNING MATERIALS OR ADVICE

Learning Methods Branch
Employment Department
Moorfoot
Sheffield S1 4PQ
(Tel: 0742–594690/753275)
NVQ/SVQ databases and other initiatives.

International Centre for Distance Learning
The Open University
Milton Keynes MK7 6AA
(Tel: 0908–653537)
Documentation centre on distance education worldwide. Its database carries details about more than 25,000 courses.

National Extension College
18 Brooklands Avenue
Cambridge CB2 2HN
(Tel: 0223–316644)
Offers a range of courses including GCSE subjects, preparatory courses for The Open University, office skills and personal development.

Open College of the Arts
Worsbrough
Barnsley
South Yorkshire S70 6TU
(Tel: 0226–730495)
Practical courses on art and design, painting, sculpture, textiles, photography and creative writing.

The Open Learning Directory
Published annually by Pergamon Press, Oxford. Details of 2000-plus packages in professional and vocational training.

Open Learning Foundation
Angel Gate
City Road
London EC1 2RS
(Tel: 071–833 3757)
Widening range of undergraduate course materials being put together by a consortium of the former polytechnics.

National Open Learning Library
BOLDU Ltd
St George's House
40–49 Price Street
Birmingham B4 6LA
(Tel: 021–359 6628)
Has 6,000 items for inspection by visitors – but no borrowing.

Open College
St Pauls
781 Wilmslow Road
Didsbury
Manchester M20 8RW
(Tel: 061–434 0007)
Offers a range of materials in such areas as accountancy, management, information technology and retailing.

The Open University and Open Business School
Milton Keynes MK7 6AA
(Tel: 0908–274066)
Many other organizations now run courses based on OU materials in undergraduate education and in vocational and professional updating courses – e.g. in management, health service and social work, teaching and technology.

REFERENCES AND FURTHER READING

Kember, D. (1991) *Writing Study Guides*, Technical and Educational Services, Bristol. Excellent advice on how to produce wraparound study guides, which itself takes the form of a study guide wrapped around Rowntree, 1990.

Lewis, R. and Paine, N. (1986) *How to Find and Adapt Materials and Select Media*, Council for Educational Technology, London. A down-to-earth guide that is still very useful despite developments in media and production technology since it first appeared.

Rowntree, D. (1990) *Teaching through Self-Instruction*, Kogan Page, London. A comprehensive collection of suggestions and examples for anyone who needs to produce open learning materials from scratch.

Rowntree, D. (1992) *Exploring Open and Distance Learning*, Kogan Page, London. An overview of the field, with chapters on varieties of openness, open learners, types of learning, learner support, media, costs, evaluation, implementation and the pros and cons of open learning, as well as the role of packaged materials.

8

Encouraging active learning: models appropriate for self-instruction

Fred Lockwood

A major characteristic of open and distance learning texts is the inclusion of activities (self-assessment questions, in-text questions, exercises, etc.), where a teacher poses a question in the text and learners formulate a response with the author providing a follow-up comment. This chapter will briefly review the rationale for the inclusion of such activities in self-instructional texts. It will describe and illustrate three models that have been developed for the design of such activities: the tutorial-in-print, reflective action guide and dialogue.

THE CONTEXT

If you were to look through examples of self-instructional material from a whole range of subject areas and types of institution you would notice that they all possess one common characteristic: they all contain activities. That is, they all pose questions in the text inviting the learner to respond in some way. Why is this so? Why do teachers and trainers in different areas and from different countries, organizations and cultures include them? Certainly, they expend considerable time and energy in devising them; why do they do this, why are activities such a characteristic of self-instructional material? Their presence in material, from the earliest stages of school to postgraduate level, from industrial to commercial training, is not mere coincidence. The writers who devise them must have sound pedagogic reasons for doing so.

When I pose these questions to teachers and trainers they argue that activities are needed to help learners to come up with their own explanations and solutions, to sort out the features of an argument, to draw inferences, to engage in controversy, to think for themselves and to apply their learning. They remark that activities provide opportunities for learners to be exposed to competing ideas and views, experience those tasks that are typical of the subject, practise important objectives, relate their own ideas and experience to the topic in question, reflect on the implications of their learning, monitor their progress and check their understanding. A common belief, strongly held, is that activities are needed to encourage learners to use the material actively. These authors do not want their learners to be merely passive readers; they want them involved in the material.

If there are good reasons for devising activities in self-instructional material, the next obvious question is how do authors devise them; what are the models upon which their design is based? I would like to describe and illustrate three different ones. The first, and one that has been extremely influential, is the concept of a 'tutorial-in-print' (Rowntree, 1973). The second, termed 'reflective action guide' (Rowntree, 1992) could be regarded as a development of the tutorial-in-print but has distinctive differences which have only recently been articulated. The third, 'dialogue' (Evans and Nation, 1989) is one that has attracted relatively little attention but one that I feel has considerable potential.

TUTORIAL-IN-PRINT

The main idea behind the concept of a tutorial-in-print is deceptively simple. It starts by asking writers to imagine they have a learner in their company for several hours and to describe the *ideal* form of teaching that would take place if a topic of their choice was to be taught as effectively and efficiently as possible; to consider simply what the teacher would be doing and what the learner would be expected to do during this time. Let me ask you. If you had a learner in your company for two hours and wished to teach a topic, idea, skill or whatever, what would you do and what would you expect your learner to do?

Although I can't know what you would do, Rowntree argued that if you really were considering the *ideal* form of teaching it was highly unlikely that you would simply talk at the learner for hour after hour; he simply didn't believe it would happen. Instead he thought you would probably regard a one-to-one tutorial as an *ideal* form of teaching and describe this form of interaction. In such a tutorial, information, source material, procedures, techniques, arguments, research findings, pictures, raw data, etc., etc., would be presented, ideas communicated and learners would be asked to respond to a variety of questions. In some cases the actual answer would be provided, in others a commentary or feedback would be provided. In such a context a learner could be asked a whole series of questions – dependent upon the nature of the topic and form the teaching was to take. The learner could be asked to recall items of information, to define concepts, draw together arguments, justify particular statements, consult other sources, interpret data, compare different interpretations of the same data, work out examples, discuss things with others and perhaps produce something themselves. In short, teachers would expect the exercise of certain study skills by which the learner constructs his or her own picture of the subject and learns to integrate what has just been taught with what had been learnt before feedback was provided. Rowntree's tutorial-in-print is simply a simulation of this tutorial process, this *ideal* form of teaching, in print.

Furthermore, the design of activities, which are consistent with the concept of a tutorial-in-print, need not be restricted to words within a specially printed study guide. Activities can contribute to learning in relation to, for example, newspapers, technical reports, video and audio recordings, periodicals and other published material, records, tapes and discs, experiments, tables, maps, charts, photographs and so on.

The tutorial-in-print tries to simulate the personal tutor but in a situation where the tutor can predict fairly accurately the sort of response a learner is likely to make. It is most appropriate when the topic in question or the body of knowledge can be clearly identified. As such it is fairly easy to identify those features associated with an activity, of the tutorial-in-print type, and the material that surrounds it. These features would probably include the following:

- *Context* – that describes or explains the topic, issue, ideas or whatever from which the activity emerges.
- *Subheading* – or the section or part of the text in which the activity occurs.
- *Typographical* – icons, student stoppers or other typographical features to flag that an activity is being posed.
- *Title* – to identify the particular activity and distinguish it from others.
- *Rationale* – to say why the activity is worthy of time and attention.
- *Time* – to indicate the scope and depth of a response (dependent, of course, on the abilities, interests and experience of the learner).
- *Instructions* – to advise the learner on the appropriate ways to format a response.
- *Example* – of appropriate or plausible but inappropriate responses.
- *Space* – in which to record a response.
- *Feedback* – on the range of response typically given and as a springboard into the next part of the teaching material.

Note: a more detailed description of these features is available elsewhere (Lockwood, 1992)

REFLECTIVE ACTION GUIDE

If I said that during a course of study much of the important learning could occur outside the self-instructional package, when a learner wasn't actually reading it, I suspect you would agree. If I said the greater proportion of study time to be devoted to a particular course may take place away from the teaching package you may still agree – but maybe less readily. If I said that during a course of study the nature of the actual activities would be so varied as to make it extremely difficult or even impossible to predict the outcome, I suspect you may begin to feel uneasy. However, this is the situation, where there isn't a clear body of knowledge to be mastered and where independent learning is encouraged, that is at the centre of the concept of the reflective action guide.

Learners have long been equipped with the information and guidelines they need to engage in a learning task away from the classroom or textbook. I am sure you can think of examples where learners have been sent off to perform a whole variety of tasks ranging from scientific fieldwork, collecting survey data via interviews, searching library archives, checking the construction and appropriateness of a bridge of their choice, monitoring the pollution of local streams and rivers to recording noise levels in a locality. However, only recently has anyone made a clear distinction between those activities that relate to a known 'body of knowledge' and those that relate to 'one's own, unique situation' – to the models of a tutorial-in-print and the reflective action guide respectively (Rowntree, 1992).

The concept of the reflective action guide is based upon several assumptions. A major one is that such activities merely offer advice and guidance to the learner's actions – actions in real and varied contexts, where some skill or ability is developed or refined, and where it is undertaken outside the confines of the printed text and which cannot be predicted. This could range from a farmer determining the balance of cereal crops, livestock and woodland for his or her own land, a trainer manager applying management techniques to his or her own department, a walker deciding which route to take between two selected points, to an industrial chemist exploring company marketing techniques.

A second feature of activities of the reflective action guide type is that the learner must be involved in thinking critically and reflectively upon his or her actions in order to guide the learning experience. It marks a major distinction between working within known parameters and setting them for oneself.

A third feature is that such activities are often demanding, time consuming and relate to the unique situation in which the learner finds him or herself. Whilst resources, guidelines and suggestions can be offered, and drawn upon as and when needed, it is virtually impossible to provide feedback that would relate to the outcome of the activity in question. Learners need to gather and assess the feedback themselves. For example, when the National Coaching Foundation, in conjunction with the Scottish Sports Council, offered self-instructional material on 'Muscle Injuries and Treatment' (Farrally, 1991) it encouraged learners to seek sportsmen and women who had received muscle injuries, provided a framework by which they could be categorized and guidelines by which treatment and rates of recovery could be assessed. There was no way in which the teacher could predict the range and nature of the information collected – but it could be assumed that it was likely to fit within the parameters and to bring the teaching to life.

DIALOGUE

Some years ago an author argued that the more explanatory and clear the exposition the less there was for the student to do; that some texts were so perfect as to stifle all real thinking. He maintained that

> If there is an inference to be drawn, the author draws it, and if there is a significant relationship to be noted, the author points it out. There are no loose ends or incomplete analyses . . . the author does all the thinking. The book never gives a clue that the author pondered (maybe even agonized) over hundreds of decisions. The result is that the creative process and the controversy of competing ideas is hidden from the students.
>
> (Sanders, 1966, p. 158)

More recently, when expressing concern about the teaching methods that writers were employing in much self-instructional material, the limiting effect of many teaching texts was again identified. The writer in question remarked that 'I have seen some brilliantly articulated and beautifully illustrated course texts, but they especially can leave the student with a feeling of inadequacy in the face of such perfection, or (even worse) uncritical contentment with having been "enlightened"' (Evans, 1989, p. 117).

Evans and fellow writer/researcher Daryl Nation have argued strongly for a greater emphasis upon dialogue in self-instructional material; for the communication that the material generates and the reflective activities that they believe should permeate the whole teaching material. In a recent article they argue strongly for students to be actively engaged in constructing meaning for themselves rather than being the mere receptacles of information supplied by the teacher. For Evans and Nation, 'dialogue involves the idea that humans in communication are engaged actively in the making and exchange of meanings, it is not merely about the *transmission* of messages' (Evans and Nation 1989, p. 37).

Dialogue involves sharing the thinking of the writer with the learner – to reproduce the form of communication that would take place between teacher and student as well as student and teacher during the process of learning. It does not assume a closed system where the boundaries of students' knowledge is set, questions posed and answers anticipated. It believes that learners, especially those studying self-instructional material, are the key persons responsible for their own learning.

Evans, Nation and others have illustrated how dialogue can permeate self-instructional material. For example, during 'An introduction to critical issues in distance education' (Evans, 1991), the writer presents his argument in a normal typeface. He then shares his own thinking with the readers, and invites them to reflect on the points raised, by counterposing material presented in *italic* print. Elsewhere a three-way discussion of the actual concept of dialogue is represented as a transcript of the discussion between colleagues (Modra, 1991); whilst a dialogue between student, teacher and writer (Nunan, 1991) illustrates how other perspectives can be brought to the topic in question. Nunan represented the three perspectives by three different typefaces: serif for the writer, italic for the student and sanserif for the teacher.

Dialogue has been exploited in teaching texts where the exchange is presented as an 'aside' (Ostwald and Chen, 1993). In their article (p. 8) Ostwald and Chen liken this 'aside' to a casual soliloquy:

> It is like the informal introduction to a presentation, or in a Shakespearian sense, when the actor turns towards the audience and delivers a private but insightful reading of the situation purely to allow the audience to understand the scene, and the play continues. It should be noted that the Shakespearian narrator always spoke in the language of the populace, thus it might be seen as a vernacular voice.

One way of deciding if the concept of dialogue is appropriate to your teaching and whether the inclusion of 'invented voices', narrators or personal revelations could contribute to your material is to spend a bit of time thinking about it and even trying to draft some material.

If you are unsure you could try discussing the concept of dialogue with a friend or colleague – even asking their opinion on the sample material you have drafted and how they would react to it. In fact, as soon as you start doing this, and documenting it, you would be on the way to producing a dialogue for the topic in question!

CONCLUSION

The three concepts influencing the design of activities are not mutually exclusive. Indeed, when training materials were assembled by the National Association of Clinical Tutors (1990) the self-instructional material included activities of both the tutorial-in-print and reflective action guide type, as well as incorporating interjections from four 'invented' clinical tutors (the medical audience for whom the self-instructional training materials were designed). Within the textual material, 40 interjections, designed to encourage reflection by the learners and foster dialogue, were positioned (in bold italics) within the text. 'Invented voices', flagged by a corresponding portrait sketch of the clinical tutor, complemented the more usual activities. However, I suspect that in any survey of teaching material you undertook you would find that activities of the tutorial-in-print type dominated, with significantly less of the reflective action guide type and relatively few examples illustrating dialogue.

The important point, however, is not the relative balance of the types of activity but rather the extent to which they succeed in enabling teachers and trainers to satisfy their aims, to involve their learners and realize the objectives or competences that have been specified. In this context I am reminded of the study conducted some time ago which explored students' reaction to the presence and absence of activities in self-instructional texts (Duchastel and Whitehead, 1980). When Duchastel and Whitehead surveyed students they concluded (p. 46): 'students value in-text questions as useful study aids . . . 60 per cent of the students believed that the absence of questions had hindered their study of the unit, and *none* claimed that the absence had helped them.' What do you think would be the reactions of your learners?

REFERENCES AND NOTES

Duchastel, P. S. and Whitehead, D. (1980) Exploring student reactions to inserted questions in texts, *Programme Learning and Educational Technology*, Vol. 17, no. 1, pp. 41–7.
Evans, T. (1989) Fiddling while the tome turns: reflections of a distance education development consultant, in M. Parer (ed.) *Development, Design and Distance Education*, Centre for Distance Learning, Gippsland Institute of Advanced Education, Churchill, Victoria.

Evans, T. (1991) An introduction to critical issues in distance education: I, in T. Evans (ed.) *Critical Issues in Distance Education*, Deakin University Press, Geelong.

Evans, T. and Nation, D. (1989) Dialogue in practice, research and theory in distance education, *Open Learning*, Vol. 4, no. 2, pp. 37–42.

Farrally, M. (1991) *An Introduction to the Structure of the Body*, National Coaching Foundation, Leeds, in conjunction with the Scottish Sports Council, Edinburgh.

Lockwood, F. G. (1992) *Activities in Self-Instructional Texts*, Kogan Page, London. In addition to providing research evidence on the role of activities in texts, the book gives a detailed description of the three models and offers a range of examples from education, commerce and industry.

Modra, H. M. (1991) On the possibility of dialogue in distance education: a dialogue, in T. Evans and B. King (eds.) *Beyond the Text: Contemporary Writing on Distance Education*, Deakin University Press, Geelong.

National Association of Clinical Tutors (1990) *NACT Training Package*, 7 St Andrews Place, London NW1 4LG.

Nunan, T. (1991) *An Introduction to Research Paradigms in Distance Education*, Deakin University Press, Geelong.

Ostwald, M. J. and Chen, S. E. (1993) Implementing problem-based learning in distance education, *Media Technology for Human Resource Development*, October.

Rowntree, D. (1973) *Student Exercises in Correspondence Texts*, Open University Institute of Educational Technology, Milton Keynes (mimeo).

Rowntree, D. (1992) *Exploring Open and Distance Learning*, Kogan Page, London.

Sanders, N. M. (1966) *Classroom Questions*, Harper & Row, New York.

9

Which team for open and distance learning materials production?

David Hawkridge

The team has become the standard method of producing self-instructional open and distance learning (ODL) materials. The internationally known but complex Open University team, which depends on leadership by subject-matter experts, can be compared with others. The transformer team is a hybrid, with subject-matter experts taking the lead initially but handing over to technologists who transform the drafts into effective ODL materials. The wraparound team assigns leadership to media specialists. The weekend team compresses creative action by a few people into a weekend or two. Which team is most appropriate for you?

INTRODUCTION

Traditionally, teachers and trainers have been expected to work on their own. Each has been expected to work without direct help from others. It isn't really surprising, then, that teachers and trainers encounter problems in working together in teams to develop ODL materials, or that they have trouble in collaborating with instructional designers and anyone else whose job it is to enhance teaching effectiveness.

The old pattern is now changing, slowly. In 'team teaching', two or more instructors share responsibility for a course, and they may even take classes together. Interdisciplinary courses have become more popular – teachers join forces to present them.

This traditional pattern is challenged sharply by open and distance education. Division of labour, within teams, is the usual way of developing ODL materials. During production, the team is the individual teacher's environment. It matters greatly how well the team is led, and how well people co-operate within it. The team can be supportive or damaging, creative or destructive.

The OU team has achieved international prominence, but others have been successful, too. Some teams are more likely to be appropriate in academic settings, others to industrial or commercial training. Which one suits your needs? How would you choose, given the human and other resources available and the constraints in your situation?

THE OU TEAM

The OU teaches about 200,000 adults annually, mainly at a distance by means of correspondence, television and radio. The course team appeared when the first four courses were developed in 1969–70. It became institutionalized and almost all OU courses are produced by quite large teams.

In the standard OU team there are five kinds of members, with distinctive tasks: subject-matter experts, media specialists (producers for television and radio, video and audio), editors, educational technologists and administrative course managers. The subject-matter experts, members of an OU faculty or consultants, prepare portions of the texts and record broadcasts. 'Writing' experts write drafts and criticize each other's, and sometimes there are 'reading' experts who only criticize. The educational technologist advises on matters such as structuring of content, clarification of objectives, media selection, student activities, self-assessment items, tests, examinations and evaluation. Media specialists (the BBC producers working with the OU) produce broadcasts and/or audio-cassettes. Editors edit the texts. The course manager keeps the production process going. The team as a whole carries responsibility for approving all ODL material. It is the author's environment.

This kind of team has survived into the 1990s, except that the average input from educational technologists and media specialists has fallen. Many teams have no educational technologist at all: there are not enough to go round. OU teams still have anything from eight to forty members, depending on whether they are interdisciplinary or interfaculty. Some have many 'reading' members. Some are for larger courses or packs than others, and so on. Perhaps surprisingly in view of the OU's socialist origins, OU teams are hierarchical. The chair, to whom is assigned considerable institutional authority, is the leader. He or she is always a subject-matter expert within the area of the course. Other subject-matter experts are expected to accept the chair's leadership for the life of the team. The media specialists are usually well qualified academically as well as commanding the making of broadcast/recorded elements. The educational technologists are members of the central academic staff and contributors to the academic products of the team. Editors and the course manager are geared to routine procedures in production. Illustrators and secretaries provide essential support.

The team changes during the university's design, production and evaluation cycle. During the design phase, the team may be enlarged temporarily by extra subject-matter experts who advise on content. In the production phase, 'reading' members, media specialists and editors join to handle the flow of production. Technicians, print designers and librarians are called in for specific purposes. The evaluation phase, when the material is actually being presented (taught) to students, sees an almost complete change of personnel: subject-matter experts leave to join new teams entering the design phase, while editors and media specialists move to teams entering production. Teams in the evaluation phase consist of a few subject-matter experts and a course manager. Evaluation is normally carried out by an educational technologist.

What are the strengths of the OU team? It aims at high quality of content by assigning leadership to subject-matter experts, and at good teaching by including media specialists, educational technologists and editors. Because it works within a complex framework, the whole team can be swept along towards completion of all the materials. At their best, team members support each other, but not uncritically. At its best, the OU production process contains many quality checks. The results are wide open to public scrutiny.

Does the OU team have weaknesses? Yes, definitely. It is slow to respond to demands for new materials: from start-up to delivery can take three years. Its timescales are rigid. It must follow bureaucratic procedures which are time consuming and costly. A weak leader can let the team wallow. Large teams are often difficult to lead, and may split into several groups, each dealing with a section of the material. Disagreement among subject-matter experts can be hard to resolve. Authors who repeatedly fail to meet deadlines can enrage the rest of the team. Pig-headed individuals can ruin well planned television or video programmes. Many team members have divided loyalties – a professional base in another unit, not the faculty where production is based. Teams can flounder and even fall apart over the long period needed to produce the OU's rather massive courses and teaching packs. Frankly, the framework can get in the way – many OU teams have stories to tell of stress and frustration. So what are the alternatives? Here are three.

THE TRANSFORMER TEAM

You don't have to adopt the OU approach. Try one of the others. For instance, there's the transformer team, with subject-matter experts taking the lead at first but handing over to educational technologists who transform the drafts into an effective set of multimedia materials. Macdonald-Ross and Waller (1976) put forward the basic idea. In its most elaborate form, there is an initiating team and a transforming team. Some members of the first team may be absorbed into the second one. The leader and members of the initiating team, all subject-matter experts, have the job of producing a set of first drafts of the ODL materials. The transforming team has to turn the drafts into a complete multimedia package that teaches effectively. An educational technologist leads this team, which may include a few of the subject-matter experts, as well as media specialists, editors and graphic designers who work side by side transforming the drafts, with perhaps a course manager.

Among the strengths of this team is its emphasis on teaching and learning, rather than subject-matter. At the OU and in many a training department, subject-matter experts' concern for content has sometimes led to neglect of instructional effectiveness. OU team meetings commonly focus on content, and members' criticisms of drafts pay too little attention to presentation techniques or student support. The same easily happens in industrial or commercial training.

Another strength of the transformer team is that most of the subject-matter experts are released early in the production cycle – they can return to research or start making a different training package. Further, this team can cope with fairly large packages, but it can be slimmed down for small ones, so that a team of two or three may be able to transform the drafts of quite a few subject-matter experts.

The transformer team has not proved popular. Why not? Perhaps its division of labour is unacceptable to those in power. Subject-matter experts may be unwilling to hand over their drafts to transformers. Even if they join the transforming team, they are outnumbered by 'technologists'. The process seems closer to book publishing than it is to course making.

Success stories can be told, however. A team of four OU educational technologists took a draft text plus a computer program on population growth (POPTRAN) and in a few weeks converted it into an undergraduate self-instructional package that could be used internationally (Henderson, Kinzett and Lockwood, 1988). It didn't matter that the program had been written originally for a different audience, in Wales. The transforming team succeeded.

If you want some advice on transforming text, turn to Melton (1990). An educational technologist, he has had wide experience, including a large project transforming materials written by experts for the International Institute of Educational Planning, part of UNESCO in Paris. His three checklists for transformers of text are comprehensive. Many of the questions can be applied to other media, too. His approach is down to earth and practical. And he supplies six examples of transformed text, to demonstrate what transformers can do.

THE WRAPAROUND TEAM

Wraparound teams started in the USA. Educational television stations in California, for example, wanted to devise distance teaching (telecourses) based on documentary or drama series broadcasts (made by teams, of course, sometimes in the UK). Today, the stations work in tandem with community colleges, where tutorials are held. To make the telecourses, they commission small teams of authors to write teaching material that is intended to 'wrap around' the broadcasts. Lightly edited, the booklets are published by the stations. Many of the telecourses have a distinct vocational flavour. College students watch the broadcasts, read the text material, attend tutorials, complete assignments and obtain credit.

This simple method is cheap and effective. The broadcasts are already paid for and taking place anyway. The writing teams do not need to be large. The students and/or the colleges pay for the text material. Tens of thousands obtain credit over the years.

Why haven't these teams gone into action everywhere else? After all, British television series such as Kenneth Clarke's *Civilization* or *Upstairs, Downstairs* each had a fine book published simultaneously. Is it that students in other countries decline to pay good money for wraparound courses based on series not intended for distance teaching as such? Is it that when the media specialists are leaders, with subject-matter experts, editors and others occupying subordinate positions, the courses perhaps overemphasize broadcast television, with wraparound texts added as an afterthought? Does education then look too much like entertainment?

The wraparound method doesn't have to use broadcasts, as Rowntree makes clear in his chapter on existing materials (Chapter 7). For example, an OU wraparound team is making a course on electronic media in distance education. The team is creating ODL materials by taking a set of already-published textbooks and other papers and writing study guides around them, with audio-cassettes added. A video-cassette of existing examples could be included, given the resources. Teams like this can make courses and packs in a wide range of subjects.

Is it possible to have a one-person wraparound team? People who advocate this are individuals who feel they know best and that they work very well by themselves. They say they know their subjects inside out and have excellent teaching skills. Why shouldn't each be a one-person production team? There is no obvious reason why a gifted individual cannot prepare a whole training package, even quite a large one. But is doing all the different tasks required the best use of that person's time and abilities? Rowntree (1990) wrote a well-known book on preparing self-instructional materials – he saw some advant-ages in working alone, but stressed the disadvantages too.

In fact, there seem to be very few instances of an individual doing it all. One person may orchestrate the making of a wraparound course for which various authors are commissioned to write. That person is not alone, though there are no team meetings and the team is virtual rather than real. And when the drafts are completed, they are often handed over to editors, illustrators and other 'technologists', on lines closer to the transformer method. Division of labour seems better in most circumstances, given the varied talents of staff. Loners can perhaps be accommodated, but the one-person team is a rarity as well as being a contradiction in terms.

THE WEEKEND TEAM

Drawn-out agonies of producing a course or training pack over several years may be inevitable when a large amount of content has to be covered, with multimedia teaching methods, but there are plenty of situations in which a single ODL handbook is all that is required, not a huge package. Try the weekend team. It consists of subject-matter experts and educational technolo-gists. The team is 'locked away' for several weekends in a country hotel, in some luxury perhaps but remote from other pressures. Under an energetic chair, it argues through the content and commissions the writers the first weekend, approves drafts the next weekend (probably several months after the first one) and, if necessary, meets a third time to finalize the handbook. Excep-tionally, almost everything is compressed into one weekend – that is how a package on coronary heart disease was produced (Lockwood, 1992). Enough to give you heart failure!

This kind of high-pressure team is best suited to preparing text-only packages. Multimedia materials are inevitably more complicated. This kind of team works best when the content is already well defined – maybe there is a set of new regulations that everybody in the company needs to know, or health advice to be taught to health workers out in the field, or a package is wanted that will introduce teachers to a new curriculum.

Weekend teams need dynamic leaders who have a very clear idea of what is required and can motivate everyone to get on with the job. That sounds a touch undemocratic compared with the OU team, but there are plenty of companies that will like the approach, and so will their trainers. Weekend teams are probably at their best if they include experienced writers, though Lockwood (*ibid.*) worked with a mixture of people.

WHICH ONE IS MOST APPROPRIATE FOR YOU?

Which team is best? That depends. It depends particularly on the following:

- How much content you want to teach, with larger packages usually requiring something close to the OU team.
- What level you want to pitch it at, with higher-level materials often needing either an OU team or a transformer team.
- How many media you think are needed, with text-only packages being more suitable for the weekend team.
- Whether you want to base the course mainly on existing video, audio or text material, in which case the wraparound team may do the job well.
- How soon you need the materials, with the weekend or wraparound team usually being the speediest.
- What expertise you can assemble, with the OU team demanding the greatest variety.
- How much money you want to spend, with the wraparound or weekend teams probably being the cheapest.

The OU team for making ODL materials may have become some sort of worldwide standard, but other teams, often simpler and cheaper to run, can be just as creative and productive. I've only considered three other kinds. Dodds (1993) suggests several more. People working in relatively small teaching and training organizations should certainly consider the alternatives. What's your situation?

REFERENCES

Dodds, T. (1993) Procedures for materials and text development in distance education. Paper prepared for the First Korea Air and Correspondence University Conference, 22–5 June, Seoul, Korea, International Extension College, Cambridge.

Henderson, E. S., Kinzett, S. and Lockwood, F. (1988) Developing POPTRAN, a population modelling package, *British Journal of Educational Technology*, Vol. 19, no. 3, pp. 184–92.

Lockwood, F. (1992) Alternative methods of materials production, *Media and Technology for Human Resource Development*, Vol. 4, no. 4, pp. 233–8.

Macdonald-Ross, M. and Waller, R. (1976) The transformer, in S. Greenwood and C. Goodacre (eds.) *The Penrose Annual*, Northwood Publications, London.

Melton, R. F. (1990) Transforming text for distance learning, *British Journal of Educational Technology*, Vol. 21, no. 3, pp. 183–95.

Rowntree, D. (1990) *Teaching through Self-Instruction: How to Develop Open Learning Materials* (revised edn), Kogan Page, London.

10

Assessing learner workload

Ellie Chambers

The amount of work learners are expected to do crucially affects their attitudes to distance and open learning courses, and their ability to complete them successfully. In this chapter some of the ways workload can be measured are discussed. A rigorous method of assessing the workload implied by a course, in advance of its publication, is outlined.

INTRODUCTION

Courses offered in distance or open learning mode usually indicate to prospective learners the study time involved – 5, 20, 60, 120 hours. The trend is evident even within conventional education, as the advent of Credit Accumulation and Transfer Schemes encourages a modular approach to course design and presentation. This must be good news for learners everywhere because, until now, 'workload' has tended to be seen as their problem.

Traditionally, teaching and training institutions have designed curricula to be covered and laid down the standards of performance required for various kinds of accreditation. The job of 'getting through' the curriculum has largely been left to the learner – whether studying for a certificate, a diploma or a degree. Often, these curricula are constructed on the principle that current learners need to know everything their teachers were taught at that level, plus the theories, knowledge and skills which have developed subsequently. Increasingly, then, learners themselves have had to make selections from the curriculum – judging how much of it needs to be covered and in what depth – whether or not they have much prior knowledge of the subject in question and with or without much help from their teachers.

By contrast, specifying the number of hours learners are expected to spend working would suggest a more rational approach to curriculum design. It implies that a course has been so designed that, if even 'beginners' apply themselves diligently for the 20, 60 or however many hours required, they can expect to cover the curriculum. However, we know that this is often not so. Many distance learning courses which specify a study time have turned out on inspection to be heavily overloaded (Blacklock, 1976; Chambers, 1989). As we shall see, it is just because such courses specify a study time that we are able to tell they are overloaded.

WHAT IS 'OVERLOAD'?

Learners are said to be overloaded when they are expected to do more work in a given period than they actually have time to complete. But this simple definition raises some tricky questions. How much time *do* learners have to give to their studies? Anyway, can we talk about learners as if they were all the same – surely, some learners need to spend much longer than others covering the same ground? What *can* 'they' be expected to achieve in a given period?

Time spent studying

In the main, study times for part-time learners have been derived from research into full-time undergraduates' patterns of study. For example, the OU based its calculations on the findings of the Hale Report (University Grants Committee, 1964), which emerged as an average of 40 hours per week during term times. Accordingly, OU undergraduates are expected to work for 14 hours per week, in each of 32 weeks over a six-year period in order to acquire a degree. (This does not include time spent attending tutorial sessions or preparing for and sitting examinations.)

In-depth studies undertaken more recently broadly support this finding, though they suggest that 40 hours per week is the average *maximum* study time (McKay, 1978; Vos, 1991). Indeed, Vos, drawing on records of all students' daily activities, argues that they *can* only work for a maximum of 7–8 hours per day given the time they need to spend on 'biologically unavoidable activities' and travelling about (Vos, 1991, p. 3). Furthermore, both researchers have found that, within this maximum period, the various activities involved compete for attention, so that if class-contact hours are increased the time spent on independent work decreases: 'students adjust their time on private study to give them a total of about 40 hours a week on their academic work' (McKay, 1978, p. 90). This was true of both arts and science students, whether in their first or third years of study. Similarly, Vos concludes (1991, p. 5): 'in terms of stimulation to study independently, curricula with low numbers of contact hours are . . . more effective than curricula with large numbers of contact hours.'

The implications of these studies are clear. First, it is pointless to construct curricula and courses which require students to work for more than 40 hours per week, or the part-time equivalent, *whatever the type or level of study*. If this is true for full-time students it almost certainly applies more strongly to part-time learners, who may also be in employment and/or have other domestic and social duties. (Indeed, according to Vos's calculations, 14 hours' study per week represents the maximum possible for most part-time students: if they have jobs and other responsibilities they must regularly be 'at work' of some kind for at least nine hours per day.) Secondly, if we do so, we actually discourage independent work. The argument that excessive workload always affects the *quality* of learning has been made elsewhere (Chambers, 1992).

Differences between learners

The answer to the second question 'Can we talk about learners as if they were all the same?' is 'no'. Clearly, individuals approach their studies in different ways and work at different rates (Morgan,Taylor and Gibbs, 1982; Entwistle and Ramsden, 1983; Marton, Hounsell and Entwistle, 1984) – whether this is due to the degree of their motivation, their preferred learning styles, their personal circumstances, or the level of their existing knowledge/skill and the ease or otherwise with which they pick up new ideas and learn new skills.

Consequently, researchers have tended to rely on methods of assessing workload that depend on learners' perceptions of it; asking individuals to rate it on a scale between 'very heavy/very light' or 'far too much work/far too little'. When large numbers of students are involved an 'average response' can then be calculated (e.g. Field, 1992). Or, striving for greater objectivity, researchers have asked students to keep a diary or log of the hours they work over a given period, either concurrently (UGC, 1964; Vos, 1991) or in retrospect (McKay, 1978). Again, the 'average hours' spent can then be calculated. However, since these methods depend on individuals' perceptions of workload, and almost certainly involve other contaminating factors, they are arguably far from reliable.

If you were a full-time student, here is a simple test: did you, and did the people you knew, regularly spend 40 hours a week working during term time? If a researcher had asked you to say how many hours you spent working, what would you have said? Or, have you ever seriously tried to make an accurate record of the time you spent on a task, excluding interruptions? Did you remember to include time spent thinking, or travelling, or on aspects of it you found very enjoyable (did these things count as 'work')? In some cases, calculation of 'average study hours' which are based on students' perceptions or records may not be just a bit inaccurate, but quite wildly so.

However, in order to get a purchase on the problem of workload within distance and open learning systems, we do have to take the *average* learner as our yardstick rather than the extremely fast or slow learner. Only by finding more reliable ways of doing so can we address the third, crucial, question: 'What *can* the (average) learner be expected to achieve within a given period?'

WHY WORRY ABOUT WORKLOAD?

We need to worry about workload, then, because there is a real limit to the number of hours even full-time students can be expected to spend working, beyond which course providers are asking them to do what cannot possibly be done – even rather badly. Furthermore, when we overload learners, the time they might otherwise spend independently (understanding ideas and applying them in new contexts, practising skills and so forth) is sacrificed to the demands of somehow getting through the course material as best they can. Clearly, study which does not allow time for thought, application or digestion does not constitute 'good learning'. On the contrary, it is unrewarding and demoralizing.

Also, if open and distance learning courses are advertised as requiring a specific 'study time', of 10, 40, 60 . . . hours, then course providers are simply duty bound to ensure that this claim is true, to the best of their ability.

Furthermore, in the context of open and distance learning for adults, a common consequence of overload is that learners vote with their feet – they 'drop out'. At the OU, Woodley and Parlett (1983) found 'a general tendency for wastage rates to increase with workload' (p. 11), and identified overload as among the most important course-related reasons for drop-out. In view of the financial and organizational penalties institutions suffer as a result, prudence alone might dictate the need for action – though we might also expect educators to be mindful of the devastating effects such 'failure' can have on learners' confidence and self-esteem.

A SYSTEM FOR ASSESSING LEARNER WORKLOAD

As we saw, methods of assessing workload such as subjective ratings, work diaries or logs are not very reliable. Also, they have usually been applied *post hoc:* at best the results enable course providers to make revisions to published courses. This is expensive, given the up-front, fixed costs involved in producing open and distance learning materials. We need to be able to assess workload and revise learning materials prior to publication. The earlier in the production process the better, since preparation of material that is ultimately surplus to requirements is wasteful too (involving extra time on the part of course planners and writers, secretarial and audio-visual media staff, critical readers and pilot-testers, editors and printers). A systematic approach to assessing workload, and more robust methods, are needed.

Secondly, we must set out to measure what the *average* learner can achieve *within a specified time period.* This involves assessing the workload implied by the whole course, including material presented through audio-visual and other means. And it must include time spent practising skills, doing exercises and preparing assignments towards accreditation.

In short, for best effect we need a *system* for assessing learner workload which is robust, timely and comprehensive. As such, it should be applicable to all the courses produced within an institution at an appropriate point in the production process. The rest of the chapter outlines such a system, by means of a case study.

WORKLOAD CALCULATION: 'HOLIDAY MAKING IN FRANCE'

This is a short section of a course in French for beginners. It is chosen because learning a language is familiar, something we have all tried to do at some time, and it is skills based. The course includes many practical exercises and uses a range of teaching media. However, the proposed system for assessing workload is in principle applicable to any open or distance learning course. Readers working in other fields will want to make appropriate substitutions for the course components and activities identified here.

The course components include a *workbook* of around 45 pages, containing 27 *practical exercises* which refer learners to extracts on *audio-* and *video-cassette*, to a separate *grammar book* and *dictionary*, and to an *evaluation and 'Corriges' section* appended to the workbook. Over a third of the exercises involve use of audiotape, some requiring learners to record themselves speaking; six require use of video; and the remainder involve some combination of reading, memorizing, speaking aloud and writing in the workbook.

The expected study time for this material, based on writers/teachers' subjective judgement, was four hours. This, then, forms the workload yardstick – the *ideal study time* identified at the top of Table 10.1. The proposed system for assessing workload consists of calculating the time it would *actually* take the average learner to study all the course material that has been prepared, and then comparing the total (in this case, approximately 6¼ hours in the box at the foot of the table) with whatever 'ideal' study time is specified. A glance will show that at first-draft stage this part of the course was overloaded.

It remains to be seen how 'average study times' were calculated for all the course components and activities involved. Looking down the table, then, we begin with the workbook, or the study of text.

Workbook

In this skills-based course the main functions of the workbook are to direct and pace the learners' work and to integrate the various activities involved.

Table 10.1 A workload chart for 'Holiday making in France'

'Ideal' study time = around 4 hours		
1 workbook	c. 4,500 words at 70 wpm	= 1 hour
2 audio and video extracts	Audio, 30 minutes playing × 2	= 1 hour
(Listen/view only)	Video, 20 minues playing × 2	= 40 mins
		= 1 hr 40 mins
3 exercises in workbook, 27	10 audio + speak/write/read (playing × 2)	= 1 hour
	6 video + write (playing × 2)	= 40 mins
	11 other (speak/read/write/refer/memorize)	= 2 hours
		= 3 hrs 40 min
Estimated average study time = c. 6¼ hours		
('Ideal' study time = c. 4 hours)		

Note: The section is overloaded by about one-third. Exercises, plus audio and video listening/viewing, are the most time-consuming elements. Rather then cutting them, and so reducing opportunities for students to apply and practise skills, consider reducing and reorganizing the curriculum – viz., cut section 6 altogether and redistribute part of this section (e.g. 'ways of expressing satisfaction') to section 3? . . . and so on.

Learners practise the skills of reading, writing and speaking in French largely 'beyond' the text: in interaction with voice/action on audio and video, and internally, as they attempt to replicate sound, rehearse, memorize and create new formulations; and by reference to the grammar book and dictionary. At intervals they return to the text to produce written evidence of learning gains and have them confirmed. However, some time has to be budgeted for the reading of instructions and short stretches of text. Close inspection of the workbook revealed that no page contains more than 130 words, and most far fewer.

The following 'rules of thumb' for calculating the time it takes the average learner to study discursive text have been developed through experimentation (Whalley, 1982; Lockwood, Williams and Roberts, 1988):

An easy read	= 100 wpm
A fairly straightforward text	= 70 wpm
A dense/difficult text	= 40 wpm

These findings concern *reading in relation to comprehension* so they are *'study rates'*, not reading speeds. They are based on the assumption that the material is unfamiliar to learners, who are anyway relatively inexperienced readers, and they allow some time for thinking and re-reading. Whether a particular text is designated 'an easy read', or whatever, is a matter of judgement, and must be negotiated and agreed by researchers and course writers/teachers.

On the basis of 70 wpm, we calculated that about an hour would be sufficient for study of the workbook (45 pages at an average 100 words per page). Although these rules have limited application in the case of language learning, they are fundamental to workload assessment in the humanities and other discursive subject-matters (Chambers, 1992). In this case, assessment centres on a range of practical exercises – in particular those related to material presented on audio- and video-cassette.

Audio and video extracts

The most objective, and basic, workload measure for these components is playing time, in this case a total of 30 and 20 minutes respectively. But when such extracts are designed to be used interactively they must be re-played – sometimes more than once. The recommended 'rule' here is that playing time for *all* such extracts should be doubled.

To ensure that sufficient time is allowed simply for listening/viewing, this 'playing time × 2' should be recorded as a separate item in the workload chart; that is, as distinct from the (extra) time it will take to do exercises that are related to the listening and viewing.

Exercises

Recent research suggests that, in general, students spend much longer working on exercises and practical activities than course writers predict (Lockwood,

1992). In this case, we anticipated that exercises based on use of audio and video extracts would be the most time consuming (Melton, 1993). They involved operating unfamiliar equipment in order to locate and re-play extracts and, in some cases, making sound recordings, as well as completing written and other work associated with listening and viewing.

From these considerations we developed the following, more objective 'rule' regarding such exercises: when audio and video extracts are used in conjunction with text, and especially when learners are asked to write about what they see, or speak (shadow) what they hear, playing time should be multiplied again (i.e. in total, 'playing time × 4'). As this suggests, each exercise has to be examined to ensure that it broadly conforms to the 'rules' – including those which are not based on audio-visual extracts, but require reading, writing or study of the grammar book. Some appropriate extra time has to be allowed for complex exercises.

Informed judgement of this kind often has to be made by researchers and teachers, as regards all kinds of exercises/practical work. (Garg, Vijayshre and Panda (1992) have also applied the system to a course in physics, focusing on the study of diagrams, on problem-solving and laboratory work.) Assessing the workload implied by such activities is undoubtedly the most tricky and time-consuming aspect of the proposed system. But another helpful 'rule' is that, whenever possible, objective measures should be preferred. For example, when an exercise requires learners to read pages of a set text and make notes, the margin for error can be reduced by calculating the 'reading time' involved separately – on the basis of 40, 70 or 100 wpm – and then adding to it the time teachers judge will be needed for note-making.

If there is serious doubt about how long an exercise might take, and especially in the case of extended exercises and project work, pilot-testing may be undertaken during the development phase of the course with a group of learners who are representative of the target group (Nathenson and Henderson, 1980). This will aid the development of further, appropriate, 'rules' for calculating workload in distance and open learning settings.

Assignments

In this case, no assignment towards accreditation is required. But this study element must not be overlooked when assessing workload. Even though the time involved is extra to the course material provided, assignments are usually among the most important and time-consuming aspects of a course from the learner's point of view (Chambers, 1992).

CONCLUSION

Clearly, this approach to assessing learner workload, through application of a system of 'rules', is not objective. In the nature of things it cannot be. But it beats pure guesswork. And if some justifiable measures can be developed, they may then be applied to the teaching materials and methods used in other similar contexts, and refined. (Garg, Vijayshre and Panda (1992) demonstrate that, so far, they are proving robust.) They can also be applied to other subject-matters and adapted for use in other contexts.

As a result, course providers will be in a better position to tell whether a course is overloaded, and where they might make cuts in course material, well before it is due to be published. Quite apart from the financial benefits noted earlier, teachers of the course may then justifiably expect learners to accomplish what is asked of them, while learners themselves have a much clearer idea of what they are expected to do.

Moreover, such workload assessment enables course providers to consider changing the balance of a proposed curriculum, so that learners may make the *best* use of the limited time available to them. The note at the foot of Table 10.1 indicates that careful accounts of learner workload can contribute to the reorganization of curricula, as well as to a reduction in their scope – which may well be overdue, especially in scientific and technological fields.

REFERENCES

Blacklock, S. (1976) *Workload: A Summary of Student Workload, 1971–1975*, Survey Research Department, Institute of Educational Technology, internal report, The Open University, Milton Keynes, pp. 1–38.

Chambers, E. A. (1989) *Student Workload and How to Assess it*, Teaching and Consultancy Centre, Institute of Educational Technology, internal report, The Open University, Arts Faculty Conference, Milton Keynes, pp. 1–12.

Chambers, E. A. (1992) Workload and the quality of student learning, *Studies in Higher Education*, Vol. 17, no. 2, pp. 141–52.

Entwistle, N. and Ramsden, P. (1983) *Understanding Student Learning*, Croom Helm, London.

Field, J. (1992) *Report on the Annual Survey of New Courses 1991*. Student Research Centre, Institute of Educational Technology, internal report, The Open University, Milton Keynes, pp. 1–18.

Garg, S., Vijayshre, and Panda, S. (1992) A preliminary study of student workload for IGNOU physics elective courses, *Indian Journal of Open Learning*, Vol. 1, no. 2, pp. 19–25.

Lockwood, F. G. (1992) *Activities in Self-Instructional Texts*, Kogan Page, London.

Lockwood, F. G., Williams, A. I. and Roberts, D. W. (1988) Improving teaching at a distance within the University of the South Pacific, *International Journal of Educational Development*, Vol. 8, no. 3, pp. 265–7.

Marton, F., Hounsell, D. and Entwistle, N. (eds.) (1984) *The Experience of Learning*, Scottish Academic Press, Edinburgh.

McKay, R. (1978) Effectiveness of learning: the place of study, in D. Warren Piper (ed.) *The Efficiency and Effectiveness of Teaching in Higher Education*, Institute of Education, University of London.

Melton, R. (1993) *Developmental Testing of a New French Course*. Teaching and Consultancy Centre, Institute of Educational Technology, internal report, The Open University, Milton Keynes, pp. 1–29.

Morgan, A. R., Taylor, E. and Gibbs, G. (1982) Variations in students' approaches to studying, *British Journal of Educational Technology*, Vol. 13, no. 2, pp. 107–13.

Nathenson, M. and Henderson, E. S. (1980) *Using Student Feedback to Improve Learning Materials*, Croom Helm, London.

University Grants Committee (1964) *Report of the Committee on University Teaching Methods*, HMSO, London.

Vos, P. (1991) Curriculum control of learning processes in higher education, *Proceedings of the 13th International Forum on Higher Education of the European Association for Institutional Research*, Edinburgh.

Whalley, P. (1982) Argument in text and the reading process, in A. Flammer and W. Kintsch (eds.) *Discourse Processing*, North Holland.

Woodley, A. and Parlett, M. (1983) Student drop-out, *Teaching at a Distance*, Vol. 24, Autumn, pp. 2–23.

11

Developing learner autonomy: project-based learning in open and distance learning

Alistair Morgan

The development of learner autonomy and independence in learning are usually cited by teachers, government bodies and employers, as one of the key aims of education at a wide range of levels. Also, with the current interest in an analysis of 'transferable skills' and how they can be developed in learners, independence and autonomy in learning are of vital importance for how we design teaching and learning in open and distance learning.

This chapter will examine some of the theoretical and pedagogical issues surrounding independence and autonomy in learning. It will also look at an example of how independence has been developed through the use of project-based learning. Although the examples are taken from higher education, they are presented so as to encourage the readers to analyse their own practice and explore the potential for developing learner autonomy in their own settings.

INTRODUCTION

Tackling questions is fundamental to teaching and learning. So an analysis of the policies, pedagogies and practice of asking questions, and more generally the nature of the learning tasks we require of our students, are the key aims of this chapter. If we do this, we shall put our curriculum practice and pedagogy under scrutiny. But first, I want to set the scene with an extract from an article entitled 'Trivial pursuit' by Laurie Taylor (1992). He questions the art of asking questions and laments that students are often not sufficiently critical of the questions they are asked:

Nowadays, students . . . are usually far too at home with the game [answering questions] ever to query its assumptions . . . And that's why there should be some sort of medal struck for Bill Kaye. Bill was a mature student when he arrived at York to study social science. One of the first seminars he attended was in the politics department. The topic was 'The British Constitution', and the lecturer, an obsessive fellow who loved nothing more than marks and grades, was quickly in his stride. 'Has everybody done the reading?' He waited patiently for the half-hearted nods. 'Right, then. Let's see how carefully you did it. Who shall we start with? Ah yes, what about you Bill Kaye. Over there in the corner. Now Bill, can you tell us how many MPs there are in the House of Commons?' Bill nodded. 'Good. And so what's the answer?' Silence. 'I'm sorry, Kaye, but do you know what the answer is? Yes or No?' Finally Bill spoke. 'Yes,' he said wearily, 'I do know what the answer is, but because it's such a stupid question, I'm not telling you.'

(Ibid., p. 21)

The form of questioning described above vividly portrays an extreme example of the type of 'trivial question' which students are often posed. However, it is questions of this type which are likely to shape students' perceptions of the sorts of knowledge and understandings which are valued by the teaching and training staff and the educational institution. They contribute to shaping the 'learning milieu' in an organization. Throughout the literature on teaching and learning, there are many studies which establish the relationship between the demands of the assessment tasks, students' approaches to learning and crucially how certain forms of assessment can induce students to take a 'surface approach' to learning (see, for example, Becker, Geer and Hughes, 1968; Entwistle and Ramsden, 1983; Ramsden, 1992).

Although in the example above, the mature student was able refuse to answer the 'stupid question', students very often do not have much choice. When questions which demand little more than memorization and the reproduction of information are part of the formal assessment for grading, students will go through the ritual of attempting to answer them, but with a disastrous impact on the quality of the learning outcomes. Certainly from the learner's perspective the assessment defines the curriculum, both in content and in terms of power relations between teachers (and the institution) and the students.

Although the dismal teaching–learning event referred to above was in a conventional classroom, some of the activities posed to students in open and distance learning for their assessment requirements amount to little more than 'scan the text to find the answer'. Certainly, many of the in-text questions incorporated into the correspondence teaching texts in open and distance learning (like the trivial question in the example) do not succeed in manipulating students' learning in the ways that course writers would imagine (Lockwood, 1992).

Course design and assessment in open and distance learning are the crucial areas for attention if we are to develop activities which will encourage learners to take a 'deep approach' to their learning and also encourage them to become more intrinsically oriented towards their learning, (Gibbs, Morgan and Taylor, 1984; Marton and Saljo, 1984; Morgan, 1993). The importance of scrutinizing our course design and assessment is that they have a direct influence on the quality of the learning outcomes.

Much of the criticism of post-compulsory education is related to the outcomes of learning. What can our students actually do – what have they really learnt? In what ways have they changed and developed as a result of their studies? How have they developed as learners over the course of their studies? Although criticism comes from a diversity of educational and political standpoints, there seems to be a common strand through the criticism about the narrowness of the curriculum, with its academic bias and little concern for the wider social context of education.

In terms of broadening the curriculum, the crucial issue is that the experience of learning from teaching or training in a wide range of settings should equip the learner to handle problems or issues that could not have been predicted in advance. Indeed, although it may sound almost hackneyed to refer to the 'accelerating rate of change' in society, people's experiences of life are now subject to change in a way previously unanticipated. Hence the urgent need for education and training to address concerns which are broader than the specific discipline area or vocational training in which learners are engaged within a particular learning activity. In short, to develop autonomy and independence in learning is an increasingly crucial aspect of 'quality in learning'.

PROJECT-BASED LEARNING

Project-based learning is an approach to course design, which can tackle some of the criticisms set out above. Although project work is an established feature of probably the majority of undergraduate courses (at least at final-year level), this is not necessarily the case in open and distance learning.

So what is project-based learning? At a general level, project-based learning can be defined as a learning activity in which students develop an understanding of a topic, issue or body of knowledge by working on actual (or simulated) problems or issues and in which students also have some degree of responsibility for designing and planning the learning activity.

Project-based learning can vary from small-scale activities up to a year's work. And in some cases the entire curriculum is structured around project-based learning. Morgan (1983) developed a conceptualization of project activities based on two key dimensions: project intention – whether it derived from academic topics or 'real-world' problems or issues; and control – whether the learning activities are teacher controlled or learner controlled.

Two examples will indicate the range of activities and the curricular issues which are raised. In the physical sciences, projects are a familiar approach, where students apply knowledge and skills already familiar to them. Students work as a sort of trainee researcher. Although they choose their topics to work on, these will be derived from the teacher's areas of interest and set out by the teacher. The methodology and approach will most likely be located in established paradigms and discipline traditions. Projects of this form are common in undergraduate science courses. So, in relation to the dimension explained above, these projects are derived from academic topics and are controlled primarily by the teacher.

Very different types of projects are common in social science and education. These are more interdisciplinary and are based around problems of contemporary issues. This sort of project will not necessarily build upon existing skills and knowledge. The methodological approaches students adopt will be less closely defined and will be derived from the requirements of the problem or issues-based topic. Students are also likely to have more freedom in their choice of topic. The project intention will be based more around 'real-world' issues and control will be located to a greater extent with the learner.

Project-based learning provides a form of educational experience which counters many of the criticisms mentioned earlier. Traditional didactic approaches to teaching (such as lectures or the specially prepared correspondence text) may be sufficient for communicating existing bodies of knowledge. Project activities, however, bring new aims into prominence. The processes of learning, autonomy and independence in learning come into focus, as well as building up an understanding of subject material.

In open learning and distance education the aims which are emphasized in project-based learning are especially important. The predominant learning material in open and distance learning is likely to be text. The problem with much of the text is that students perceive it as an authoritative academic monologue. Although this may not necessarily be the author's intentions, the style of the presentation can imply a certainty about the knowledge and the perfection of the presentation does not draw the student into dialogue with the author. Harris (1987), in probably the most substantial critique of The Open University in the UK, refers to this problem as the explicit pedagogy in the text and how this leads to 'closure' in education. When students are confronted with teaching texts which do little to take them into the processes and debates which produced them, together with the contested and conjectural nature of much of the knowledge, students can easily be induced into adopting reproducing strategies in their studies. Although this critique is based on the OU, it seems to be relevant to the majority of distance teaching institutions, in view of the likely complex division of labour in the knowledge production and distribution processes.

The critique by Freire (1972) of much of traditional education can act as a salutory reminder for us in open and distance learning as we engage in our course design and development work. Although he was working in a particular context of adult literacy in a developing country, his analysis of the 'banking concept' of education can serve as a powerful reminder to distance educators, who sometimes get overenthusiastic about the value of their instructional packages.

In contrast to 'banking' knowledge, project-based learning involves students to some extent in designing their own learning activities – they are involved in a very different type of activity compared to traditional methods, with the emphasis on transmission modes of teaching. The learning activities encourage students to develop a degree of independence and autonomy in their learning.

INDEPENDENCE AND AUTONOMY IN LEARNING

So far, I have made a brief reference to independence and autonomy in learning, but with little elaboration of these concepts. Independent learning is a much-used term in educational debates, particularly in distance education and open learning. As Nation (1991, p. 102) explains lucidly,

> It [independent learning] creates a warm glow within and without its many
> users, who use it happily and frequently; it is even shared by those who
> disagree with each other theoretically and practically. Like 'democracy',
> 'freedom' and 'education' itself, few eschew its use. Its meaning is both
> shared and contested.

Two contrasting meanings of independent learning can be identified in the
literature. One view of independent learning is that of students working away
by themselves on various activities which have been produced for them by the
teaching institution – independence is a basic characteristic of distance education with the separation of teacher and learner. The other view means something quite different –namely students taking more responsibility for what they
learn and how they learn it. This means that students take greater control of
learning – they are more self-directed and autonomous learners.

Project-based learning is an important approach to teaching and learning
and provides a unique contribution to the curriculum as it encourages student
autonomy in learning and independence in learning (in terms of responsibility
in learning).

PUTTING PROJECT-BASED LEARNING INTO PRACTICE

Following on from the analysis above, what are the possibilities for using
project-based learning in open and distance learning? The contested meanings
of 'independent learning' are closely linked to contested views about the curriculum and the aims of education, which will emerge in the course design work
involved in developing project activities in open and distance education. So the
debate will focus around questions such as: 'Are the students sufficiently prepared for projects? Will they gain enough of the discipline knowledge through
doing projects? How can we grade students' work reliably? How do we keep
control over their learning? How will the tutors cope with supporting students?' etc., etc.

The potential for project work and independent study raises many important issues about the nature of the curriculum and how it relates to the learners'
experiences. As O' Reilly (1991, p. 11) claims, using independent study to
mean autonomy in learning:

> I would see almost irresistible educational arguments for including indepen-
> dent study as an element in educational provision for adult learners. Enab-
> ling students to plan and negotiate their learning brings tremendous energy
> and committment into the learning process. For non-traditional students,
> the process of building a learning contract from previous experience as a
> bridge between that person's personal, social and cultural realities and the
> realities of higher education.

O'Reilly's reference to non-traditional students is of particular importance
when there are efforts in all areas of post-compulsory education and training
to increase participation rates and to widen access. To build the learning

experiences around the adult student's experience of life seems to be a very powerful approach to make the curriculum relevant to non-traditional students.

PROJECT WORK: AN EXAMPLE FROM DISTANCE EDUCATION

Although the following example is taken from the OU, it is only provided as a basis from which to identify some of the key design issues and the key questions which need to be addressed, as a more general framework for putting project-based learning into practice in open and distance learning.

In the 'Environment' course (U206, a full credit, second level, interdisciplinary course) there are three broad aims which inform the course, albeit at a very general level: awareness, analysis and action. It is in the context of this third aim, action, that the course team (of which I was a member) embarked on the design of a project. A project component in the course, where students could examine an issue of environmental concern in their own locality, seemed an appropriate course design for students to tackle in parallel to the more conventionally taught part of the course contained in specially produced textbooks.

The guidance for the project component is all contained in a substantial project handbook, which students receive at the start of the course. The introduction to this handbook conveys the aims of the project as follows:

> Your project will be a major part of achieving the third of the course aims: evaluating desirable courses of action. It would be improper for the course team to tell you how to act, or even that you should act, but we are asking you to develop skills by behaving as if you were going to act. We are asking you to investigate a local environmental issue, to write a short report and to draft a letter to an appropriate decision-making body advocating a particular outcome . . . Most students who do projects find that they generate much stronger feelings than the more passive learning elsewhere in the OU system. The job of this Project Handbook is to provide a framework to help you to take on this challenge successfully, so you can emerge with strong positive feelings rather than the disappointment that can result when projects go wrong. We have written this booklet and scheduled feedback from your tutor to minimize the opportunities for error, but *the nature of a project is that the ultimate responsibility is yours.*
>
> (Open University, 1991, p. 2, emphasis added)

I have used this quote from the introduction to the project handbook as it conveys how different the project is from the rest of the course (and also the orthodoxy in open and distance learning of the self-instructional text). The overriding aim in designing the project component is to allow students some degree of control and responsibility for deciding what they learnt and how they learnt it. At the same time the framework within the project handbook was set out so as to encourage a series of interactions between the student and tutor (correspondence tuition) to minimize the chance that students would get 'stuck' with their project activities.

As well as allowing students this responsibility in learning, we also wanted to encourage and facilitate their 'reflection in learning' and 'learning from experience'; these approaches to adult learning seemed especially appropriate in view of the local focus of the project topics. The course design set out to adapt the concept of 'experiential learning' as a basis for structuring the project, derived from the work of Lewin and the Kolb 'experiential learning cycle' (Kolb and Fry, 1975).

To encourage students to engage with the concept of experiential learning, the first assignment relates to their project topic (where they set out their initial ideas and choice of topic) and requires them to go through the various stages of the experiential learning cycle. The project handbook sets out the four-stage model as follows: experience, observation, conceptualization, experiment. It provides explanation of the ideas underlying the stages of the cycle. So, for example, under 'conceptualization' students are asked to consider issues of power in society, what is driving environmental change, who serves to benefit from a particular change and what are the conflicts of interest involved.

The assessment requirements for the project are structured through four of the nine assignments of the course in the following way (TMA = tutor-marked assignment):

- Choosing a topic (TMA 01).
- Planning your investigation (TMA 03).
- Collecting and interpreting information (TMA 05).
- Reporting your findings – recommendations for action (TMA 07).

The aim of assessment structure is to ensure that students are in contact with their tutor at the various stages throughout their project. The project handbook provides students with guidance for each stage of their work. So, for example, to help students to choose a topic and to convey to them the 'feel' of possible project topics, three 'ways in' to getting started are explained. The aim of this project handbook is to stimulate students' ideas and teach them about the notion of experiential learning, rather than provide a set of ready-made projects. To summarize briefly then, for each stage of the student's work, the handbook provides support and guidance.

From this brief description of the course design, we can see that the underlying assumptions and the demands of the learning tasks for students are very different from those involved in studying the highly structured correspondence teaching text, which I have called the 'orthodoxy' in distance teaching and open learning.

DESIGNING PROJECT-BASED LEARNING

Although it would be contrary to the philosophy of the curriculum design to derive a sort of 'blueprint' for designing project activities in open and distance learning, a set of key questions can be derived from the above example.

First, the stages of 'doing a project', which are addressed in each of the assignments above, need to be considered explicitly in the guidance and support provided for the learners. This is particularly important in relation to 'choosing a topic' and 'getting going'. It is this stage where students probably require the most help, as they grapple with taking a degree of responsibility for their own learning, and 'sussing out' what a project consists of.

Secondly, helping students to 'focus down' sufficiently within the scope of their own studies is a crucial area for support and guidance. Finally, in terms of designing project-based learning in a wide range of education and training settings, to structure formally the existing experiences of the adult learner into a course or training provision based on the ideas derived from experiential learning is a way to relate education and training to the wider concerns of the learner and the learners' lives in the workplace and in society.

CONCLUSIONS

The example discussed above indicates some of the potential for project-based learning in open and distance education. Project work is not merely a 'method'. It is an approach to the curriculum which raises fundamental question about the aims of education and the sorts of outcomes we want to develop in our learners. More importantly, project-based learning is an approach to course design in open and distance learning which does encourage the development of autonomy and independence in learners – for many people these are the outcomes of learning which are crucial in debates on quality in learning.

REFERENCES

Becker, H., Geer, B. and Hughes, E. C. (1968) *Making the Grade: The Academic Side of College Life*, Wiley, New York.

Entwistle, N. and Ramsden, P. (1983) *Understanding Student Learning*, Croom Helm, London.

Freire, P. (1972) *Pedagogy of the Oppressed*, Penguin Books, Harmondsworth.

Gibbs, G., Morgan, A. and Taylor, E. (1984) The world of the learner, in F. Marton, D. Hounsell and N. Enwistle (eds.) *The Experience of Learning*, Scottish Academic Press, Edinburgh.

Harris, D. (1987) *Openness and Closure in Distance Education*, Falmer Press, Lewes.

Kolb, D. A. and Fry, R. (1975) Towards an applied theory of experiential learning, in C. L. Cooper (ed.) *Theory of Group Processes*, Wiley, London.

Lockwood, F. (1992) *Activities in Self-Instructional Texts*, Kogan Page, London.

Marton, F. and Saljo, R. (1984) Approaches to learning, in F. Marton, D. Hounsell and N. Entwistle (eds.) *The Experience of Learning*, Scottish Academic Press, Edinburgh.

Morgan, A. (1983) Theoretical aspects of project-based learning in higher education, *British Journal of Educational Technology*, Vol. 14, no. 1, pp. 66–78.

Morgan, A. (1993) *Improving your Students' Learning: Reflections on the Experience of Study*, Kogan Page, London.

Nation, D. (1991) Teaching texts and independent learning, in T. Evans and B. King (eds.) *Beyond the Text*, Deakin University Press, Geelong.

The Open University (1991) Environment (Course code U206), *Project Handbook*,
    Milton Keynes.
O'Reilly, D. (1991) Developing opportunities for independent learners, *Open Learning*,
    Vol. 6, no. 3., pp. 3–13.
Ramsden, P. (1992) *Learning to Teach in Higher Education*, Routledge, London.
Taylor, L. (1992) Trivial pursuit, *New Statesman and Society*, 5 June.

12

Developmental testing: monitoring academic quality and teaching effectiveness

Hossein Zand

A face-to-face teacher can respond immediately to students' questions, repeat arguments and, if greeted by blank expressions, can do some remedial teaching in the next session. In self-instructional materials such options are seldom available and so producers of open and distance learning materials need to control the quality by other means – developmental testing is a strategy for doing this.

In this chapter the concept of developmental testing (DT) is introduced, preparation for DT is described, methods and strategies for the collection of suitable data are outlined, data collection in practice is explored and the reporting of results is finally discussed.

INTRODUCTION

Are you producing self-instructional materials for a small audience, or an extensive course for hundreds of learners? How would you describe your organization? Is it relatively small, producing specially designed courses for clients in business and industry, or is it relatively large, producing courses in a variety of subjects? Whatever your situation may be, once you have produced a draft of your learning materials, you will probably be asking such questions as:

- What will other subject specialists think of the materials?
- Do the materials enable learners to achieve the objectives of the course and, if not, why not?
- Will clients who might have commissioned the materials be satisfied?

Providing answers to such questions, and incorporating these into the course production, are likely to ensure the quality of learning material. This in turn serves other important purposes. First, since production costs can be very high, ineffective learning material wastes financial resources. Secondly, a course production group may require a variety of expertise, and forming a coherent team takes time and effort. Thirdly, a successful course invariably brings professional satisfaction to all concerned, and of course enhances your reputation as a producer.

THE CONCEPT OF DEVELOPMENTAL TESTING

Developmental testing is a type of formative evaluation which aims to find answers to such questions as listed above. Answers usually come from the following sources:

- The results of field testing of the teaching materials on a group of learners with a view to collecting feedback that can be used to improve the teaching.
- Discussions in the production group, where members, having studied each other's contributions, explore ways to improve the materials.
- The comments of subject experts who are invited to evaluate the completeness, currency, accuracy and technical quality of the learning materials, and how they can be improved further.
- Evaluation of the materials by your colleagues who have experience teaching the subject and may be familiar with potential learners.
- Evaluation by those who might have commissioned the materials, e.g. by an employer for staff training, to see whether the materials fulfil their requirements.

Developmental testing can be conducted by a member of the production team, called the evaluator, who plans the exercise, designs questionnaires and helps with data collection and analysis. You can begin your DT by giving a draft of your materials to one or two subject experts and one or two of your experienced colleagues. Ask them to read the materials critically. It is possible they will identify possible errors, better ways of presenting particular concepts, more appropriate activities, better assessment questions and so on. You can discuss their comments and incorporate them to produce an updated draft. You can then field test this draft on a group of learners, called testers. The main purpose of this is to see the material from the testers' perspective. You can ask them a variety of questions, for example which activities were too difficult, which examples were not sufficiently helpful, etc. The evaluator, with input from authors, can analyse the data collected and suggest a plan of action for improving the materials. However, acting on this plan requires the full commitment of the authors to the entire process of DT.

If this commitment can be established, the new draft can be sent to anyone else whose evaluation is to be taken into account; the final draft can be produced in the light of their comments, thus completing the DT exercise.

PREPARATION FOR DEVELOPMENTAL TESTING

Choosing testers

The testers should be a representative sample of the target audience. Just a handful of testers can help reduce major weaknesses in the materials, such as inappropriate diagrams, exercises that cannot be done, etc. Furthermore, such testing is cheap and relatively easily organized (Hodgson, 1993). However, if there are uncertainties about the teaching effectiveness of the materials, a larger group of testers may be needed to collect more extensive data. Although 10–40 testers cannot generally be representative of the target audience in the statistical sense, unless the audience is fairly homogeneous, they are adequate for most purposes (Henderson and Nathenson, 1980).

The actual selection of testers depends on your particular situation; however, you may find the following suggestions useful:

- *Prerequisites*. Testers should possess the background knowledge required to study the materials. This can be verified in a selection interview, or by inspection of past training records or college transcripts.
- *Ability*. Is it possible to predict the range of ability in your population of learners? If so, can you specify it? When possible, it would be prudent to include one or two learners at the extremes of this range with rather more around the middle – whatever the middle may be.
- *Interest*. Testers should show a reasonable amount of motivation to learn the course (Tessmer, 1993) and willingness to go through various steps involved in field testing.

Other possible criteria for the selection of testers include gender, race, geographic region, reasons for wishing to participate in the field testing, etc., to see if any particular problems arise with the materials for these groups.

The method of rewarding testers will depend on your circumstances. Options include acknowledgement of their contribution; offering an academic credit; a free copy of the learning materials; and, although a poor motivator, the payment of a fee.

Which draft to test

For ease of reference, let us assume that the learning materials are divided into a sequence of similarly structured 'modules'. The module drafts become ready for testing after the comments of the subject experts and other teachers of the subject are incorporated, and should contain the following items:

- *The list of objectives*. These are statements which identify as clearly as possible what learners should be able to do to demonstrate their learning. A correspondence between the objectives and the structure of the learning materials can help learners (and also represents a useful discipline for authors in their writing).
- *All activities* (also called *self-assessment questions*). Activities give learners a chance to engage with the learning materials in an active way; to think for themselves, scrutinize definitions and arguments, practise objectives and construct their own understanding in the process.
- *The assessment* (also called *evaluation) questions for the module*. Learners' performance on these questions is a good indicator of their success in achieving the objectives for the module. A clear correspondence between these

questions and the objectives not only helps the learners but it is also crucial in data analysis.

METHODS AND STRATEGIES FOR DATA COLLECTION

Methods of data collection

The main methods of collecting data in DT include questionnaires, expert reviews, interviews and the use of audiotapes.

Questionnaires can be used to collect data on the process and the outcome of learning. The questions can be posed by the evaluator or by individual authors and try to anticipate learners' problems. The questionnaires can be interleaved at strategic points in the module, e.g. after an important activity, after a complicated argument or at the end of a section.

The *expert review* 'is an intrinsic evaluation of the instruction, meaning that the instruction is evaluated in terms of intrinsic merits such as content accuracy or technical quality' (Tessmer, 1993). In addition, experts can provide information about completeness and currency of the content, and indicate whether the materials are suitable for their purposes, e.g. consistency with the examination requirements of professional bodies such as the Institute of Chartered Accountants, etc.

Interviews allow learners to describe aspects of their learning experience which questionnaires may not capture. However, they should be non-threatening and non-judgemental. Care should be taken not to allow the feedback to be skewed towards the experiences of one or two more outspoken participants. Participation in interviews can be a threatening experience for authors, as they may feel that their work is being adversely criticized. However, firsthand information may give them useful ideas for improvement of their contributions: 'In addition to freeing learners from any restriction imposed by handwriting, the use of [self-recorded audiotape] would enable them to respond freely to the questions posed and talk whilst referring to the [text] and personal notes' (Lockwood, 1991).

Strategies of data collection

The main strategies of data collection include home-based and tutorial-based study.

During *home-based study* modules are sent to testers together with a description of what they are expected to do, and a timetable for returning completed questionnaires, activities and assessment questions. The advantage of doing this is that testers can work at their own pace and can choose when to study. The disadvantage is that it takes time before feedback reaches the production team.

In *tutorial-based study* all testers gather in a convenient location and study the materials, complete questionnaires, etc., while you and the relevant members of the production group are present. (Many computer software producers test their products this way.) The advantage is that it allows immediate feedback and face-to-face discussions. The disadvantage is that some testers may feel that they are working under pressure, thus unable to do their best.

Questionnaire design

Questionnaire design is a skill which develops with practice. It involves asking the right questions and presenting them in a format which will ensure that the sought data are actually collected and interpreted unambiguously. Questions used in questionnaires are either 'closed ended' where the response must be chosen from a given list of options, or 'open ended' where the respondents are allowed to give their own responses.

Closed-ended questions may be of the dichotomous 'yes-no' type, or offer a longer list of options. Closed-ended questions are easy to process but they constrain the respondents to a limited choice of options, and prevent them from providing valuable information not anticipated by the evaluator. Open-ended questions, although they may be extremely time consuming to analyse, give respondents a chance to explain the nature of their problems and thus yield more valuable information.

DATA COLLECTION IN PRACTICE

Whom to ask

From *experts* and other *experienced colleagues* we need answers to questions like the following:

- Are there any technical errors in the materials?
- Are the proposed activities and the assessment questions suitable? If not can they suggest better ones?
- Do the materials meet the purposes for which they are written?

From *clients* we need answers to questions like the following:

- Do the materials fulfil their expectations?
- Do they find them consistent with their training requirements?
- Are their customers, e.g. trainees, likely to be satisfied with the products?

As far as the *learners* are concerned Henderson and Nathenson (1980) identify the following five types of data:

1. Data on clarity are concerned with such questions as whether the language and style of presentation of the materials are clear, whether students can perceive the relative importance of the various sections of the material, whether any tables or diagrams are clearly presented, etc.

2. Problems of level include such questions as whether students with little experience of the subject-matter encounter any particular difficulties and whether the most able students feel that they have been given the opportunity to pursue the subject-matter at an adequate depth.

3. Action data are required to discover what students actually do with the materials. For example, if the materials include self-assessment questions or other types of activities, do students do them? If optional routes are provided through the material, do students use them?

4. Data on attitude are concerned with such questions as whether students are motivated by the material, how students feel about answering self-assessment questions, or engaging in activities, or proceed through any optional routes which are provided, etc.

5. Data are also required on the time students spend studying the materials, including how they distribute their total study time between various sections or components of the materials.

These data are concerned with what actually happens during the learning process. In addition, there are other data which can help us to see the course from the learners' perspective. For example, a common expression used by learners of mathematics, sciences and engineering, or any learning material which involves formulas, etc., is to describe it as 'difficult to follow'. All such sections of the materials need to be identified. However, 'difficulty' is a blanket term which can point to deficiencies such as inadequacy of explanation. Therefore appropriate open-ended questions can discover what is meant by 'difficult' in each case. Inner feelings of learners during learning can affect the learning itself. For example, many mathematics learners experience various levels of anxiety affecting their study (Burt and Zand, 1989). Data may reveal whether learners felt excessive levels of anxiety and stress, and indicate why.

To evaluate the outcome of learning, a very useful piece of data is the testers' performance on the assessment questions for each module.

What questions to ask

After identifying the individuals or groups who will provide the data, we need to devise questions which will provide the information we require. A checklist of questions, offered by Henderson and Nathenson (1980) is given below to illustrate the kind of questions that you may wish to pose.

Most distance teaching materials can be divided into three distinct parts: preliminary organizers, the main body of learning material and the retrospective organizers.

Preliminary organizers

They direct the learners to what is coming in the course and include a list of objectives, prerequisites and the study guide. Questions you may wish to consider about objectives include the following:

- Are the objectives expressed clearly in terms familiar to the learners?
- Do the learners find them helpful?
- What do learners do with the objectives – ignore them, read them carefully, or what?
- What do the learners suggest about the objectives – delete them, present them differently or what?

Prerequisites are terms and concepts which learners are assumed to be familiar with, either from previous texts or from their general knowledge. This will communicate to learners what needs to be known before studying the materials. Questions you may wish to consider about objectives include the following:

- Can the prerequisites be realistically assumed?
- Is the list of prerequisites complete?
- What can learners do if they find certain terms unfamiliar?
- Do the learners have any suggestions for improving the list of prerequisites?

The study guide is a document which describes the structure of the teaching materials, informs learners about assessment, comments on how the course can be tackled, etc. Questions to consider include the following:

- Does the study guide fulfil its function?
- If the materials are multimedia, does it explain adequately the teaching function of the various media?
- Is there any information missing from the study guide?
- Do the learners have any suggestions on how to improve the study guide?

The main body of the learning materials

The kind of questions that you should be concerned with in relation to the main body of the text are illustrated by the following checklist of questions (Henderson and Nathenson, 1980):

1. *Problems of performance*

   - To what extent do students realize the objectives, their expectations of the course, etc.?
   - Can students identify the main line of an argument?
   - What answers do students provide to self-assessment questions?

2. *Problems of clarity*

   - Are the language and style of presentation of the materials clear to students?
   - Is the relationship between the purposes of major sections and the overall objectives clear to students?
   - If the materials include tables, illustrations, figures, photographs, diagrams, charts or maps, do students find these clearly presented?

3. *Problems of level*

   - Are the materials pitched at an appropriate level for students?
   - Do students with little previous experience of the subject-matter encounter particular difficulties?
   - Do students answer self-assessment questions in ways which are not anticipated by the specimen answers?

4. *Problems of action*

   - How do students react to self-assessment questions?
   - What do students do if they get a self-assessment question wrong?
   - If optional routes are provided through the materials, how do students use them?

5. *Problems of attitude*

   - Are students motivated by the materials?
   - How do students feel about the density of data or ideas in the materials?
   - Where examples have been given, do students feel that they illuminate the concept or principle they are meant to illuminate?

6. *Problems of time*

   - Do students know how much time to devote to various sections of the materials?
   - How much time do students spend answering self-assessment questions?
   - How much time do students spend on tables, illustrations, figures, photographs, charts, maps, etc.?

7. *Difficulty:*

   - Which items in the text do students find difficult?
   - What do students mean when they label something 'difficult'?
   - How does orientation to learning and ability influence what is found difficult?

8. *Inner feelings:*

   - Do students experience anxiety, frustration or stress during their study of the text?
   - Which particular items in the text generate such feelings?
   - Does the text adequately signpost the intellectually challenging parts?

Retrospective organizers

Post-study assessment questions, summaries and the list of new terms are the main types of retrospective organizers. Ideally, the assessment questions should directly correspond to the objectives and thus to the main body of the module, and the learners' performance thus provides a good diagnosis of the problem areas in the main body of the text. With regard to assessment questions the evaluator should be concerned with such questions as:

- Did the assessment items contain any terms, concepts, etc., which were not defined in the text?
- How difficult were these items?
- Were the assessment items found effective in assessing learners' knowledge?
- What do learners suggest for improvements of the assessment items?

REPORTING RESULTS

The aim of DT is to improve the academic quality and teaching effectiveness of the material – not to antagonize authors. A good DT report must be constructive. In this vein the following suggestions can be helpful:

- Always acknowledge what is commendable in a module before embarking on points of contention.
- Report with tact and sensitivity, especially if testers' comments are very negative.
- Be as specific as possible about the nature of any problems.
- When reporting a problem suggest how to improve it.
- Let the authors see your report before you make it public.

SUMMARY

In this chapter we have seen how the quality and effectiveness of open and distance learning materials can be ensured by developmental testing, and we have explored the main practical aspects of running such a test. In testing your own materials, you may find some of the suggestions made here useful, but you will need to modify and interpret them to suit your own particular situation.

REFERENCES AND NOTES

Burt, G. J. and Zand, H. (1989) Social and emotional dimensions of continuing education in mathematics, *Educational Training and Teaching International*, Vol. 26, no. 1, pp. 50–55.

Evans, T. and Lockwood, F. (1991) *Using Self-Recorded Interviews in Distance Teaching Research*, audio-cassette, M905, IDE806 and UDE606, Research in Distance Education, Institute of Distance Education, Deakin University and the University of South Australia.

Henderson, E. S. and Nathenson, M. B. (1980) *Using Student Feedback to Improve Learning Material*, Croom Helm, London. This book covers many theoretical and historical aspects of using students' feedback to improve open and distance teaching materials, and offers many examples which practitioners can find very useful.

Hodgson, B. (1993) *Key Terms and Issues in Open and Distance Learning*, Kogan Page, London.

Lockwood, F. (1991) *Data Collection in Distance-Education Research, the Use of Self-Recorded Audiotape*, IDE806 and UDE606, Research in Distance Education, Institute of Distance Education, Deakin University and the University of South Australia. This paper and tape explore the use of activities in open and distance teaching materials, which producers of self-instructional texts can find extremely useful in the design and the production of their texts.

Tessmer, M. (1993) *Planning and Conducting Formative Evaluation*, Kogan Page, London. Tessmer's text covers many theoretical aspects of formative evaluation and offers a variety of practical questions which practitioners, after suitable adaptation, can find very useful.

PART 3
PRESENTATION

Overview

Janet Jenkins

Issues of presentation are central to the effectiveness of open and distance learning. The term 'presentation' is used to cover all aspects of delivery and operation of a course, in which learning materials are a key component. How do learners access the material? How is their learning to be assessed? What support for learning do they receive? What forms of interaction are available to provide feedback or deal with queries? How is the effectiveness of the learning process to be monitored? The answers to such questions, addressed in the chapters that follow, affect the quality of course reception, support and operation.

These issues are naturally of importance for tutors, mentors, managers – all those whose primary concern is course delivery. But they also matter to course designers – all those involved in course development, whether they plan, write, edit or produce learning material. The process and environment of learning complement the materials, and the challenge for open and distance education is to create conditions for effective learning.

Different arrangements for teaching and learning are appropriate in different circumstances, and excellent learning materials may have only limited impact if support for learning is inadequate, inappropriate or absent. With open and distance learning being used in an ever-greater variety of situations, it is an increasingly complex task to design a teaching and learning system which maximizes the potential in each case.

Readers could usefully focus their thoughts on the learner. How do the information and ideas in each chapter relate to learning effectiveness? How could they affect course design and development, in support of effective learning? What effect might awareness of learners' different environments – home, workplace, educational institution – have on course design?

Course designers may usefully have an influence on course presentation. Those involved in the design and development of a course become thoroughly familiar with it and are well placed to brief tutors and help set up the delivery system. There is a particular weakness in much workplace learning: managers recognize the value of open learning, but often introduce it without understanding the implications of doing so, and the need to design and resource a support system. Course designers may be called on to advise in such situations, to avoid wasted effort. Poor presentation arrangements can kill a course, as Hilary Temple shows in her first chapter in the section (Chapter 15).

The opening chapter in this part, Peter Raggatt's 'Outcomes and assessment in open and distance education' (Chapter 13), draws attention to how the nature of assessment provision affects the nature of the learning environment. In traditional open and distance learning we expect to see a combination of formative assessment, which helps learners check progress and develop their understanding through activities, and summative assessment, which evaluates learners' achievement. Self-assessment is used alongside tutor-marked assignments to provide both formative and summative feedback, with the occasional use of peer-group activity and face-to-face tuition. The rising prominence of competence-based learning is forcing a rethink. The emphasis on summative assessment of outcomes has to be reconciled with the need to support the process of learning; and the requirement on learners to demonstrate their achievement of complete sets of competences, in contrast to the traditional academic approach of selective demonstration of acquisition of knowledge, means that the assessment strategy must cater for a variety of different types of outcome. In particular the strategy will usually need to include assessment of performance in realistic working environments. While not all open and distance learning is competence based, the approach discussed leads to re-evaluation of assessment strategy in open and distance learning and provides ideas for its broadening. The implementation of such a strategy will be a challenge that makes new demands on learners and their tutors as well as on course developers.

Such demands will be in addition to those that already exist for all newcomers to distance and open learning. Most people at first find it difficult to grasp the different nature of delivery and assessment. Learners need guidance in how to use their course material, which tutors are generally expected to provide. But new tutors do not themselves necessarily understand the issues. Mary Thorpe's chapter, 'Planning for learner support and the facilitator role' (Chapter 14), explores the role of the tutor as a bridge between learner and materials. The materials are common to all students on a course, while the tutor responds to the learner as an individual. Since materials and tutor are complementary, it is essential for course designers to concern themselves with both, to make decisions about the precise role of the tutor at the course planning stage, and to take these into account in developing the learning material. Further, an agenda for tutor training demonstrates that course developers are ideally involved in that training.

Hilary Temple's chapter, 'Workplace learners: learning in "unconventional" settings' (Chapter 15), identifies the various issues that have to be faced and demonstrates the particular difficulties of providing support in the workplace. She explores the benefits of open learning as a method for workplace training, and suggests that it is most effective if the workplace itself is perceived as a learning environment, where on-the-job learning is reinforced by directed learning. The importance of the mentor is stressed, and we may soon see on the agenda the joint and complementary training of mentors and tutors, particularly to address the assessment strategies of the future set out in Peter Raggatt's chapter (Chapter 13). Indeed, if competence-based approaches to learning continue to grow in importance, the workplace may rapidly become a standard, rather than unconventional, setting for much open and distance learning.

As Mary Thorpe points out, it is not just learners who need learning materials. Tutors and mentors also need briefing materials. Desk-top publishing has brought flexibility to course production that makes it easier to provide a range of text resources within a limited period of time. Paul Lefrere's chapter, 'The technology and management of desk-top publishing' (Chapter 16), removes the mystique and explains what DTP is and what it can do for you. It can help course developers control output and can contribute to quality. The shortened span necessary between final editing and print and the ease of handling means that it is possible to incorporate last minute changes or produce additional material, without missing deadlines. Among its strengths is speed of delivery, important when one of the great weaknesses of open and distance learning is late distribution of material.

Printed text is still the main medium of instruction for open and distance learning. But other media are regularly used and interest is high in new technologies both for teaching material and for delivery. New technologies are all too often enthusiastically embraced and tried without full consideration of the needs of learners and the context of use. Hilary Temple's second chapter, on managing open learning (Chapter 17), provides a systematic approach to the design and operation of an open learning system tailored to each different situation. She draws attention to planning issues essential to consider before decisions on learning technologies can sensibly be made.

This position is uncompromising but common sense. The bottom line is that learners must have access to learning, and technology must be used in a way that enables rather than impedes. Bernadette Robinson's chapter on quality assurance (Chapter 18) also takes a commonsense approach, again putting learners first. While acknowledging the value of procedures for assuring quality, she suggests that their application does not guarantee a good result, showing the shortcomings of a mechanistic approach. Taking the line that quality results from attention not only to the whole process of teaching and learning but also to each and every part of that process, she offers practical advice for progress towards excellence.

The final chapter in this part, Judith Calder's on course evaluation (Chapter 19), explores how evaluation during presentation can provide insight for course development. The notion of academic quality is closely linked with learner satisfaction. The chapter sets out suggestions for course evaluation techniques which provide an opportunity to examine the process of learning and explore how learners perceive it. Conclusions drawn from such evaluation can usefully feed back into course revision and the design of new courses. Importantly also, evaluation contributes to a detailed understanding of what makes open and distance learning effective in an increasing variety of different settings. We come full circle, with the views of learners informing course design.

FINAL WORD

You may come to this part of the book after reading the first two. But I hope that you have arrived here before you have done your course planning and production. I hope too that this overview convinces you that it is worth reading on before you get to work on your course, although you may also wish to come back to the section for reference later.

The book is about open and distance learning, that is learning which takes place without much face-to-face contact. But the learners are the central interest throughout. This part places them firmly in an environment supportive of learning. What are the characteristics of such an environment? Only good understanding of your learners can enable you to define these. I would like to urge you, before you progress your own work in open and distance learning, to make contact with some learners in a typical environment. Try to arrange a visit to an open learning centre or an Open University study centre. If you are new to the field, you will find that this will place in perspective this part, and much of what you have read in the book; if you are already experienced, it will refresh your vision.

13

Outcomes and assessment in open and distance education

Peter Raggatt

In most open and distance learning organizations assessment and learning have enjoyed a close and intimate relationship. Assessment has not simply been the end point of learning but has been an important component in the design of the learning process itself, an essential tool in facilitating learning. That relationship and the belief on which it rests is now being severely tested by the movement towards an outcomes model for education and training. This chapter begins by acknowledging the conventional relationship between learning and assessment which lies at the heart of much good practice in open and distance learning and then examines the outcomes approach and its implications for assessment.

ASSESSMENT AND LEARNING

Formative and summative assessment

In open and distance learning, much effort is expended on the design of learning materials, on the selection of content, the preparation of texts and on tutorial and other forms of learner support. Assessment cannot escape this strong and pervasive orientation to planning effective learning. It is not then simply that assessment is a necessary feature if certification is to be awarded but that much of it is also specifically designed to aid learning. This may be made explicit as it is in the formal distinction between formative and summative assessment.

Formative assessment is designed to uncover where learners are experiencing difficulties or have an incomplete understanding, i.e. it is concerned with *how* learners understand a concept or procedure rather than how much they know or have achieved (Murphy, 1988). Formative assessment often focuses on the more difficult concepts and ideas and is designed to ensure feedback and improve learners' understanding before they progress to dependent areas of study.

Activities and questions which are incorporated into texts and followed by a commentary from the author are a common example. Learners are able to check their own comments (and understanding) against yours. They are able to 'see how they are doing' and where they may need some additional help from you or through further focused study. In a similar vein where evaluation suggests that there is an area of particular difficulty, a formative assignment may be set to guarantee a teaching input.

By contrast summative assignments are formally graded and recorded. They are designed to assess *what* is known (and what is not known). They may include a formative stage, i.e. the assignment is submitted at a planning stage to get feedback and advice. The learner can then use the feedback to develop the assignment for the final summative submission.

Pacing learning

In open and distance learning it is all too easy for learners working largely independently to fall behind in their studies. Other work, domestic difficulties and spending too long on earlier sections of the materials all conspire to subvert the best intentions. For those who do fall behind, the difficulties involved in *'catching up'* may seem insurmountable and may result in dropping out. A well planned assessment schedule which helps learners pace their learning can reduce this risk. An early assignment will ensure that the learner makes an early contact with you and that he or she quickly understands the demands of the course. Carefully planned dates for the submission of assignments provide an external source of discipline for learners and will alert you to potential difficulties in instances when learners are late with their assignments. More exacting assignments can be introduced as the course progresses with a weighting to reflect the differing demands. Later assignments may require learners to integrate concepts from different parts of the course or to apply and evaluate different models for the analysis of a context, case study or problem. Again the link between learning and assessment is an important feature underpinning the design of the course and the assessment strategy.

Assessment, then, is a key feature in open and distance learning. It fulfils a number of functions. It may be formative, enabling a learner or you to check the response against criteria; it may be diagnostic, enabling at least an initial identification of strengths and potential areas of learning difficulty; it will be used to provide guidance and feedback; it may be summative, providing a grade which contributes to the final award; and it may be the source of necessary external discipline without which a learner would fall too far behind in his or her studies. Assessment can also help to motivate learners through the admission of personal experience as a relevant source of learning and of data for assignments and through the feedback from you which can help learners to develop self-esteem and confidence in their development.

THE OUTCOMES APPROACH: THE NEW CHALLENGE

The origins of the outcomes approach can be traced to the New Training Initiative (Employment Department, 1981) which introduced the notion of standards (of occupational competence) on which vocational qualifications and training and are now largely based but the same concept underpins the approach to the National Curriculum and has been signalled for 'A' level (Department of Education and Science, 1991). It has been slower to take root in higher education but there are now strong signs of a steady growth notably in professional and applied areas such as management and in the Enterprise in Higher Education Initiative now present in over 60 universities.

At its simplest the outcomes model asserts that successful participants, employers and other interested parties should know what a qualification or a successful learning experience means in terms of what the holder should know, understand and be able to do. Outcomes provide the criteria against which learners are assessed, but they make no prescriptions about the modes of learning or where it should take place. It opens the way for learners to present evidence of successful learning however or wherever it has been achieved. Depending on the particular outcomes, evidence may be accummulated in a variety of contexts. Assessment and learning are thus separated and the learner has greater autonomy both in relation to the learning process and to assessment.

The specification of learning outcomes also makes it easier for learners to understand what is expected of them and to choose between learning opportunities with different learning outcomes. It establishes targets and provides a clear focus for learning and assessment.

The specificity of these targets varies across education and training. Occupational competences as manifested in National/Scottish Vocational Qualifications (N/SVQs) provide examples of explicit targets. In order to achieve an N/SVQ candidates must demonstrate competent performance in all elements of competence. In contrast, educational targets tend to be more general and are concerned with the development of intellectual and personal skills, such as communication, and with values. In practice, there is considerable overlap between the two areas and there are many examples of ways in which occupational competences contribute to intellectual and personal development and in which education contributes to occupational competence.

This becomes apparent as we progress to higher-level N/SVQs which are increasingly being offered in colleges and universities. While all N/SVQs 'unreservedly concentrate on the ability to perform effectively' (Mitchell, 1993), effective performance also depends on individuals having a body of knowledge, theory, principles and cognitive skills on which to draw. It is this that stabilizes performance enabling it to be sustained over time and in different contexts. This body of underpinning knowledge and understanding is very substantial at higher levels and is reflected in different forms of assessment used at different levels.

The characteristics of higher-level roles (or those likely to occur at level 4 or 5 of the N/SVQ framework) have been summarized by Mitchell (1993, p. 6) as those where:

- action is based on considerable bodies of underpinning knowledge and understanding – facts, views, theories, concepts etc.
- much action can be viewed as 'knowledge in action' – an individual's performance within an occupation often revolves around rapid cognitive

processing – the outcomes of action are the results of this cognitive processing

- initiation and origination of work for others are likely to be key competences at this level and will involve individuals in synthesizing information in new ways to offer one or more solutions to problems
- action takes place over a wide range of contexts which are subject to wide variation and uncertainty and are often complex in nature
- the results or outcomes of action are likely to be long term or have long-term consequences with actions tending to be future focused rather than concerned with the here and now
- the results or outcomes involve high degrees of criticality, either in terms of value or for their personal and/or social consequences
- process outcomes tend to be more predominant than product outcomes
- the work tends to involve interactions with environments and systems outside the employing organization
- individuals have a high degree of autonomy and usually take final responsibility for the consequences of their actions.

Whilst such facets characterize higher level roles, they are not restricted to them . . . Level 5 is distinguished by the greater likelihood of occurrence of these characteristics and their occurrence in combination.

Mitchell has been quoted at length not simply because she provides a clear articulation of the importance of an extensive knowledge base at higher levels and illustrates the overlap with many intended outcomes of higher education but also because, by inference, she draws attention to the wide array of criteria that will underpin competence at higher levels which need to be encompassed in the assessment strategies used in colleges and universities.

OUTCOMES AND ASSESSMENT

The specification of learning in terms of outcomes necessarily focuses attention on the validity of assessment and raises questions about existing assessment practice. In education, assessment has typically been based on sampling learners' knowledge and understanding. In addition, assessment has included the principle of compensation, i.e. learners have been allowed to compensate for poor answers on some questions with good scores on others. But are these practices tenable, are they valid, in an outcomes approach? In certificating a learner the institution is making a public statement that the learner can do to an acceptable level of performance whatever is specified in the learning outcomes. It does not mean that the learner can perform successfully at *some* of the stated outcomes but against all of them. It would be no good giving a pilot a certificate of competence because he or she can do most parts of the job very well but has difficulty in landing. For assessment to be valid all learning outcomes must be assessed. Moreover, the assessment methods must be appropriate to the learning outcomes.

In the past, educational institutions have relied heavily on written forms of assessment. These work well enough for certain forms of performance, notably those assessing knowledge and the skills of academic discourse. But there are many other important forms of performance – practical skills and procedures in science laboratories, engineering workshops and restaurants, landing a plane, the ability to apply theories, principles and ideas in new situations, interpersonal and negotiating skills – which cannot be assessed using written tests. It is not valid to exclude such skills from assessment if they are intended learning outcomes, nor is it valid to assess such skills through written questions. They require realistic situations where the skills can be demonstrated. To meet this obligation a wider range of assessment techniques is needed than is customarily used by educational institutions. Some will be difficult to implement unless an institution is prepared to share responsibility for assessment with other groups.

Direct observation is a case in point. There are many instances where direct observation of performance is necessary, notably where an institution is working in vocational and professional areas. Discussing this point, Eraut and Cole (1993) cite recent research involving 11 professional bodies where they found 'no dissent from the NCVQ/SCOTVEC principle that evidence based directly on performance in the workplace should be given a high priority' (p. 10). In professions where there is a high level of personal interaction with clients and a premium on interpersonal skills and communication, as occurs in counselling, social work and teaching, observation of performance is the most valid form of assessment for some aspects of the work role. This is difficult for an open and distance learning organization to deliver cost effectively unless it is done in collaboration with others – which raises the issue of who owns and controls assessment.

Over the next few years we can anticipate much closer working relationships between educational organizations and employers. Employers are likely to be involved increasingly in supporting learning and assessment. One example of this approach is provided by the Personal and Career Development course at The Open University. The course is primarily concerned with the development of transferable skills, particularly communication, interpersonal and problem-solving skills. The materials provide a structure through which learners undertake a process of self-assessment, goal setting or action planning, skills development and reflection. In most instances learners design and undertake a project to demonstrate the development of transferable skills within the workplace (though other contexts and roles are entirely acceptable). Employers participate by providing the learner/employee with the advice and support of a mentor and, perhaps, by creating new responsibilities or situations where the skills can be practised and demonstrated. Learners are assessed largely through a project report in which they are required to describe and explain their development of transferable skills and how it is linked to their action plan. As yet employers are not directly involved in assessment though the course offers this potential. Other courses – in management and child care – have gone further in involving employers in the assessment process and include, for example, witness testimony (written accounts of the activities and performance of the learner/candidate), authentication that the work products, candidate reports, etc., are the candidate's own work.

The shift to an outcomes approach will have major implications for assessment. It is not possible to develop the issues here but the main points are summarized below:

- It has separated assessment from learning.
- It has potentially separated qualifications from the education and training process.
- Credit will be dependent on learners achieving a satisfactory level of performance (competence) against all specified learning outcomes.
- There will be a growing demand for an assessment-only option and for the accreditation of prior learning (APL).
- There will be a greater emphasis on the validity of assessment.
- A wider range of assessment methods will be used.
- The relative importance of assessing for underpinning knowledge and understanding will increase as the knowledge base increases but tests of knowledge will need to be supplemented by other forms of assessment including assessment of performance under realistic working conditions.
- The responsibility for assessment will be shared with other bodies.
- There will be a need for effective verification and a quality assurance system including the use of competent assessors.

IMPLICATIONS FOR OPEN AND DISTANCE EDUCATION

The implications and responses of open and distance education institutions will range across a continuum. Immediate changes in academic areas which have no direct relationship to occupations will be small. Assessments will continue to focus on knowledge and understanding and written assignments and examinations will continue to have an important role. Even here, however, we can expect to see a broader range of assessment methods with formal examinations coming under closer scrutiny – is it a valid way of assessing performance? Other possibilities such as learning files, portfolios, presentation of case studies and reflective accounts of the cognitive processes – for example, outlining how judgements were made – may be explored. The further questions that you and your institution will have to address is whether to offer an assessment-only option and whether assessment can be available on demand, i.e. when individual learners are ready for it.

The greater changes will be in those areas which are more obviously concerned with the application of knowledge. In FE colleges where open learning, or resource-based learning, is being introduced to support the development of knowledge and understanding for N/SVQs, a range of internal facilities (salons, kitchens, restaurants, construction and engineering workshops, etc.) and external facilities (industrial placements) is normally available which enables them to deliver a complete range of assessment. At Chippenham College, for example, in some departments very little class teaching is now provided. Unit-specific texts provide the underpinning knowledge and this is consolidated through one-to-one teaching in practical contexts, e.g. in the salon in relation to the service needed by a client. Assessment is initiated by learners when they judge they are ready (i.e. competent). More assessment is likely to be undertaken in the workplace as the number of competent and qualified assessors increases – the college is providing assessor training for companies.

Similar developments are occurring in higher education with management leading the way. This is impelled by the need to provide assessment under realistic working conditions for N/SVQ Levels 4 and 5. The Open University which, as a distance learning organization, has greater difficulty than most in using observation of performance, is training assessors in companies who will then assess the performance of learners in the workplace on behalf of the university. The university will provide the necessary quality-assurance procedures to ensure that the required national standards are being sustained. The care area is also developing an assessment strategy that includes assessment in the workplace.

Many other departments in higher education also have a substantial applied element in their learning programmes – the sciences which teach laboratory skills used throughout scientific industries, mathematics, computing and systems which have wide applications in industry, social sciences which are used in many applied forms such as local administration, the health services, urban planning, land management, social work, environmental health and so on. They clearly have a choice. They can decide to restrict learning materials to knowledge and understanding and use written methods of assessment, or they can develop a broader strategy for assessment and include the assessment of performance in realistic working environments.

If the former option is adopted and learners wish to achieve an N/SVQ they could use parallel or subsequent work experience to develop evidence of practical skills through a portfolio of evidence. They could submit this to, say, an NVQ awarding body or to SCOTVEC along with the proof of competence in underpinning knowledge and understanding from the course they have taken. This would provide a useful facility for many learners who are not yet in a work role which enables performance to be assessed. In the short term this may be an attractive option for many departments and learners, perhaps especially those engaged in continuing professional development.

If the latter option of delivering learning materials and assessment is adopted the organization will either need to deliver assessment with a partner who can provide performance assessment in the workplace, for example through industrial placements, or it must develop the necessary systems on its own. Either way it will involve a considerable extension of the typical assessment repertoire of educational institutions and new quality-assurance systems.

AN ASSESSMENT STRATEGY

Eraut and Cole's (1993) paper on the assessment of competence in higher-level occupations offers a useful insight into the forms of assessment that are used by professional bodies and could be more widely employed. They include performance evidence: direct and indirect (audio and video recordings and photographic evidence), observation in the workplace, observation of simplified practice and role playing; simulations (competency tests, skills tests, proficiency tests, projects and assignments); extracted examples from work roles (computer programs, case studies, evaluations of marketing strategies, an audit report, blueprints, lesson plans, etc.); reflective reports on work by the candidate; work logs and other portfolio evidence; and project reports and assignments. In some instances the evidence produced will have to be authenticated by a company representative as the work of the individual learner. Supplementary evidence may be obtained through oral and written questions, essays, witness testimony and mentor reports.

Some learning outcomes need to be assessed through direct observation of performance. Many of these come in the area of the core skills such as communication and interpersonal skills but also relate to values. In more practical terms they refer to the ability to work with others, to negotiate, to provide leadership and to counsel others. At one level they are important abilities in teaching, social work, child care, management and other professional work. At another level they are relevant personal and citizenship skills required by all. Some evidence of achievement can be demonstrated indirectly through audio and video recordings or through simulation.

Drawing these ideas together anyone planning an assessment strategy would find it helpful to plot learning outcomes against possible assessment methods as shown in Table 13.1.

Table 13.1 Learning outcomes and assessment methods

Learning outcomes or objectives	Written examinations	Written assignments	Project reports	Work-based (practical) project	Simulation, role play	Work product	Work logs, diaries	Reflective account of practice	Witness testimony	Indirect observation	Direct observation	Oral questioning	APL
1.1													
1.2													
1.3													
1.4													
2.1													
2.2													
2.3													
3.1													
3.2													
3.3													
etc.													

The use of a grid of this sort would facilitate reliability and validity in designing assessment – several assessment methods can be used for each outcome to enhance reliability and the methods can be readily checked for validity. Moreover, the grid could be made available to learners and APL candidates who could then be given greater responsibility and autonomy for deciding, perhaps in consultation with you or an adviser, which forms of assessment are most appropriate to their situation. The evidence could be presented in portfolio form possibly with reflective accounts of activities – depending on the learning outcomes specified for the course – the cognitive processes used in reaching judgements and so on.

Your role in this system becomes one of advising and guiding on the collection and organization of evidence, its suitability, sufficiency and currency. You may or may not also act as assessor but you will have an important role in authenticating that the evidence in the portfolio is the learner's own work.

SUMMARY

Over the years open and distance education institutions have developed imaginative and effective methods of teaching and learning. They will now have to be equally imaginative and effective in developing a wide range of assessment methods. Organizations, departments and tutors must face many issues of policy: should an assessment-only option be offered or is taking the course a requirement? To what extent can responsibility for assessment be shared with other organizations? What new quality-assurance systems will be needed? There will also be numerous technical questions: What evidence do we need? How shall we collect it? How can we ensure its authenticity? Whatever the individual decisions the outcome for open and distance organizations will be a much wider range of assessment methods.

REFERENCES AND NOTES

Department of Education and Science (1991) *Education and Training for the 21st Century*, HMSO, London.

Employment Department (1981) *The New Training Initiative: A Programme for Action*, HMSO, London.

Eraut, M. and Cole, G. (1993) Assessment of competence in higher level occupations, *Competence and Assessment*, Issue 21, Sheffield, Employment Department. *Competence and Assessment* is a free quarterly issued by the Employment Department (TEED). It provides a range of short articles concerned with assessing for competence.

Mitchell, L. (1993) NVQs/SVQs at higher levels: a discussion paper, *Competence and Assessment*, briefing paper no. 8, Sheffield Employment Department.

Murphy, P. (1988) TGAT: a conflict of purpose, *Curriculum*, Vol. 9, no. 3, pp. 152–8.

For an up-to-date discussion of outcomes, learning and curriculum matters and related assessment issues, see Burke, J. (ed.) (1994). *Outcomes, Learning and the Curriculum*, Falmer, Brighton.

14

Planning for learner support and the facilitator role

Mary Thorpe

It is a common experience among learners in open and distance learning that interaction with other learners, and with a tutor or facilitator, is highly valued. Materials producers need to design systems which can respond to the varying demands for interaction among those using their materials. Central to many such systems is the tutor or facilitator – titles may differ, but mediation between learners and the goals set by the materials, and meeting the learners' interpersonal learning needs, are central to this role. Specialist and generalist roles of facilitators can be distinguished. Materials producers need to make explicit decisions about the facilitator role at the design stage, so that materials and guidance to students can incorporate this perspective into their learning experience. Launching the materials also requires briefing and explanatory material for facilitators and the content of meetings and documentation are suggested in outline. Facilitators also have a continuing role through assessment and evaluation, and communication should be maintained through the life of a course.

INTRODUCTION

Learning is a socially constructed activity. From the earliest moment, what and how we learn is a product of our social context and of the immediate social relationships through which we are learning. In the case of learning to achieve a particular goal, such as work-related training or study, social interaction continues to play a role (to different degrees for different people) in successful learning. Even when learners are not experiencing difficulty, and even more so when they are, they are likely to want to share their interpretation of course materials, and to find out how well they are understanding and achieving the goals set by the course. Some comments illustrating this point and made by users of distance-taught courses in both industry and education are included below: the first two extracts are from an industrial training context, the next two are from students studying psychology majors by distance learning at Gippsland Institute, Australia (Parer and Benson, 1989) and the last two are from Open University students.

Employees in work-related open learning
It doesn't stick in my head as well as attending a course; I've just attended a five-day training course, where the tutor really brought to life each of the topics, and I can really remember what he said about different things. A

package is so dry – even with different layouts and cartoons which help to alleviate the effort you have to put into it – but still a lot of it just doesn't stick, so retention isn't as good as with a good face-to-face course. Also the group helps. When you do exercises they make an input and you miss that with exercises you do on your own. You're never sure you've done it right and you miss the input of other people.

It would be better if someone read these books out on video or in the room to us – not relying on us to read and digest all the facts. It is too much for us to digest in [*sic*] and starts to get boring. I do not like reading.

Psychology students in higher education
Every day I wish I had another student somewhere locally to talk over problems with. This to me is the most difficult area of external study . . . I can barely think of examples when asked to at the end of a section, yet when I can discuss it with someone – often one mind seems to get the other up and running.

I wish I had someone with whom to talk over different theories so I can get my own views sorted out . . . I really miss having other students to chat with – that used to help me more [*re.* analysis rather than absorption of facts].

Students studying for a professional diploma
It's only really when you actually got to the group tutorials that you realized the sort of things you were short of. So that wasn't as useful, not because [the tutor] wasn't very helpful on the phone, but I just found it wasn't as helpful as face-to-face tutorials and the group working sessions.

I suppose I went through from the beginning and worked through, and if I didn't understand things, I rang [the tutor] and said 'I'm really not in the slightest bit interested in this mathematical diagram to do with learning' and then she made me look at it in different ways, and when I went back to it, I discovered that I had understood it and knew all about it, and I'd just been a bit stupid.

This desire to relate learning to our direct experience and for a response from others is not, of course, equally developed in all who learn, and we could add to the list above remarks from some who prefer to learn on their own. Practical experience at The Open University, for example, has shown that a small minority of students value the distance element in open and distance learning (ODL) for its own sake – they choose it precisely because they want to distance themselves from others. But to varying degrees, others want contact with a trainer or facilitator, and with other learners whether face to face or by other means, in the real time of their learning process. For some, a single effective conversation may be enough; for others a regular schedule of meetings may be necessary. And one of the issues which materials producers need to address, therefore, is the establishment of systems which can respond to these varying demands for interaction from those using their materials.

This point can be argued as a general issue, about the nature of learning, irrespective of the effectiveness of particular materials or the learners in ques-

tion. But, as the opening selection of quotations suggests, both materials and the institutional arrangements within which they are used create a range of difficulties and challenges which require interaction with others if they are to be resolved positively.

This introduces one of the most important outcomes of practical experience in ODL, which is that, even where materials of proven high quality are created, many learners still require the flexible and individual attention that only a person can provide in order to achieve their intended learning goals. In some cases, whether because of the difficulties experienced or because of the high demands made by the course, effective progress can only be made with the expertise and assistance of a person who can listen and speak to the learner, using a language which effectively 'bridges the gap' between learner and material.

This is the central role of the tutor or facilitator in being able to converse with learners and help them understand what they are having difficulty with, or to challenge and extend an early, provisional grasp of course materials. In addition, tutor or trainer contact may be the only way in which certain skills can be developed, through modelling of the correct way, and feedback immediately to the student on the effectiveness of their own efforts. Many learners also value social interaction with peers as well as with tutors because it stimulates a sense of the wider, social purposes of learning, and helps strengthen motivation and commitment.

Learner support has come to be used as the phrase summing up this area, although it is not entirely successful in indicating the wide range of both content and learning-specific issues which it covers in practice. It has been defined as 'all those aspects of an ODL system able to respond to a known individual learner' (Thorpe, 1988). This is to distinguish it therefore from interactive devices embedded in materials which, however successful they may be in generating a personal response from the learner, cannot respond to that learner as a known individual, during the process of learning itself – the learner can only be known as an abstract identity before learning begins, however effective the market research and surveys we undertake. We can never *wholly* predict the actual response of our learners and provide for it in advance.

Materials producers may need to set up complete systems through which materials are distributed to users and trainers/tutors are effectively prepared to support the materials in use. A full treatment of this topic, encompassing as it does issues such as study centres, residential schools, telephone communication, computer-mediated or face-to-face tutorials, assessment and counselling generally, is well beyond the scope of a single chapter. In many circumstances, however, it is the person who acts as facilitator who plays the key role in meeting interpersonal learning needs. I have focused therefore on the role of the facilitator (a title which encompasses both trainer and tutor roles) and on issues which require planning and preparation by materials producers.

The nature of planning and action required depends upon the relationship between what is to be taught, to whom and in what circumstances. Materials producers therefore cannot pick prescriptions off the shelf, but must analyse what is required successfully to achieve the goals of their course. In doing so, it may be helpful to consider the distinction between specialist and generalist definitions of the role of facilitators.

FACILITATORS WITH SPECIALIST TEACHING ROLES

This approach allocates to the facilitator only, the role of teaching some aspect of course content or of achieving specific course outcomes. The facilitator is in effect treated as one of the teaching media alongside others, whether text alone, or with audio-, video- and computer-based instruction. A facilitator may be given a specific role to teach certain elements in a course which it is felt can only be taught, or can best be taught, using the human teachers in a system. This may reflect the fact that other interactive media are not available or feasible, or a judgement about the relative merits of particular media for the learners concerned. ODL technology has more easily taken the place of lectures, for example, than of demonstration, workshop and laboratory course work. To exploit the role of facilitators, many organizations mount residential schools to teach those things which it is felt cannot be taught in any other way. Morgan and Thorpe (1993) have outlined the rationale for such schools in detail and they emphasize the role of direct contact with tutors and other learners in bringing about major conceptual change, attitude change and skill learning, particularly motor-skill learning where there is no substitute for role play and try out, with immediate feedback from an expert.

This approach to facilitators as a specialized teaching medium requires decision-making at the stage of materials design and production. The decision may also reflect the relative costs of using existing staff rather than creating new materials. It has often been noted, for example, that computer-based training and other expensive technologies are unlikely to be developed by small- and medium-sized enterprises, because they require highly skilled staff and expensive facilities to produce. Where small numbers of learners are concerned, human tutors and trainers may still be the most cost-effective medium for some kinds of learning, working in tandem with print and other media (see Henry, Chapter 1).

FACILITATORS WITH A GENERALIST ROLE

Here the primary role of the facilitator is to create a relationship with the learner(s) which is productive for their learning, and through this relationship to provide a back-up to all the other media of the course. This approach to the role provides an illustration of the points made above concerning the social, interactive nature of learning. The facilitator provides something the materials by definition cannot provide – a relationship with and a response to a known learner. This role places the facilitator in the position of an intermediary, perceiving the interests and requirements of both materials package and of the learners. It is the facilitator who must articulate these different requirements and establish a dialogue between them (Thorpe, 1979).

This distinction between specialist and generalist roles for the facilitator is not always easy to separate out in practice, and a combination of the two may often be in play, as where the facilitator also assesses learners. Assessment creates a specialist role since it is only through the judgements of the facilitator that learners are accredited. This can be integrated with the generalist role where the facilitator also seeks to support other aspects of the learners' needs in using the materials.

IMPLICATIONS FOR MATERIALS PRODUCERS

A strong case has been made for the positive effects on learning using self-instructional materials, when these are combined with (limited forms of) social interaction, particularly between facilitators and learners. Although materials producers are likely to be dominated by the production process, they can also contribute to effective learner support in a number of ways. They can make explicit decisions about the role(s) of tutors in their course, they can reflect this role in the content of materials produced and they can provide an effective introduction for facilitators, both to the course and to the role they will play. Each of these areas for action is discussed in turn.

Specifying the facilitator role and resources for tuition

Materials producers need to decide whether any of the course aims or outcomes is to be taught primarily via the facilitator. If so, materials designed specifically for facilitator use will probably be necessary. Decisions will also be required about the frequency and length of contacts with learners, and guidelines on how such resource might be scheduled through the duration of materials use. This may be very much a guestimate, and flexibility should be built into the system, allowing adjustments to be made in the light of experience. The producers could use trainers or teachers experienced in the topic to review the course outline and offer judgements about the scheduling of contact or group sessions.

Course evaluation should also be designed to include feedback from learners on the amount and kinds of support they need. Flexibility is desirable even year on year; for example, some learners manage on four hours' contact with a facilitator for a course which others find requires a minimum of eight hours or more.

Producing materials which 'cue' the facilitator role

Facilitation is at its most effective where learners are proactive and make demands, rather than wait to be helped. Materials producers can foster this orientation in a number of ways. They can suggest that activities in the materials be discussed with the facilitator or raised at a group session. A flexible assignment structure can allow learners to negotiate their assignment topics with their facilitator, who thereby plays a larger role in the learners' learning. The timing of group sessions can also be devolved to facilitators to negotiate with the group to suit their immediate needs.

In some cases, the role of a facilitator may be closely defined by the design of the materials. The example in Figure 14.1 shows a small section of the pack produced by British Gas for the co-ordinators of a video-led training programme, introducing changes in company policy on central heating servicing.

Running the training

Where do I start?

Introduce the session by briefing the trainees on:

- the reasons for the future policy.

- the advantages to the company.

- the importance of involving the customer.

- the use of the Marketing Pack.

Section 1 of the workbook contains a number of exercises covering each of the major points.

Running Part 1 of the video

Introduce the video by explaining its function (see "Package components").

"Bye"

Run Part 1 of the video and stop the action after approximately eight minutes when this frame appears.

Ask the group to consider the importance of creating a good first impression and the ways to achieve this. Note the answers on the flipchart.

Discuss the merits of each answer. Emphasise the following:

- uniform.

- identity card.

- preparation of tools and equipment.

Figure 14.1 Extract from notes prepared for the facilitator of a video-based British Gas training pack

Could this approach be adapted to situations where the content of the learning is less clear cut – or where there is no one right answer? It is also likely that facilitators will need material outlining their role on the course as a whole, and this is taken up in the next section.

Launching the course and keeping in touch

The final implication for materials developers is that their products need to be effectively launched – for facilitators just as much as for learners. This *launching* process can be done via materials as well as meetings, but it is often desirable to begin with a meeting. People who have met, if only briefly, seem much better able to sustain communication at a distance than if they have never met.

One of the challenges materials developers face when setting about this task is that they find it difficult to adopt the perspective of the facilitator and speak primarily to their needs and interests in supporting learners. There is a risk that materials producers spend virtually all their time explaining to facilitators what they have done, and what is in *their* course, rather than helping the facilitators see what it is that they will be required to do, and how best to do it. Although facilitators do need to know about the materials, they also need other things, as they face the prospect of supporting learners on a course they have not produced themselves. A list of requirements which course briefings for facilitators should fulfil is offered as a starting point:

- A map of the course components and how they fit together.
- An overview of the concepts/content of each major component.
- An understanding of the teaching and learning assumptions made by the materials producers and embodied in the materials.
- The implications of these assumptions for what facilitators will be required to do.
- A timetable for the scheduling of learning, including assessment, from start to finish.
- Some idea of the likely difficulties learners might face, including preferences (where known) for some media over others, learning styles, etc.
- A guide to the criteria for assessment and to the standards required in marking learners' work.
- Procedures and documentation for systems of communication between facilitators, learners and institution – whether mail, telephone, computer-mediated communication or a combination of these methods.
- Procedures for course evaluation, especially any facilitator involvement.

Materials producers need to consider how best to draw on the technologies at their disposal to meet these requirements for briefing facilitators. Some can be most effectively met by preparing material and activities to do before the meeting, particularly to avoid the tendency to cram too much into the face-to-face session. The constraints on these meetings are not unlike those facing facilitators supporting their learners. There is often too much information to communicate effectively to learners; *telling* is perhaps not the best use of time, and yet the pressures often lead to precisely that. Briefing facilitators therefore is an opportunity to demonstrate the value of role plays, small-group discussions and other approaches which lead to active participation and variety. The materials producers should role model the desired approach and activities of the facilitator. It is important therefore that the team does not fall back on *chalk and talk* methods, and that it demonstrates interpersonal responsiveness and openness towards facilitators.

Good relationships established at the launch of a course can be maintained during its use, and it is desirable to arrange contact between producers and facilitators at a point where early experience can be checked and adjustments made. The establishment of common criteria and standards in assessment, for example, is much more likely where facilitators can discuss their grading or marking at the time it is done, and compare reactions and judgements. This is also reassuring, and a very common reaction among facilitators new to a course is to feel uncertain about whether their approach to assessment is what is required. Keeping in touch over these issues is valued, and likely to lead to positive commitments to the learners and the course.

Facilitators also have an important role to play in course evaluation (see Thorpe, 1993, and Calder, Chapter 19, for a discussion of this topic) and the results of both learner and facilitator surveys can be summarized and provide useful feedback about general course-progress issues overall. The materials-production staff should not see their role as finished once the materials are in use.

CONCLUSION

The effectiveness of course materials can undoubtedly be enhanced by constructive *thinking forwards* to the kinds of help and interaction learners are likely to need. Materials producers can provide guidance and support to the person whose role is to facilitate learning, and should plan to maintain contact during the use of materials, particularly over assessment and standards. The effectiveness of the relationship between materials producers and facilitators feeds through to the effectiveness of learning and thus to the quality of the course as experienced.

REFERENCES AND NOTES

Kelly, P. and Swift, B. (1983) *Tuition at Post-Foundation Level in The Open University*, SRD paper no. 253, Institute of Educational Technology, The Open University, Milton Keynes.

Morgan, A. and Thorpe, M. (1993) Residential schools in open and distance education: quality time for quality learning?, in T. Evans and D. Nation (eds.) *Reforming Open and Distance Education: Critical Reflections from Practice*, Kogan Page, London. This chapter outlines the general rationale for extended face-to-face teaching, as in residential schools, but applicable also to training courses. It is, therefore, a useful review of the learning goals which such events are often intended to achieve, such as major attitudinal change, synthesis of large conceptual frameworks, integration of practical and conceptual understanding and so on.

Parer, M. and Benson, R. (1989) *Professional Training by Distance Education*, Centre for Distance Learning, Gippsland Institute, Victoria.

Thorpe, M. (1979) When is a course not a course?, *Teaching at a Distance*, no. 16, pp. 13–18.

Thorpe, M. (1988) Learner support, in *Open Learning*, Module 2 of the Post-Compulsory Diploma in Education, The Open University, Milton Keynes, p. 54.

Thorpe, M. (1993) *Evaluating Open and Distance Learning*, Longman, Harlow. This provides a general introduction to evaluation for practitioners in open and distance learning, with emphasis on the organization of effective contexts for the use of findings. Also includes case studies and examples of different issues and approaches to data collection, in relation to tuition, counselling/guidance, courses and student self-evaluation.

15

Workplace learners: learners learning in 'unconventional' settings

Hilary Temple

In this chapter we shall look at the situation of learners who use open learning outside conventional teaching or training settings. In other words they are learning in surroundings which are not primarily established to be learning environments. These learners may or may not be volunteers, but they can be assumed to be learning mainly at the behest of the organization. To avoid the use of negatives like 'non-academic', I have chosen the term 'workplace learners', though this does not imply that all their studying is necessarily carried out in the workplace.

LEARNING AT WORK

'The days when we used to hang our brains up with our coats on the way into work are over now' says a manager in a chemical company. Work-based and workplace learning are more than buzz-phrases: increasingly they are regarded by companies as essential to their survival. Why is this? There seem to be two kinds of pressure operating on organizations to change the way they develop their employees.

The first is the internal logic imposed by the market-place. In every part of industry, commerce and the public sector, quality improvements are needed in order to meet the demands of ever more critical and articulate customers. Nothing stands still for long:

- Markets change (even without the impetus of one-off structural transformations like the Single European Market).
- Technology not only changes but also changes at an increasing rate, requiring organizations to speed up their response time.
- There are changes in the nature of work which mean that few low-skilled jobs remain compared with 20 years ago.
- As a corollary to this, a larger percentage of workers are becoming 'knowledge workers'.
- A profound change, particularly in the public service, has occurred in the relationship between those providing goods or services and those receiving them. There is an increasing tendency to regard services as products and to apply to them the same kinds of quality criteria that one would to a physical product. Customer charters and similar measures are the outward signs of this transformation, which can genuinely reverse the accepted hierarchy. A

large motor vehicle manufacturer, for example, now puts in order of importance its customers at the top, the people making the cars next and management at the bottom. You may be able to think of similar developments in
organizations with which you are familiar.

The consequence of all this is the greatly heightened need for constant development and redevelopment of staff in the light of constantly changing work
requirements. The volume and pace of this is such that no longer can training
be regarded as a separate event: it is a major strand that has to be woven into
the fabric of the working day.

The second type of pressure is external: a sustained government initiative to
change the structure of industrial training and to recognize competent performance through vocational qualifications. (Roger Lewis (Chapter 3) discusses
National Vocational Qualifications.) Essentially they entail assessment of competence in actually performing in a job role – which in its turn means that, in
the first instance at least, line managers have to carry out quite specific assessments to national standards as part of their everyday work. You may have
views on the strengths and weaknesses of such a system.

Just as a typical first-line manager now has to take on the unaccustomed role
of assessor, so the typical workplace now has to take on the additional role of
being a learning environment. But can it cope? Thinking about the various
contexts in which teaching and training takes place in the workplace is one
way to start exploring this question. What is your mental picture when you
read phrases like 'the workplace as a learning environment'? Perhaps you
visualized a noisy factory floor with a frantic learner, fingers stuffed in ears,
trying to read a distance learning pack in a corner? Or perhaps you envisaged a
workplace learning centre, neatly fitted out with computers and boxes of
learning materials? Or perhaps, most interestingly, you reflected briefly on
your own experience of learning at work, which might have been through
formal training sessions, reading the papers that wafted across your desk,
reading the papers on other people's desks, not intended for you, talking to
colleagues and visitors? The possibilities are almost infinite.

You might want to pause to think about the various learning environments
that your organization sets up – and those other places where learning takes
place. In case you have simply read through the paragraph above without
pausing for reflection, consider what the following situations show about how,
when and where learning takes place in the workplace:

1. Pat is trying to photocopy two sides of A4 back to back on a single sheet.
   Chris, passing by, sees the problem and demonstrates. (Pat is a senior
   manager and Chris a youth trainee.)
2. The new administrative assistant comes out of the manager's office apoplec-
   tic with fury, having taken in an apparently reasonable report and had it
   rejected out of hand. 'Oh, he's always the same on Thursday afternoons',
   says a more senior assistant. 'He sits on the Bench on Thursday mornings
   and it leaves him a bit het up.'

3. Dalwinder is on a management training course and is undertaking a study of potential hazards in the warehouse. 'I don't know where to begin.' 'Go across there this afternoon and talk to Geoff, he'll put you on the right track', advises her line manager.

You might agree from this and from your own experience that:

- a lot of learning goes on in the workplace;
- learning in the workplace does not have to be labelled formally as such;
- it need not involve books, or training materials of any kind;
- people are a vital resource to help other people learn; and
- such supporters of learning may be peers, bosses, colleagues who happen to be in the right place at the right time.

OPEN LEARNING AT WORK

If all this sounds to you as if work is some kind of Utopia, with discovery learning going on all over the place and employees basking in the resultant warm glow, this would be far from the reality. Of course, work sites are fertile sources of learning, but a substantial part of it has to be learning which is directed in some way to achieve business objectives. At one time this would have meant sending employees on a course. Now there is more choice of mode.

There is an ever-growing number of work-oriented learning packages and an increasing awareness of open and distance learning among training managers and others who make decisions about developing the workforce. Open learning has a number of attractions which need to be thought out in the context of each organization's or individual's needs. What do you think the benefits of open learning could be for your organization or some of the people in it?

Benefits often cited by managers include: being able to train small numbers of employees who do not constitute a viable classroom group; being able to train large groups of people whom it would be impossible to release from work for conventional training courses; training to consistent standards, perhaps on many sites in different parts of the country (or of the world); economy – being able to buy exactly those modules that are needed; and the capability to train key personnel without needing to release them from work at set times, thus allowing for peaks and troughs in workloads.

You can perhaps think of some disadvantages to set against these benefits. If you will need to argue the case for open learning it will be important for you to be clear about these; part of the 'down-side' of open learning is shown in the following true story:

A training manager decided that the evening course for training supervisors was unsatisfactory. Changes of shift and domestic difficulties led to drop-out. The firm bought some sets of open learning modules that closely re-flected the classroom-delivered syllabus. A dozen or so potential and actual supervisors were given the modules one bright May morning and told that they had till September to complete about 180 study hours. They'd agreed to do this in their own time, being under pressure at work. They met the tutor who would mark the assignment at the end of each module and had a phone number to contact her if necessary.

By September, one learner was halfway through the programme and another had completed about one-third. The rest had made virtually no progress and didn't want to continue. Perhaps the materials were at fault?

The training manager reviewed the reasons. One supervisor said, 'I thought I'd be able to put in about six to eight hours a week – it didn't sound very much. The week after we got the books, the World Cup started. It was on the TV every night, and most of the blokes naturally wanted to follow it: even those that didn't usually had kids who wanted to watch. So straightaway we were lagging. The books sat in a heap and I kept thinking "I must get on with that". I started one of them, then we had our annual shut-down. Well, holidays are no time for studying, are they? So at work it was "How are you getting on, then?" "I can't seem to get stuck in." One bloke did three of the books, he's a young chap living with his parents. He rang the tutor once, but she was on holiday in August. For the rest of us who've been out of school for a good few years it didn't seem worth starting. I wouldn't mind trying again, but most of them think they'd rather go on a proper course where you don't have to do it all yourself.'

This is possibly a classic way *not* to introduce open learning. We need to be aware that workplace open learners may face particular tensions and challenges. You may have come across examples to add to this list:

- Learning being regarded as a 'wimpish' activity in comparison with *real work*.
- Clash between openness/flexibility in a particular programme and closedness/rigidity in the organizational culture as a whole.
- Pressure to meet customers' needs overriding learning needs.
- Lip-service being paid to open learning – lack of strategic support from senior management.
- Inadequate preparation for those engaging in open learning programmes, perhaps through absence of strategic planning or because the realities of open learning are misunderstood.
- Mismatch between learners' needs and the materials chosen.
- Employees not on learning programmes being reluctant to give help to those who are.
- Family and friends resenting leisure time eroded by open learning (which may be seen as being mainly for the benefit of the employer).
- Uncomfortable awareness of skill deficiency (frequently found in older learners).
- Sense of being a guinea pig when open learning is new to the organization.
- Sense that open learning is second rate compared with a proper classroom-based course (perhaps because the organization has laid undue emphasis upon open learning as cost-cutting).
- Fear of falling behind on a corporately negotiated programme.

PLANNING OPEN LEARNING AT WORK

If you had to draw up a checklist for the training manager to try again, what key elements might it include? You might find it useful to consider the adverse features listed above and how you might turn them into positive features. If you did this, what broad categories would you identify?

I would suggest that these could include:

- motivating;
- preparation: developing skills and techniques, organizing the context/ environment, scheduling;
- briefing: all those involved;
- active tutor input;
- monitoring progress; and
- evaluating outcomes.

Specifically, I think any manager would want to check that the following are covered before the learners are let loose anywhere near open learning materials:

- Brief each learner's line manager beforehand about the scheme – what is expected of them and of the learner.
- Check that learners have the prerequisite skills to undertake the programme: if they haven't, provide developmental materials *before* the programme starts.
- Make clear to learners what they and the organization get from the open learning – even a distant goal can motivate so long as there are defined staging-posts along the way. It is possible to generate a sense of excitement about the programme while retaining realism.
- Brief learners about successful study techniques: a place to study, review and practise, short, frequent study sessions.
- Negotiate and agree individual study schedules and set up a mechanism for monitoring them – and varying them if necessary.
- Make alternative study provision (at work or elsewhere) for those with uncongenial facilities at home.
- Give feedback to learners often enough to be formative and in such a way as to be motivating.
- Clearly define the tutor's role and make sure that a positive relationship is formed with learners.
- Build in support apart from that offered by the learning materials, the training department, the line manager and the tutor. Give proper guidance on how to get the best out of these other sources. (This is such an important element that we will dissect it further on in the chapter.)
- Acknowledge and celebrate successive stages of achievement.
- Obtain feedback from learners in such a way as to get genuine views – and use it to improve future programmes.

Assailed by lists of things to avoid and things to ensure, perhaps some workplace open-learning advocates wonder why they ever embarked on the idea. It is sad but true that enthusiasm on its own is not enough to enable successful workplace open learning to happen. Organizations need to learn how to use open learning. There seems to be a natural evolution of thinking, from *open learning as a learning package*, through *open learning as a package plus support*, to *open learning as a learner plus support*. Fortunately an increasing number of organizations are learning from others' experience and omitting the first stage.

SUPPORTING LEARNERS AT WORK

Let's finish by looking more closely, as we said we would, at sources of support for learners. The prime source will be the learning materials, which may (or may not) be good at encouraging users to use what they already know from experience as well as to apply their new learning to their work situation. A tutor can assist this process but may lack detailed knowledge of the particular work environment. Who else can help a work-based learner, apart from tutors and trainers whose main function it is to share their subject expertise and impart effective learning techniques? This is worth thinking about, since you may want to add to the list as you encounter new models of open learning programme.

Your list may include other learners who have just been through the programme (not possible in the case of a pilot, like the example above); the learners themselves setting up small study groups; family and friends (perhaps for trying out ideas, practising presentations, reading through written work); a learning centre and its staff if available; and a mentor who is not the learner's line manager.

Those whom I have come across include the following:

Learning centre staff. They can offer the learner

- an organized and uncritical environment;
- expertise in the use of systems (catalogues, computer equipment, reference sources);
- their experience of supporting a range of abilities and learning styles; and
- (possibly) networking with other learners.

A peer group. This can be very supportive of its members, but it needs to be stimulated into functioning. Open learners may actually feel that the solitariness inherent in individual learning is part of the experience. They may retain values from school associated with not 'cheating' or 'copying' (or infringing the teacher's prerogative by helping!). They may be reluctant to admit to difficulties in front of peers who they feel are in competition with them. A useful part of the tutor's role is to launch such a group, with some suggestions for activities in the early stages and a more or less rapid move to full autonomy depending on the confidence of the learners. Fellow learners can offer

- the sense of a shared experience which can be more powerful even than a sense of personal achievement;
- a sounding-board;
- saving in time and effort;
- a context ('I'm not thick – he didn't understand page 40 either', 'I'm not the only one who didn't think they would make it'); and
- a sense of purpose, especially if organized on a seminar basis so that learners take turns in leading the group through a topic.

Learners who are one or two jumps ahead can offer some of these benefits together with a perspective which has the advantage of being seen as relevant and immediate, and role modelling of a kind which an expert cannot emulate.

Families and friends. Although they are more difficult to organize from the employer's point of view, companies have successfully involved partners, for instance, in initial briefings on open learning programmes (to explain the commitment required) and in awards ceremonies for successful completion. A few large companies also make their learning resources available to families, though this usually has to remain fairly limited in scope. At any rate, workplace learners can be alerted to the possibilities of using such a resource.

Mentors. Mentoring is well established in some specialized areas such as the professional development of engineers or the induction of graduate recruits. It has recently, however, become much more widely used at work. 'If it works for new graduates, who are bright and are going to cope anyway, it ought to work even better for the less high fliers' is a typical comment from a training manager. It can be a system peculiarly well suited to the support of open learners, since it can open up 'softer' lines of communication in the organization.

MENTORING WORKPLACE LEARNERS

So what does a mentor offer? You may have experience of a particular system or a range of systems whose features you can compare with each other and with my list below:

- The main role of the mentor is to be on the learner's side.
- Mentors are usually not the learner's line manager (the main exceptions are in engineering where there is a formal requirement for those seeking membership of a professional body to have a senior member as a mentor, and in very small organizations where there is little choice of suitable individuals). This enables the support of the learner to be clearly distinguished from the appraisal, pay and promotion structure and makes the relationship an unthreatening one in what may be a very competitive work environment.
- The mentor can give a learner access to parts of the organization that it would be difficult to reach on their own, for instance by introducing them to key individuals who can further their learning.

- Since the mentor is usually someone with considerable experience of the organization they can help speed up learning by passing on some of their own wisdom. Part of the training of mentors should cover encouragement of independence in learners.
- With experience, mentors can offer their skills as sounding-boards or devil's advocates, depending on the needs of their learners, enabling them to practise new things in a risk-free setting.
- The non-judgemental support offered by a mentor can improve retention rates in study programmes, especially those of long duration where motivation is all-important.

The mentor–learner relationship is potentially a very powerful one, so its introduction requires the same careful planning that an open learning system does. Provision has to be made for:

- adequate briefing about the scope of the mentoring scheme (for mentors, learners and the line managers of each);
- changing pairings that do not work (without blame on either side);
- limiting the learner load of any one mentor, if necessary by extending the scheme to involve more mentors; and
- ending the relationship at an appropriate stage, which may have different degrees of negotiability depending on the organization and the purpose of the mentoring.

Even those organizations with considerable experience of mentoring seem to undertake little evaluation of its cost benefits. This may be because they suspect that it occupies a great deal of management time. Nevertheless it is unfortunate if information is not available since (in terms of open learning) prevention of drop-out alone may well save the costs of mentoring – quite apart from the less easily quantified benefits of improved learning and motivation.

At the beginning I said that organizations were not primarily in business to be learning environments. It could, of course, be argued that their main functions (of survival and growth) can only be sustained through learning in a myriad of forms – and that in all likelihood it is the 'learning company' that will set the tone for post-industrial employment into the twenty-first century.

FURTHER READING

Lewis, R. (1984) *How to Tutor and Support Learners*, National Council for Educational Technology, Coventry. One of a series of open learning guides, which though now ageing contains many ideas which are still highly current. The text encourages a lot of activity in the reader and focuses on important issues such as the different kinds of support needed at different stages of the learning programme.

The Open College (1992) *Mentoring*, The Open College, Manchester. Very much a how-to-do-it guide, with separate packs for the manager responsible for introducing mentoring, the mentor and the learner. An audiotape gives firsthand accounts by users of how their mentoring scheme has helped them and their organization.

Pedler, M., Burgoyne, J. and Boydell, T. (1991) *The Learning Company*, McGraw-Hill, Maidenhead. If learning is to be built into employees' everyday experience, what effect does this have on the organization – can it learn as well? Development work is currently being done to examine the features that a 'learning company' (a title deliberately chosen for the warmth of the term 'company' in contrast to 'organization') has at different stages and how real organizations are working towards the ideal.

Temple, H. (1991) *Open Learning in Industry*, Longman, Harlow. Contains case studies of open learning in action in a range of occupational settings as well as examinations of the usefulness of learning centres and the various technological ways of supporting learning.

16

The technology and management of desk-top publishing

Paul Lefrere

This chapter looks at desk-top publishing (DTP) and related technologies in relation to current and prospective planning and production methods in open and distance learning. Most of this chapter is concerned with the use of DTP by individuals and small teams, particularly for the production of printed study material. Brief details are given of the trend towards using DTP for non-printed material, such as courses delivered on CD-ROM. DTP has gained prominence because it has the potential to cut production times and printing costs dramatically, compared to conventional publishing methods. This can make print-like quality economic even for courses with low numbers. With care and some familiarity with the basics of information design, even people who are working alone and new to DTP can achieve acceptable results.

WHAT IS DTP?

The term 'desk-top publishing' refers to the use of computers to integrate text and graphics in electronic form. That integration allows the creation of multi-page documents, in which text and graphics can be sized up, juxtaposed and precisely aligned anywhere on a page. Changes can be simple and fast. Illustrations can be moved nearer to where they are mentioned or, if space is a problem, illustrations can be altered to suit the space or text can be edited to fit. Text can be in a variety of styles and sizes. Pages can incorporate tables, formulae and common types of graphics such as charts, graphs, half-tone photographs and line art.

By using DTP, you can eliminate much of the handwork associated with traditional approaches to producing camera-ready copy. The result can be huge reductions in costs and in production time, possibly accompanied by improvements in the visual appeal of the material. Further, making changes is easy, so you can more readily update a course. You can also reuse material in other courses or in a different context. In the not too distant future, this will include creating entries for searchable, selective electronic versions of catalogues of open and distance learning material.

At the heart of any DTP system there is a small ('desk-top') personal computer with software – either a single all-purpose DTP program, or separate programs, for wordprocessing, creating and editing graphics, and laying out text and graphics on a page. In addition to a computer and software, a basic DTP system comprises a laser printer and some means of capturing existing graphics or photographs, such as a scanner. Your own organization may well have most of that equipment; if not, each component is relatively inexpensive.

Options for final output

Most users of DTP find that a laser printer is entirely adequate for routine work. If you have a low-enrolment course, you can use the laser printer to run off individual sets of printed pages for immediate distribution ('on-demand printing'). The cost drops if your laser printer can print on both sides of a sheet. With more than about 20 students, you can treat the laser output as camera-ready copy, and reprograph from it on a photocopier or digital duplicator. As your use of DTP grows, you may be able to justify the cost of a copier which can reproduce two or more colours, and also bind or hole-punch printed pages. For prestige work you can output to a photosetter and print on offset-litho presses.

TYPES OF DTP SOFTWARE

Although all DTP software allows text and graphics to be integrated, any particular program will impose a bias on users: it will be either page or document oriented. A page-oriented program, like PageMaker or CorelDraw, is better for producing double-page spreads (pairs of facing pages). Here, diagrams can be placed anywhere on a left or right page, or even across two pages, quite independently of any text on the page. Text can be split into blocks and proportioned and positioned appropriately and aesthetically. When they use a page-oriented system, designers can find it quick to lay out a double-page spread. However, authors or small teams may not have the skill or inclination to take the many small design decisions needed on each page. With such systems, it can be difficult to adhere to a 'house style'. Also, even skilled users can find it laborious to alter the document's overall design or to add or remove text or graphics, as may happen if you update a course. This is because in page-oriented programs, a document is generally split at the layout stage into more than one 'text flow'. This makes it impossible to select all of the text and the graphics as a single object, to which a global change can be applied.

A document-oriented program like Ventura or Word is better for straightforward documents, with few pictures per page. Here, you set the overall appearance of the document by using a 'style sheet' (see below). The program then lays out each page according to the specifications in the style sheet. With such a program, it is trivial to alter the document's overall design. It can be hard to achieve fine control over the layout of individual pages, so you will have little control over the layout of particular 'double-page spreads'.

If you have to produce material in collaboration with people who use a different DTP program, you are more likely to encounter compatibility problems if each of you uses a page-oriented program. Although it is possible to move text and graphics from one page-oriented program to another, it is very unlikely that you will be able to retain information about the layout of any page.

INTEGRATING OTHER PROGRAMS WITH DTP

Whichever kind of DTP program you use, you can link it to other programs or add ancillary 'extensions' to the DTP program to reduce inconsistencies, save time and increase your control of the content and appearance of your material.

One useful extension to a DTP program is 'Multiple Undo' or 'Multiple Version'. This lets you reverse previous decisions or see the effect of possible changes in layout. You might use this to handle a problem which is revealed only in careful editing: you find it necessary to revise the previously edited elements in a linked series. This could be the result of poor organization of the ideas in your draft; mechanical inconsistencies (e.g. abbreviations, spelling and other aspects of house style); and content inconsistencies (e.g. the use of technical terms).

A 'Multiple Version' feature can help if you need to make large changes to the order and the content of text, perhaps as a result of comments on drafts from students. Such changes are facilitated by exporting the DTP text to a wordprocessor and an outliner program or planning aid, then re-importing the text to the DTP program. To eliminate those export/import iterations, you should keep the text out of the DTP program, by using 'external links' from the DTP program to files produced by a wordprocessor.

If you use a document-oriented DTP program, you will be able to integrate it with an outliner program. An outliner diverts attention from the appearance of the text and directs it towards content, order and structure. Although at first sight this is the opposite of what DTP does, it should be seen as an essential component of DTP. This is because outliners require you to identify relationships between parts of a document. If those relationships are explicit, this makes it far easier to spot inconsistencies and far easier to change the status of text (e.g. from a heading to a subheading).

You could reduce textual inconsistencies by adding extensions to automatically renumber paragraphs, diagrams or tables after changes; to update cross-references and citations; to create an index or table of contents; and to keep track of which changes have been made. Without such facilities, you have to undertake those tasks manually, which gives rise to errors and makes it cumbersome to explore alternatives and encourages premature commitment to a particular plan (Williams, 1991).

As your use of DTP increases, it is likely that you and your colleagues will create a collection of graphics, including bought-in 'clip-art', that you will want to reuse in different courses. However, if those graphics vary in style, this can confuse students. You should therefore create all your graphics with a drawing program, linked to your DTP program, that groups graphical attributes into styles. This will let you quickly impose some consistency over the illustrations in any document, by re-rendering the text styles, colours and line widths for all the illustrations at once.

Other programs you may find useful as adjuncts to DTP include: a glossary generator; programs to evaluate surface features of text such as word use; on-line reference guides to editorial and design conventions; and programs to annotate drafts.

PREPARING FOR DTP

The introduction of DTP should be in response to an educational need that is not being met or which can no longer be afforded using traditional technology. Its adoption needs to be handled as carefully as any other major innovation. Adopting DTP could benefit or harm everyone involved in the production and consumption of educational material, from authors to students to budget holders.

In this connection, your organization might consider some form of initial support from a consultant (see Pickering, 1989). That support might include guidelines in basic visual grammar, to raise authors' sensitivity to design issues or guidelines to help them to recognize DTP work which cannot reasonably be undertaken by unskilled users.

Where DTP is adopted by teams, it is likely to require changes in the roles of team members, changes which may be problematical wherever demarcation is an issue. Many such teams do not include professional designers, editors, typographers and typesetters. Problems often arise if those professional skills are not available in some form at some stage. This is especially obvious where DTP is adopted by small teams or lone authors who lack any formal training in graphic design. If they also lack intuitive design skills, they may overuse some of the facilities in DTP systems and produce ineffective documents. Examples of this include filling up all available space on a page, using too many graphic devices within the same document and using graphic devices inconsistently within that document or across related documents.

DTP IN RELATION TO STUDENT NEEDS

The key issue here is one of accessibility. Open learning material should be affordable, available and easy to use and learn from. Taking each of these in turn, DTP can save time and money at every stage of origination and production, especially if material goes through multiple drafts. It makes it easier to reuse parts of existing work for new purposes or new audiences, and to produce draft versions for critical commenting or for questionnaire-based try-outs with learners. This may translate into lower-cost courses, or make open learning courses feasible for smaller numbers. By using DTP, it may be easier to meet deadlines for printing and distribution, which helps availability.

The ease of use and 'learnability' of a document depends on its content and on the match between form (appearance) and content. There are all too many ineffective documents, in which form is not matched to content. Often, that mismatch can be seen at arm's length, because such documents typically

Interpolation and Extrapolation

We can use the equations in the previous section for calculating values not on the measured scale. If we look back at equation (1) $F = 1.8C + 32$, our measured range of temperature was $32°\ F$ to $212°\ F$ (freezing to boiling). If we required the centigrade equivalent of a Fahrenheit value between these two limits we can INTERPOLATE using the equation. Therefore if we need to know the temperature of the human body in $°C$ ($98.6°F$) our calculation would look like this:

Temperature of human body in $°F = 98.6$

from before; $F = 1.8C + 32$

transpose to make C the subject.

$$\therefore F - 32 = 1.8C$$

$$\therefore \frac{F - 32}{1.8} = C$$

$$\therefore \frac{98.6 - 32}{1.8} = C = 37°C$$

This is known as **interpolation**, because $98.6°F$ lies inside the measured range $32°\ F \rightarrow 212°F$. If we require a value outside this range we can also use the same equation.

The boiling point of sulphur is a commonly used reference temperature ($444.44°\ C$). If the Fahrenheit equivalent is required we may EXTRAPOLATE this value from the measured range using equation (1).

Boiling point of sulphur $°C = 444.44$

$$\therefore \text{ as } F = 1.8C + 32$$

$$\therefore F = 1.8 \times 444.44 + 32$$

$$\therefore F = 799.992 + 32$$

$$\therefore F = 831.992°\ F$$

This is known as **extrapolation** because $444.44°C$ lies **outside** the measured range $0°C \rightarrow 100°C$.

Self-Assessed Question

Using the following data derive an equation that relates the length of a spring (cm) to the load applied (kg).

Load applied, K (Kg)	2	4	6	8	10
Length, L (cm)	50	70	90	110	130

Using the derived equation find the load applied or the length of the spring that corresponds to the following:

(a) 3.5 *kg*   (b) 97 *cm*   (c) 11 *kg*   (d) 40 *cm*

State whether these values are found by extrapolation or interpolation.

Figure 16.1 (above and opposite) Facing pages from a 1982 self-study course for first-year students in integrated engineering, developed by South Bank University

overuse the graphic facilities in DTP systems. Even where the day-to-day users of DTP are not professional designers or editors, they can come to recognize such shortcomings. They are then better placed to be able to use DTP to clarify the implicit structure of teaching material and raise its general usability.

In experienced hands, DTP can be used to create layouts which are effective for less academic students who prefer the 'busy' page layouts of magazines. You could keep some parts of a page blank ('white space'); add diagrams and illustrations, including photographs; and use several columns of text, a variety of fonts and type styles, two colours and patterned or shaded backgrounds. These are not options for beginners.

Effective communication through print is partly a matter of capitalizing upon readers' expectations, such as the expectation that documents have a structure. DTP provides many graphic devices which you can use for this. Examples include:

- indenting paragraphs or numbering them (Figure 16.2), to make a document's structure explicit (this is appropriate for relatively sophisticated students, as in this example);
- using bullets (e.g. ● or ◊) to mark important points (Figure 16.2); and
- drawing attention to certain components of the document by using larger type, bold type or a different font (Figure 16.1); by using horizontal or vertical 'rules' and shading (Figure 16.2); and by using the margin for comments (Figure 16.2) or special symbols (Figure 16.1: a pointing finger denotes examples; exercises are denoted by a hand holding a pen; space is left for tackling exercises and making notes).

Judicious and economical use of those graphic devices can help you to clarify your intentions to the reader and make your documents easier to study. Such

COMMENT *Obviously I cannot comment on your institution. However what I have observed and read suggests that many developing countries continue to be very closely tied to developed countries particularly if they were once colonies. We only have to ask:*

- *To what extent are newly formed international partnerships equal?*
- *How are common goals and the means of achieving them defined ?*
- *Who is paying for a technology and on what basis?*

to realise that these issues are intensely political and complex. We shall consider some of these issues in more detail later when we look at the Ivory Coast Television Project.

4   Models of collaboration

Over the thirty years from 1960 to 1990, despite efforts to change things, the pattern of material and people exchange continued to be predominantly from north to south, and west to east. A look at any international trade figures or conference register is likely to confirm this. It is a sobering thought that in 1981, six developed countries, with one tenth of the world's population, controlled two-thirds of the world's trade.

In 1979 the British Open University held an international conference to celebrate its tenth anniversary. One of the special themes of the conference was collaboration (for further details see Neill, 1979). During the conference, several models for collaborative exchange were put forward. One particularly interesting one was proposed by Tony Kaye (1979), then deputy director of the British Open University's international consultancy service. Kaye developed an analytical model of collaborative experience by distinguishing between three broad elements:

- type of exchange (transfer or pooling)
- level of development
- source of finance.

In the case of the transfer and pooling of expertise, information and materials, Kaye suggested that running a training course for staff in institution X by a specialist from institution Y would constitute transfer. The joint production of a series of radio programmes by institutions X and Y would constitute **pooling.** Transfer implies a one-way flow and pooling implies a two-way movement.

The second element, level of development, is largely based on the economic differences between states. Different kinds of regions are paired together - for example, developed-developing.

The third element was the source of finance for the collaboration. Kaye divided this into two broad categories:

- internally funded, from the institutions themselves or their governments
- externally funded, from international aid agencies or private foundations.

A summary matrix combining these three elements – level of development, source of finance and type of exchange – is shown in Figure 2.

Figure 2: Models of collaboration and transfer

Development pair / Source of finance	Transfer		Pooling	
	Internal	External	Internal	External
I Developed Developing	1	2	3	4
II Developing Developing	5	6	7	8
III Developing Developed	9	10	11	12
IV Developed Developed	13	14	15	16

ACTIVITY 4

You should spend about 20 minutes on this activity. Which kind of collaboration and transfer would you say were the mos tcommon? Which kinds do you think are the least common? There are 16 boxes int hematrix. Which of the following terms would you place in each box?

- most frequent
- occasional
- rare

For example, if you feel that the most common collaborative schemes are transfers between developed and developing countries, and are externally financed you would write 'most frequent' in box 2. You may not want to fill in every box. Can you give any reasons ror your answers? Can you think of any dimensions that Kaye didn't include? Can you think of any weaknesses of the model?

COMMENT

The most frequent schemes tend to be transfers from developed countries to developing countries financed by external aid. However you may be surprised to know that many of the loans made by international agencies which involve repayment with interest are classified as aid. There have been some moves towards transfer and pooling between developing countries financed both externally and internally. Transfers from developing regions to developed areas are as you might imagine quite rare.

Models such as Kaye's help us to categorise and analyse the examples of collaboration that we find. This may help us to develop general rules that may be applied across different cultural settings. How helpful did you find it for your own thinking?

ACTIVITY 5

You should spend about one and a half hours on this activity. Read the extract by Hugues Koné and Janet Jenkins in your set reader (chapter 21), entitled 'The programme for educational television in the Ivory Coast'. This is an account of a collaborative educational television project in the Ivory Coast. The project, which ran from 1968 to 1981, was established to try to accelerate the process of modernisation and economic growth in the country through the development of primary and adult education. Read the article carefully in the light of what we have discussed so far in this unit (referring back in particular to the section on

Figure 16.2 (Above and opposite) Facing pages from a 1991 postgraduate external diploma in distance education, developed by the University of London Institute of Education and the International Extension College

issues are covered at length in books on information design, some of which are listed in Duffy and Waller (1985) and Hartley (1992).

PRODUCTIVE DTP FOR A SMALL TEAM OR LONE AUTHOR

Possible measures of productive use of DTP include the teaching effectiveness of those pages, as well as more readily quantifiable measures such as the number of finished pages produced for student use, or time or cost savings.

The point was made above that creating an effective teaching document requires careful matching of form and content to capitalize upon readers' expectations. It helps to establish and reinforce those expectations if you set out pages in a consistent fashion, according to a house style which is carried over from one course to another. How easy this is will depend on your graphic skills and on the DTP program you use.

In the days before DTP, the matching of form and content was carried out by editors, designers, page layout artists and typesetters, who would interpret the intentions of the author and transform raw text into a final publishable document. Typically, this required much hand work. For example, the editor briefed the typesetter by marking up each figure, caption and heading. The designer then briefed the typesetter on the required appearance of each component. In this way, they imposed a consistent type style and use of white space above and below headings.

Similar results can be obtained by a single user in DTP, through the use of 'style sheets' – definitions of the type style and layout of each class of paragraph in a document. The pros and cons of style sheets are considered at length elsewhere (e.g. Kember, 1992). The most relevant observation here is that if an author uses DTP only on a casual, infrequent basis, then it is sensible to use a document-oriented DTP program to minimize layout decisions, and to make the style sheets as sparse as possible, to minimize the mental effort involved in their creation and use. Achieving an effective overall design requires considerable design skill. Authors can either use a commercial off-the-peg style sheet for the document, or commission a bespoke style sheet and house style from a design professional.

PRODUCTIVE DTP FOR A LARGER TEAM

If a team contains an editor and a designer, then it may be sensible for authors to delegate page layout and detailed editing to those colleagues, who can be expected to be more consistent and also more productive at using programs designed for those tasks. However, in large or bureaucratic teams it is equally sensible to avoid demarcation disputes by specifying the conditions under which it is acceptable for authors to carry out their own page layout and editing. It is also appropriate to use programs which make it easier for every member of the team to collaborate with the rest of the team and to annotate text or diagrams or to spot changes made by others. Regardless of how comments are made – on disc or on paper – it should be possible to amalgamate them. This can be done using a wordprocessor or, preferably, by the DTP system itself, automatically.

USING DTP FOR NON-PRINTED MATERIAL

There is a trend towards using DTP as a means of matching form to content in non-printed material, such as courses delivered on CD-ROM. This allows students to view material on screen and then use selected parts as they want. For example, they might choose to treat the CD-ROM as a library. 'Books' could be inspected and pages could be 'photocopied' for later reference, perhaps to quote in essays. Larger organizations such as The Open University are already requiring students to do this on some courses, both working individually and in groups.

One practical problem with the use of DTP in that way concerns the facilities which students have. If they have to buy their own computer, it is unreasonable to assume that they will each have the same printer, DTP program and typefaces, or even the same kind of computer or operating system. At present, there is no standard way to exchange DTP documents between users who lack identical facilities, although several vendors have proposed solutions. For planning purposes, it is reasonable to expect that, by the late 1990s, students will be able to view, edit, search or print any DTP files you provide them with, and add cross-references and comments.

REFERENCES AND NOTES

Duffy, T. M. and Waller, R. (eds.) (1985) *Designing Usable Texts*, Academic Press, Orlando, FL and London. Although this book has no explicit references to DTP, the effectiveness of DTP can be greatly enhanced by an appreciation of the issues it raises about usability and how to improve usability by training authors and editors and by testing design alternatives. The examples include textbook design, job performance aids, information mapping, manuals, illustrations, algorithms and open and distance learning material.

Kember, D. (1992) Using style sheets, templates and the features of publishing software to facilitate the development of printed study materials, in J. Hartley (ed.) *Technology and Writing: Readings in the Psychology of Written Communication*, Jessica Kingsley Publishers, London and Philadelphia, PA. This is a relatively brief tutorial guide to the use of style sheets in producing self-study materials. All examples use features in Microsoft Word, which is a document-oriented program. The other chapters in this book cover various topics in information design, which may be of interest but which are not central to DTP.

Pickering, T. (1989) *Desk Top Publishing Training Handbook*, Training Agency, Sheffield. This offers useful guidance on DTP consultants and on how to choose and use a DTP system.

Williams, N. (1991) *The Computer, the Writer and the Learner*, Springer-Verlag, London. This book discusses how computers can help to support the entire writing process, from assembling of notes to editing, printing and publishing. It includes chapters on DTP, hypertext and collaborative projects.

17

Managing open learning: designing and operating the system

Hilary Temple

However carefully we design our open learning materials they usually cannot provide all the support a learner needs. What strategic and practical steps can we take to ensure the materials function as part of a system? In this chapter we look at introducing open learning for the first time (within or outside an organizational context), administering the system, developing staff appropriately to support learners and evaluating the results.

OPEN LEARNING AS STRATEGIC CHANGE

Open learning materials do not exist in isolation: even while they are being created their relationship with learners is being built in. But this is not a one-to-one relationship: they operate as part of a system. Consequently they need managing, whether they are being introduced into an organization or to an individual learner. In fact open learning needs managing even before any learner lays hands on the materials.

If you have ever studied the management of strategic change you may find some parallels in this chapter. The manager (or potential manager) of the use of distance and open learning is an agent for change, because open learning is so fundamentally different from conventional education and training. Before continuing you might want to pause for a minute or two and think about some of the connotations that the word 'change' has for you. When I have done this in the past I've found that most people's responses tend to fall into 'good' and 'bad' categories. For instance the good or positive responses are associated with excitement, opportunity, growth and adaptation. Bad or negative responses focus on restlessness, discomfort, unfamiliarity and people getting mown down or left behind.

So any or all of these 'good and bad vibrations' surround open learning when it is first introduced, just as they do any other kind of change. Open learning enthusiasts sometimes forget that ideas which have become acceptable and even commonplace for them (such as 'learner centredness') are still novel and may even seem threatening to other people. And, oddly enough, even beneficial change produces some stress. When you plan the introduction of open learning you need to take these ideas on board, otherwise you risk becoming counterproductive.

Whatever kind of open/distance learning system you are planning, even if it is of very limited scope in the initial stages, you need a strategy to manage its:

- introduction,
- implementation and
- evaluation.

This seems a logical order in which to consider the phases.

INTRODUCING OPEN AND DISTANCE LEARNING

You may find it helpful to use the following as a checklist at the planning stage, adding extra items to suit your own situation. Although the language describes a strategy for an organization, you can equally well use the ideas to introduce open learning to individual learners.

Question	Comment
• How would we describe our organization's culture? What elements of openness are in it already?	It is quite possible to introduce open learning into a very rigid and hierarchical culture, but efforts to do so often remain marginalized. Remember that different parts of an organization can have quite different cultures: start with the most open if you have a choice! Features you might look for include the amount of bottom-up and lateral communication; how authoritarian the style of managers is; how new ideas are received in the organization.
• Are we clear about our reasons for introducing open learning? What do we want it to achieve and with whom? What policies/initiatives regarding teaching and training are under way, planned – or being abandoned?	
• Do we have the backing of make-or-break figures such as senior managers?	How will they manifest it (e.g. by personal messages to potential participants; taking part themselves)?
• Where will the opposition come from? Can we defuse it or go round it? If so, how?	

Question	Comment
• Where will our support come from? How can we best harness it?	Consider particularly the people with greatest influence in the organization – not necessarily those who have the greatest status.
• What resources will be required? What constraints can we identify?	Budget, staffing, time, premises? When are they available, and how does this affect the timing of the introduction?
• What internal marketing is needed?	E.g. do we need to encourage people to join the scheme, or are we only informing them of its existence? What incentive will they have? Improved work performance? Skill development? More money?
• What media can we use?	Leaflets? Posters? Billboards? Newsletters? Staff/union representatives?
• When and how will those affected (learners, their line managers, learner supporters) be briefed?	
• What other liaison is needed?	E.g. with services staff, security, reception.
• Will anyone not under our direct control be involved? How do we manage them?	These may include tutors and other external contractors such as printing firms.
• How will we demonstrate the effectiveness of the system? To whom? When?	Broad strategy only is needed here – the detail can come later. The important thing is that your evaluation must be built in at the beginning, not bolted on later.

You cannot help but notice that some of these are large questions that probably need more than one person to answer them; you may also be able to put in extra questions that relate to your own situation, which is unique. A surprising number of open learning systems come into being as the result of one person's drive, but it is notable that the most successful are those initiated by good co-operation and good lobbyists!

IMPLEMENTING THE PLAN

The details of implementation will vary depending on what sort of system you have. Will it be freestanding and require little physical resource, as when a 'package plus tutorial support' is bought in from an external supplier for a limited number of learners? Will it require the setting up of a bank of materials to be distributed to certain learners on negotiated programmes of study? Or does it aim to open up opportunities to a wide range of learners – perhaps the whole population, such as a workforce or the college student body and require premises, staffing during what may be quite long opening hours and learning materials in a variety of media?

Whichever structure you choose it must relate both to identified need and to the resources available at the time. It is discouraging to everyone concerned if facilities fail to match demand. For instance, one company sought to offer a drop-in centre where anyone connected with the firm, such as a relative of an employee, could learn in their own time, but demand from the core workforce prevented the plan from being carried out. Another organization offered an informal drop-in centre to users but found that it was impossible to meet the demands for equipment and materials at peak times and had to resort to a booking system. (You may feel that there is nothing wrong with this: after all, we accept the need to book driving lessons in advance. But it was an unfortunate start to an initiative that had been promoted very much as a flexible resource.) It is probably more satisfactory to start with an undertaking which can be fulfilled, even if its scope is somewhat restricted. An excess of demand over supply can do wonders for the reputation of the system as well as being a good argument for increased resourcing!

Consider (and reject if irrelevant) any of the following questions and add your own:

Question	Comment
• Who is responsible for: — management? — administration? — tutoring? — other support such as mentoring? — staff development (in skills such as materials writing and adaptation, advising and guiding, tutoring)? — monitoring and evaluation?	One person may carry out more than one of these roles. For instance, an administrator will often collect information for monitoring, a manager may carry out both staff development and evaluation.
• What arrangements can be made to meet learners' practical requirements, e.g: — quiet place to study? — friendly place for discussion? — availability of these (e.g. if in other use)? — adaptation of workstations so that learning can take place there?	Learners may need space, equipment and time to learn in the workplace. Even if most of the learning has been scheduled to be carried out at home, there is usually some overlap into the workplace – and rightly so. It is best to acknowledge from the outset that pressures may be put on learners to give up study time to work on pressing tasks ('You can do

Question	Comment
— 'learning' equipment such as computers, video and audio?	that another day, this stuff has got to get out of the door!').
— workplace equipment used for production (e.g. machine tools, computers)?	We discussed earlier the need to have an accurate assessment of demand: this is not just to meet the needs of
— appropriate worksurfaces (e.g. for using practical kit, spreading out documents)?	the learning hordes, but can work the other way round. We have no doubt all visited empty learning
— any special needs (e.g. of learners with disabilities)?	centres and wondered where the clients were!
• What materials are to be bought/ developed/adapted?	Developing your own materials, though exciting, can be more trouble than it is worth if a reasonable fit can be found between learning needs and existing materials. Learning to work with other people's materials is in itself a development exercise for tutors and managers.
• How will they be stored and retrieved?	They are often quite bulky and need deeper shelves than books. (If production is under your control, is it possible to keep storage to a minimum by calling off copies from a publishing system at need?)
• How will they be distributed?	If by post, is special packaging necessary? If yours is a commercial operation, is the financial management system appropriate?
• What assessment will take place?	Examples include computer-marked assignments, unseen written examination, practical assessments of competence.
• Is an external awarding body involved? What are the resulting administrative arrangements required?	Their timetable and administrative arrangements will affect the management of your own scheme. Even if a full qualification is not being awarded, might candidates use the programme to gain credits towards a qualification (e.g. an NVQ)?) If so, they will need to collect evidence of their achievement.

Question	Comment
• What is the system for learners to contact tutors and vice versa?	Tutors vary in their willingness to be available outside conventional hours. Contact need not, of course, be direct if you have sufficient administrative back-up to operate a message service, perhaps by telephone, fax machine, e-mail or personal pigeonhole.
• What system will we use to keep track of learners' progress?	This needs to be more than a class register. It needs to record significant activities such as returning assignments, requesting new materials, logging on in the learning centre. The test of effectiveness is: will it give early warning of difficulties so that action can be taken before a learner hits serious problems?
• What other monitoring do we need to do?	What sorts of data will the organization need to be confident that the scheme is being properly managed?
• What arrangements for acknowledging achievement do we need to make?	This is irrespective of the award of a qualification or credit towards one. It is an important part of your management role to ensure that learners receive, as soon as possible after completion of a programme, acknowledgement of the effort and time (one might almost say 'risk') involved in any form of self-development.

SKILLS DEVELOPMENT IN LEARNER SUPPORT

You probably already have a pretty clear idea about the skills needed by those staffing your open learning system. First of all you need to be quite clear about what roles are needed and the extent to which they will be new to the people involved. It is worth taking some time to list these roles briefly here so that nobody (least of all you) gets taken by surprise when the system is in full swing.

Most people think first of the roles of tutoring open and distance learners. (Mary Thorpe goes into this in Chapter 14.) Other roles include those of:

• administrators and managers of the scheme/a learning centre;

- materials writers (in what media?);
- materials designers and producers;
- reception staff and switchboard operators;
- marketing staff;
- line managers of open learners;
- mentors; and
- counsellors.

(You might even argue that the learners themselves are involved here, since they plainly have responsibilities within the system. They are perhaps a slightly different case, since their skills will mainly be for achieving their own learning objectives. There is a note about learners supporting other learners in Chapter 15.)

What new skills do these people need to develop? How do you know if someone working in your open learning system is good at their job or not? Unfortunately, both education and training have a history of being casual about the standards of those supporting learners. An irresistible move to rectify this is under way, however, and may already be taking place within your organization. Are staff appraisal systems in place or about to be introduced, for instance?

If there is no sign of a system being introduced for the people who need it, the Training and Development Lead Body standards, although difficult in terms of structure and language, offer a basis for ensuring competence. Even if you suspect that those involved will not be interested in gaining a qualification, the standards do at least give a way of thinking about what people in the various roles ought to be doing. There are similar standards for office-related occupations.

The kinds of skill that are needed by all these people are, you might well think, only those that should be exhibited by anyone involved in education or training in those roles, particularly with adult learners. Here is a list of some of them. Use this as a basis to add to, prioritize or cluster to see how many people need each kind. You can even put individual names to them:

- Identifying learning needs correctly.
- Guiding and advising learners.
- Knowing the system and being able to explain it to others.
- Knowing the roles and responsibilities of colleagues and being able to explain them and to refer learners as necessary.
- Designing specifications for learning materials.
- Adapting existing learning materials for a particular purpose.
- Writing materials (paper based, computer based, audio, video . . .)
- Reviewing materials.
- Piloting materials.
- Developing open and distance learners' study skills.
- Tutoring open learners (e.g. by telephone, post).
- Carrying out assessment in such a way as to contribute to learning.

- Carrying out administrative tasks efficiently and courteously.
- Managing the system's finances, if necessary in line with the system of the host organization.
- Developing staff.
- Promoting the programme.
- Monitoring the programme.
- Evaluating the programme.

EVALUATING EFFECTIVENESS

We said earlier that evaluation arrangements need to be built in at the beginning of the system's installation if possible. Just as assessment requirements have to be linked to learning objectives in the development of learning materials, it is logical if you take a similar approach to the management of your open learning scheme. Working in it will, after all, be a learning experience for everyone concerned, so everyone needs to know at the outset what they are aiming to do and how it will be measured. Also you need to be sure you will be collecting the right information from the beginning: it can be very difficult to backtrack. You might need to refer back to your criteria for success.

Few organizations using open learning make any detailed and systematic attempts at evaluating its effectiveness. This is less surprising when you reflect how rarely in the past conventional training and education have been evaluated, beyond the 'happy sheets' completed by participants which are of only limited usefulness. To be fair, it is also true that many open learning schemes have had a good case made out for them beforehand, which presumably increases the organization's confidence in them. Nevertheless, the absence of clear performance criteria and evaluation mechanisms make the open learning innovator vulnerable to criticism.

Have you considered what constitutes effectiveness for your open learning system? What will convince the powers that be that the system is worth continuing? What does 'quality' really mean in your organization? Take into consideration what the long-range aims are for your scheme. Do you, for instance, want to expand it rapidly in the near future? If so, what proofs will be needed to attract more resources? (Detailed examinations of quality in materials, quality-assurance systems and course evaluation are covered in other chapters.)

Existing scheme managers' responses included:

For us effectiveness is less attendance time at college: that's what our MD wants to know about.

At the moment, all we need to prove is that running costs are cheaper. But as part of our quality drive we shall, I know, in a year or two's time have to show that the learning is better or quicker. Then we shall have to do much more detailed measurement, before and after the course.

We shall have justified our existence if we open up access to people who wouldn't normally dream of taking a course.

This is a large organization, so economies of scale are a principal criterion of success. We've made a massive investment in interactive video, and my business plan shows a payback within two years.

The experience of the learners is probably the obvious start point. Crude measures such as numbers of learners enrolled and completing the course are usually needed to give a general idea of the volume of activity. Savings per head over similar conventional courses (especially where travel and subsistence are major cost factors) can also readily be identified. It is harder to collect data about how many 'hours' worth of learning' each person represents. It is even more difficult to measure cost benefit to the individual. For instance learners may appear to drop out of a study programme before completing all the modules, but this may be a sign of achievement rather than failure; or a longitudinal study may be needed (which may show better retention and application of the content of an open learning programme than an equivalent conventional course). Cost benefits to the learner's organization are the most difficult to quantify: they may not be observable in the short term and you cannot always be sure that a particular phenomenon results directly and solely from a learning programme. Not all the information need be quantitative, of course: it is always useful to ask open-ended questions relating to whether the learners enjoyed their experience, what action planning has resulted and what they would change next time round, so that their experience can be used genuinely to improve the course for others.

Tutor and trainer feedback can also afford useful management information. Their view of the learner experience is valuable for 'triangulation' (if we can borrow this analogy for getting a measure from more than one standpoint of the learner's state), as is evaluation of the learning materials, the administrative arrangements and other support facilities such as learning centres, the equipment within them and other support roles such as that of line managers.

Line managers are the obvious source of information on improved learner performance as the result of the development programme. Their feedback is most useful when they have been clearly briefed about its purpose, so that they know what they are looking for. Timing is important and depends on the nature of the learning: it needs to be soon enough after the programme for the effects to be clearly seen, but long enough afterwards for the full results to have emerged.

Mentors are better placed to give you information about the processes that the learner has gone through. Some of the detail may be confidential and needs to be safeguarded if shared.

Learning centre managers, administrators and receptionists can carry out detailed monitoring during the programme to ensure proper control (for example, of finances) and to enable modifications to be made as you go along, but you also need them to give an overview of the effectiveness of the system.

Depending on the strategic purpose of the evaluation, it may also be useful to get feedback from people who are not directly involved but know about the scheme such as senior managers or learners on other programmes. It may also be revealing to get someone from outside the organization to carry out the evaluation.

The way in which you use the information that you gather is all-important. Consider the following questions and amend them or add any of your own:

- Who will receive the report? There may be an immediate and a wider audience – reports get circulated!
- Is timing important (e.g. in preparation for a new planning cycle)?
- What should be its format? Might you need different formats for different audiences, such as summaries for the busier and more remote people?
- How should data be presented?
- How are the issues to be identified and drawn out?
- Will you make a practice of referring back the data to those who provided it to get their reactions and comments?

The open learning system not only offers a framework within which learning materials can be used but it also complements them to ensure that learners get maximum benefit from them. A well managed, flexible system can offer an almost infinite degree of responsiveness to individual needs that even the best open learning materials cannot yet do.

REFERENCES AND NOTES

Lewis, R. (1985) *How to Develop and Manage an Open-Learning Scheme*, National Council for Educational Technology, Coventry. One of the series of open learning guides which fits a great deal into a small format, including activities and case studies, with detail on material resources required, schedules and checklists.

National Extension College (1989) *Implementing Open Learning in Colleges*, National Extension College, Cambridge. Despite the title this mixed-media pack (three workbooks, user guide, video, audio, computer disc) has general applicability and focuses on planning rather than implementation. It contains good working definitions of open learning, and plenty of emphasis on initial research, costing (with a computer program to help) and preparing a proposal.

The Open College (1991) *Managing Open Learning* and *Administering Open Learning*. (Blueprints series), The Open College, Manchester. Both these packs use an open learning approach for managers and administrators who are either starting an open learning scheme or want to improve an existing one. The way in which objectives and activities are laid out incidentally assist the user who wishes to collect evidence of competence for a vocational qualification.

Paine, N. *et al.* (1987) *Open Learning in Industry: A Guide for Practitioners*. Flex Training, Baldock. A pack containing video, audio and, most usefully, workbooks and job aids (documents for completion as you go along) which cover every planning stage for the different elements that make up an open learning system.

Training and Development Lead Body (1992) *National Standards for Training and Development*, Cambertown Ltd, Commercial Road, Goldthorpe Industrial Estate, Goldthorpe, nr Rotherham S63 9BL. Strictly for those who wish to investigate a competence-based approach to professionalism or to implement a National Vocational Qualifications structure. There is now a qualification within this framework for those working in open learning. The pack contains the occupational standards themselves, an executive summary, a description of the qualifications structure and guidelines for implementation.

18

Assuring quality in open and distance learning

Bernadette Robinson

Quality in open and distance learning is most often thought of in terms of the learning materials (the printed texts and other media). These are the pivot on which the whole learning enterprise turns. However, the quality of open or distance learning relies on more than the quality of the learning materials alone. It also depends on how effectively the delivery and learner support systems function, and how well they all integrate in operational terms. Together, they create the conditions for learning. So how do you ensure good quality? How do you manage the processes effectively? This chapter looks at the role that quality assurance can play.

FAILURES OF QUALITY

Failures of quality in open and distance learning are easily recognizable, as these two experiences show. I expect you'll have examples of your own which spring to mind too. At the end of the chapter I hope you will be in a position not just to recognize failures but also to institute procedures to identify their sources and resolve them:

> A student wrote 112 letters to a distance teaching institution in a continuing attempt to get the course materials for which she had registered and paid. This achieved no result. She finally obtained them after the course had begun and after travelling over 100 miles to the headquarters of the institution, with her parents, to make a personal appeal.

> The assessment of a part-time professional course was by course work and examination. A mature learner, living 70 miles from the institution, submitted her assignments by the due dates throughout the year but received no feedback on them, could not find out what marks they had earned and did not get them back to assist her in revision for the examinations. Afterwards, her assignments were returned, with grades and an amount of helpful tutor comment on them. No one on the staff could or would explain why they had not been returned earlier or what system was in place to ensure the timely return of assignments to the learners.

Failures of quality can often be traced to failures in systems. In the first case, the learning materials were well designed but failure in the delivery system to deliver them on time and to remedy the error of non-delivery quickly enough prevented the student from obtaining them when needed and as promised. The cause of failure lay in a combination of a poor records system, lack of specified time for dispatching materials after receipt of registration information, lack of a monitoring system and unclear designation of responsibility for checking performance. Tracking further back, the source of the problem lay in late production of the materials, created by late handover by writers and a haphazard contracting relationship with external printers.

In the second case, the organization did not implement and monitor routine and reliable mechanisms for giving learners feedback on their work in time for them to make use of it. Nor did any individual member of staff apparently have the designated responsibility for ensuring that procedures for returning work to learners were followed. There was also infrequent communication and lack of co-ordination between the staff teaching the course. The learner did not know what her entitlement was nor what routes to use to remedy the situation in time. No written advice was provided.

The point of these examples is to identify quality (or lack of it) and make it concrete. What they illustrate is a failure of the organizations to manage and regulate their internal processes in order to create conditions for learning. 'Conditions for learning' are here interpreted as being broader than the act of engagement with the learning materials. 'Quality' lies in the totality of products, delivery, services and general ethos (Normann, 1984; Robinson, 1992); all combine to affect the quality of the learning experience.

What causes lapses of quality? What has been your own experience? In mine, some lapses of quality may be due to lack of human or financial resources. Some are attributable to inadequate rewards for staff. More are due to neglect of training. Many are due to failures of systems in some way. So what can you do to ensure that systems are sound enough to support the production of learning materials and delivery of support services? How can you ensure good quality in their functioning? How can you avoid the kinds of problems illustrated above? One approach is quality assurance.

ENSURING QUALITY

Quality and quality assurance

Although everyone agrees on the desirability of quality, there is less agreement on what it is and still less on how to measure it. This is because 'quality' does not exist in isolation from its context of use and judgements differ according to whose views are being sought. The differences stem from the amalgam of different meanings under the label of 'quality' and variety of perspectives of stakeholders. Different views on quality may also be held simultaneously by different functional areas within a single organization. The priorities will vary according to who is making the assessment and for what purposes.

To unscramble the main features you may find it helpful to regard 'quality' as a characteristic, however you define it, and 'quality assurance' as a process directed towards achieving the characteristic. It is one way (others are quality control and total quality management or TQM) of managing an enterprise in order to achieve a stated standard or quality of performance. Quality assurance is the set of activities that an organization undertakes to ensure that standards are specified and reached consistently for a product or service. It has as its goal the avoidance of faulty products or services whereas quality control operates retrospectively, 'inspecting out' or discarding faulty products which fail to conform to a predetermined standard. Quality control and quality assurance, together with the assessment of quality systems (that is, the monitoring, evaluation and audit of procedures) are overlapping functions in regulating how an organization or venture works. They all have a role in quality management approaches, the best known of which is TQM (Oakland, 1989; Sallis, 1993).

Quality assurance focuses attention on operational processes and systems. It is a simple idea with three main elements:

1. You set standards for a product or service.
2. You organize the production or delivery of a product or service so that the standards are consistently met.
3. As a consequence, you create confidence in the client or recipient that what is promised is what will happen.

It sounds easy and straightforward but they are not so simple to implement. I suspect your experience of quality assurance will vary according whether you are working in a large or small organization or are freelance, and whether you are a materials developer or learner-services provider, or both. Whatever your context, the basic framework applies though it needs adaptation. In the checklist below I have provided a series of questions, under key headings, that I hope will help you to begin questioning the quality assurance system you have in operation – or which you may establish. Needless to say the questions are illustrative, not exhaustive, and you will no doubt want to omit or amend some questions and generate others.

Checking your quality-assurance system

1. *Quality policy and plan* Has your organization developed a policy on quality which all staff are familiar with? Has this been translated into a practical plan?
2. *Specification of standards* Are there specified and clearly defined standards in place? Have they been communicated to all concerned? Are they specified for key activities? Are they achievable, reasonable and measurable?
3. *Identifying critical functions* Have the critical functions for achieving the standards been identified? Have they taken the learner as the starting point for some of these? Have the procedures to achieve them been analysed?
4. *Documentation* Are the procedures to be followed clearly documented? Are they explicit? Do they represent fact (practice as it happens) or fiction (an idealized version?) Are they consistent in different documents? Are they concentrated on essential procedures? Are they in a readable and user-friendly form? Do all those who need them have access to copies?

5. *Staff involvement*   Have all staff been involved in the development of quality-assurance systems in your organization? Have their suggestions been built in? Has enough time been given to this process?

6. *Monitoring*   Are there systematic monitoring mechanisms for critical functions? Do they check whether standards are being met and procedures followed? How do you know? (What is their product and impact?) Are the findings disseminated? Are they harnessed to appropriate action? Do they result in improved performance or a review of practice, or a reappraisal of standards? Do they provide effective feedback loops between providers of products and services and learners or clients?

7. *Involvement of users*   Have learners and clients and staff been involved in setting and monitoring standards? Have staff made an input as 'internal customers' or clients?

8. *Training*   Is there adequate provision of training and staff development? Is this linked to the achievement of standards? Are there effective mechanisms for assessing training needs? Are these reviewed regularly? Are there resources allocated to meet them?

9. *Costs*   Is there a strategy for monitoring the costs of implementing and maintaining quality-assurance activities? Does this take account of human and financial costs? Are the costs greater than the benefits? Is there a review process to find out?

Using formal (published) standards

You don't need to use formal standards such as BS 5750 (British Standards Institution) in order to have a quality-assurance system (you can construct your own) though you may choose to do so for some of the reasons given below. Standards aim to state clearly the way in which an activity is to be performed and how it is to be measured, verified or evaluated. Basically, they encompass the simple cycle of 'plan, do, check, act' and aim to bring consistency to products, services or processes. They ensure that what is specified is what you get – they say nothing about the quality of a product itself. In the references and notes I have given details of handbooks and published standards and offer brief comments on them.

The origins of published standards is in manufacturing and their application to education and training is not straightforward; the language and concepts are somewhat alien, and not all the categories in the standards transfer or apply easily to open learning (as Freeman, 1991, describes).

However, they can prove to be useful in:

• providing a framework for an organization's own system for managing quality;
• providing an external reference point;
• enabling comparisons to be drawn between stated policy and actual practice;

- communication in transactions;
- regularizing procedures;
- clarifying expectations and contracts;
- assisting in the definition of roles and responsibilities;
- identifying ownership of processes and the accountability of individuals for them;
- reducing uncertainty;
- offering a framework for audit and review (either internal or external); and
- carrying external validation and recognition (formal certification).

Unfortunately they also have limitations in that they:

- may fail to provide a holistic view of an organization's quality assurance management;
- may be mechanistically implemented, resulting in a reductionist view of quality;
- can involve too much paperwork so that documentation becomes an end in itself;
- may omit some important aspects;
- are no guarantee of the quality of the product;
- may fail to take sufficient account of professional judgement and expertise;
- are static while needs and the environment are not;
- involve a heavy investment of staff time; and
- can create a checklist culture.

Many who have used these standards comment that much of their value may lie in the experience of trying to adopt and adapt them. They also offer some structure for evaluation of practice and reflection on it.

Quality assurance for services

Open and distance learning involves both products and services, though these may not be offered by the same provider. Research and experience show that causes of poor quality are different for services and products. In contrast to the production of materials (texts, videos, computer software), services such as advising, tutoring, counselling, coaching, responding to enquiries:

- are less tangible, more difficult to measure;
- can't be separated from the persons involved in the transaction;
- are transient, ephemeral, can't be stored ('of the moment');
- have a strong client presence (often face to face or voice to voice);
- need a delivery system which is highly user-friendly and accessible;
- are judged more by client satisfaction measures and perceptions;
- need to fit client convenience more closely (access and timeliness);
- require strong record control and documentation; and
- require a stance of not only 'right first time' if possible but also good recovery from errors.

Quality-assurance systems for the service elements of open learning need to reflect these differences if they are to be appropriate. The BS 5750 standards for quality production systems have proved inappropriate for service systems; the recently produced service provider's version (BSI Draft Document 90/971000) is more relevant.

The most common failures of quality in the provision of services are failure to understand or test assumptions about learners' needs, an inappropriate specification for service quality, insufficient resource, failures of equipment or people to reach the stated standards of service delivery and poor comunication. These would be good focal points for examining the systems assuring the quality of services you offer. Evaluation can be done using the familiar approaches from social science (questionnaires, group and individual interviews, observational data) to produce both quantitative and qualitative information, as well as some of the tools below.

FIVE TOOLS FOR IMPROVING QUALITY

At a practical level 'doing' quality assurance involves a continuous cycle of:

- setting standards for a key activity;
- carrying out the activity;
- judging achievements against the standards (measuring the gap between policy or plan and practice or performance);
- planning for improvement; and
- taking action to implement desired changes.

Here are five tools which you may find useful.

1   Flow diagrams

In any quality-assurance system, processes need to be thoroughly mapped and understood. Flow diagrams are a useful tool for this. They provide a way of tracking and displaying how quality is shaped through several stages or phases. They are useful for:

- systematically recording steps, decisions and activities required in a sequence;
- providing a clear diagrammatic representation of a process as a way of sharing information about what happens;
- identifying critical points or bottlenecks;
- displaying the consequences of planned change;
- standardizing practice (it can be the basis of written procedures);
- training; and
- tracking and diagnosing the sources of failure.

2 Pareto analysis

An economist called Pareto suggested that 80 per cent of problems arise from 20 per cent of causes. If you track the causes that create most failures of quality, you can concentrate your efforts on those areas which pay the most dividends. To apply this you need to identify the problems and try to quantify them (for example, categorize the nature of complaints from learners and record their frequency). This information can then be used to make a simple bar chart which ranks the categories. It will show where most of the problems lie and indicate priorities for action.

3   Tracking the source: 'five whys'

The first reason given for a failure of quality may not get to the heart of a problem, yet typically this is where most questioning stops. The reasons need to be tracked back to source. One simple technique is to ask 'why?' five times (or more if necessary) in answer to each response to uncover the point at which the problem arises and to get to a deeper level of understanding and analysis.

Problem: the learner failed to receive feedback on her assignments before the examinations:

Q1   Why ?
A   Because no one returned her assignments to her.
Q2   Why?
A   We don't know . . . no one knows what's supposed to happen . . . each tutor passed the request on to someone else.
Q3   Why?
A   Because there's no set procedure or guidelines for doing it.
Q4   Why?
A   Because it's nobody's job to see that there is.
Q5   Why?
A   Because giving learners timely feedback isn't seen as a high priority in our organization.

And so on.

4   Ishikawa or 'fishbone' diagram

This maps in a structured way the causes (major and minor) of a problem, the effects and factors involved. It is useful in helping to diagnose and analyse problems with colleagues, especially when there is more than one cause. To use this you need to:

- identify the problem in a few words and put this as the head of the fishbone;
- identify the main issues or causes (four is a manageable number);
- under each of these four, explore the component factors or sub-causes (you can use brainstorming or the 'five whys' for this); and

- discuss the completed diagram; try to distinguish between symptoms and causes; agree on the one main cause and highlight it so that plans for remedies are focused on this (remember Pareto's rule).

Problem: the learner (along with numbers of others) failed to get a response to her request for the course materials after registration (Figure 18.1).

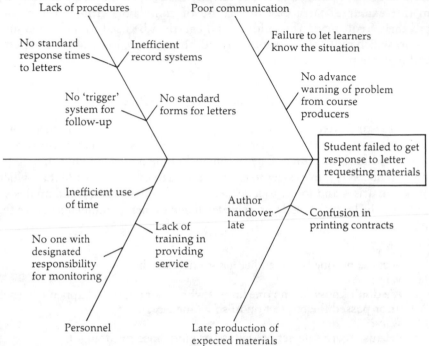

Figure 18.1 Exploring why a lack of response

5 Milestones and barriers

This charts the learner's progress through an institution, course or training programme to identify key milestones and barriers. Once identified, the processes that converge on these milestones or barriers are mapped and examined in detail with the goal of reviewing or evaluating them. This is a way of highlighting critical points in systems, including the learner's point of view. The same can be done for other key players in an open learning venture (external writers, corporate clients, tutors and support staff). The points of interface or handover between stages or players (such as the handover of texts to editors or printers) are often critical barriers or milestones (Figure 18.2).

CONCLUSIONS

Quality-assurance systems should not be seen as a recipe for perfect open learning every time. It is possible to have effective quality-assurance systems

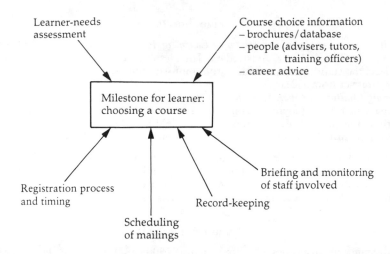

Figure 18.2   Processes converging on the learner

which deliver poorly designed courses. They can, however, assist in improving operational aspects of an open or distance learning (ODL) organization and can reduce *ad hoc* practice, uncertainty, lack of co-ordination, inconsistency in performance as well as improving communication between all the parties involved. What they can't easily do is create the culture of commitment which separates the excellent from the adequate, for

> simply delineating the elements of a quality assurance system, and promulgating timetables for action, will not secure in themselves a higher quality of services and activities. For that, the staff have to be engaged, intellectually. They have to take on the idea of quality maintenance for themselves, and become committed to it themselves.
>
> (Barnett, 1992, p. 80)

REFERENCES AND NOTES

Barnett, R. (1992) *Improving Higher Education: Total Quality Care*, the Society for Research into Higher Education and Open University Press, Buckingham.

Freeman, R. (1991) Quality assurance in learning materials production, *Open Learning*, Vol. 6, no. 3, pp. 24–31.

Normann, R. (1984, revised 1992) *Service Management: Strategy and Leadership in Service Businesses*, Wiley, Chichester.

Oakland, J. S. (1989) *Total Quality Management*, Butterworth-Heinemann, Oxford.

Robinson, B.(1992) Applying quality standards in open and distance learning. Paper presented at the European Distance Teaching Universities/Swedish Association of Distance Education International Conference on Quality, Standards and Research in European Distance Education, University of Umeå Sweden, March.

Sallis, E. (1993) *Total Quality Management in Education*, Kogan Page, London.

RESOURCES ON QUALITY ASSURANCE

Handbooks

Quality Guide for Open and Distance Learning 1991, available from SATURN, Keisersgracht 756, 1017 EZ Amsterdam, The Netherlands. Identifies key questions and reflects the standpoint of different roles: information provider, developer, deliverer, corporate customer, learner.

Ensuring Quality in Open Learning: A Handbook for Action. (revised edition 1990), Department of Employment Training Agency, available from the Training and Education Directorate (TEED), Moorfoot, Sheffield S1 4PQ. Provides a code of practice which the British Association of Open Learning require members to adhere to.

Both handbooks try to interpret BS 5750 (ISO 9000) standards for ODL and marry them to quality management approaches. They adopt a checklist form to guide users and indicate the processes for developing quality-assurance systems, including the learner's role in improving the quality of provision.

Published standards

British Standards Institution Quality Systems 5750 (1987), Parts 1–3; Part 4 1990. BSI, London.

British Standards Institution BS 5750, *Guidance Notes for Application to Education and Training*, BSI, Milton Keynes (February 1991).

British Standards Institution BS 7850, *Guide to Total Quality Management*, Part 1, Management Processes; Part 2, Quality Improvement (both applicable to education and training).

British Standards Institution Draft Document 90/971000 on services and service quality management (1993).

BS 5750 is a series of British standards for quality management. The standards also exist as EN 29000 (European Norm) or in international version (ISO 9000). Some of the standards in the series provide definitions and guidelines, others (such as ISO 9001, ISO 9002, ISO 9003) are used for external quality-assurance purposes (i.e. certification). All versions are more or less equivalent.

19

Course evaluation: improving academic quality and teaching effectiveness

Judith Calder

The quality of open and distance learning courses is one of the issues which most concerns those who organize or use open and distance learning methods in their work. The challenge lies in establishing what we mean by quality in the context of open and distance learning; how we go about measuring it, and what criteria should be used and, just as importantly, how we go about using the information we collect in order to maintain or improve course quality. This chapter will look at all these issues, guiding you through different course evaluation models from which you can select the approach which is most appropriate for your needs.

QUALITY IN THE CONTEXT OF OPEN AND DISTANCE LEARNING

Quality is one of those words, like 'beauty' or 'poverty', which people happily use, but which prove difficult to get hold of when you try to define them. We usually use it when we want to imply some element of comparison, or claim some form of excellence – a 'quality' product, 'high-quality service'.

In education and training through open and distance methods, we often use the term quality in relation to course materials and services to indicate their 'fitness for the purpose intended'. This definition raises the question of whose purpose we are talking about. With any course, there are a number of different interested parties, or stakeholders: there are the course designers, the programme managers, the organization providing the course, the funders or sponsors of the course, the students themselves and, increasingly, their employers.

The major concerns of each of these stakeholders may well differ from each other. They will cover academic, pedagogic and vocational issues as well as the learning experience as a whole. For example:

- Course designers have worked hard to produce a course package which might use a number of different media, and which will have a variety of teaching strategies and devices within it. They will probably be principally concerned about the teaching effectiveness of the course.
- The programme managers and the organization providing the course will be concerned that the course at least covers its costs, and that the funding agency feels that it has received value for money.
- The funders' criteria are perhaps the least predictable in that the range of possible funders is so wide. It may be that the funding body is an employer, a

government agency, a charitable trust or the students themselves who are paying the full cost of the course. Each of these groups will have different criteria which may or may not include such aspects as the type of person recruited as a student (e.g. courses for the unemployed), the numbers recruited, who successfully completes the course and the knowledge, skills and personal qualities they expect those who complete the course to have acquired in the course of their studies.

- Students' criteria for judging a course are likely to focus on the process of learning as well as the outcomes from it – whether or not they grew in confidence as learners, the extent to which they found the experience pleasurable, the balance between the costs of study (financial and personal) and the perceived benefits, the usefulness of the qualifications or the skills and knowledge gained and the quality of the learning experience.

- Employers will be more concerned with the output from the course – the skills, knowledge and the personal qualities students acquire.

All stakeholders are also likely to be concerned about the student survival and pass rates, about whether the course reaches the standards agreed with its accrediting body, and whether the students find their learning experience a satisfactory one.

HOW WE MEASURE QUALITY

The purpose of the evaluation

Given that people with a stake in open and distance learning courses can hold a range of different aims and intended outcomes, how can we best assess the 'fitness' of the courses for those purposes? In part it will depend on what you want to achieve. If you intend to draw a conclusion or make a judgement about either the relative or absolute merits of the course or course components being evaluated, such as in deciding whether or not to go ahead with the introduction of a new open learning course, then your evaluation would have a *summative* purpose. If your intention is to improve or develop the course further, such as with developmental testing, then your evaluation would have a *formative* purpose. Realistically, in evaluating courses in order to establish 'fitness for purpose' you often use the evaluation data both summatively and formatively.

For example, consider the situation where you were buying in courses developed elsewhere. You might want to pilot them initially before deciding whether to include them in your programme. The summative role would be necessary in order to make the decision about whether or not to include the course in the programme, but the evidence collected might suggest that, with some modifications, the course would be a useful addition to the programme. In other words, we would also be using the evaluation data in a formative role.

IN-DEPTH APPROACHES

If you are introducing a radically new kind of course, or one which, if adopted more widely, would require major capital expenditure such as the purchase of microcomputers or CD-ROM drives, then you are likely to be thinking of a full in-depth evaluation. Two major models which have been developed in order to evaluate major innovations are the illuminative approach and the CIPP approach.

The illuminative approach

This approach was developed by Parlett and Hamilton in the early 1970s (Parlett and Hamilton, 1972/81). Before that the emphasis in course evaluation had been on input and output, and the measurement of the difference which different courses or new approaches made to students' learning. In other words, on the achievement of specific goals and outcomes. Parlett and Hamilton felt that if the evaluation was going to play any sort of formative or developmental role an understanding of the actual processes which students went through during their course studies should be the major focus. They were concerned with describing the course as a whole, to show what it was like for the student and for the tutors who were participating. Thus illuminative evaluation involves interpreting data gathered in a range of different ways from different sources rather than in the simple measurement of achievement and prediction of outcomes.

The CIPP approach

This approach, developed by Daniel Stufflebeam at around the same time as the illuminative approach, also involves examining the process which takes place during the presentation of the course and the context in which the course is being used (Stufflebeam, *et al.*, 1971). However it retains aspects of measurement in relation to intended outcomes. The acronym which describes this approach comes from 'Context, Input, Process and Products'. The inclusion of all four aspects are seen as essential to a complete evaluation of any educational innovation. There are clearly overlaps with the illuminative approach but the main differences are related to the range of methodologies which are used, the perceived role of the evaluation (CIPP can play a summative role in a way which would be difficult for illuminative evaluation) and the importance assigned to the evaluation of the context with the CIPP approach.

Look at the following example:

An extensive and multidimensional evaluation project was set up involving a number of linked projects examining the experiences and reactions not only of students but also of the academics who developed the course materials, computing support staff, local tutors and other staff. The data-collecting tools of the evaluation were large-scale student surveys, student journals and interviews with staff and students.

(Jones, Kirkup and Kirkwood, 1992, p. 58)

This extract from a published evaluation of a major educational innovation is an example of an illuminative approach. The students' and the staff's view of what happened is the central focus. Outcomes were investigated, but not in terms of measured performance. The costs of the project and the way in which it was managed are not part of the evaluation, so although there was a discussion of the institutional context within which this innovation was introduced, it was not at the detailed level which would lead us to view the evaluation as using a CIPP-type approach.

While full examples of the CIPP approach are somewhat hard to come by, the following may give you a flavour of the difference in the range of emphases of the CIPP-type approach from the illuminative approach:

An evaluation programme for an Appraisal and Counselling course using interactive video (IV), was devised to examine four main factors:

- Learning effectiveness
- User-machine interaction
- Organizational impact
- Cost-effectiveness.

(Brown, 1990, p. 5)

The study was divided into two phases. Phase one comprised a 'study of the distance learning components, interviews with senior managers on the aims of the course and expectations, observation of managers using the IV in BT districts and attending the follow-up workshop' (ibid.). A series of interviews with and questionnaire surveys of trainees and district trainers was also carried out. In phase two, a study of the appraisal and counselling processes in practice was carried out, together with studies on perceptions of changes in the quality of the recording and performance practices of responsible staff, together with an investigation into comparative production and delivery costs of both the old course and the new IV course.

In this example, there are several different aspects. While the views of trainers and trainees are important, there is also a clear attempt to measure the outcomes, to identify costs and to examine the institutional context within which the course was being introduced.

MONITORING AND FEEDBACK APPROACHES

Depending on the approach selected, in-depth approaches do allow for the concerns of the major stakeholders to be investigated. However their major drawback is the time they take and the costs which such approaches incur. If your concern is mainly to establish that your courses meet a minimum standard, or conform to a common standard – say, equal to those achieved by other courses you already offer – then a process evaluation may be a more appropriate approach. With this approach, the students' learning experiences and tutors' perceptions of the pedagogical effectiveness of the course are monitored. There are a whole variety of different ways in which this kind of monitoring can be operated. The main differentiating features, however, are:

- the level of detail at which the course is being investigated;
- the timing of the approaches to staff and students; and
- the frequency of monitoring any one particular course.

The level of detail of the investigation

The level of detail wanted in the feedback is likely to vary depending on who are the principal users of the data from the feedback. If the course designers are the principal users, then they are likely to be interested in using the data formatively, and so will want relatively detailed feedback from students. If the principal clients for the data are the managers of the programme, then they are more likely to be interested in the overall quality of the course, and will want summary data for the course as a whole:

> It's not practical for me to take a detailed interest in the individual courses and packs. I pass any [feedback research reports] straight to [the responsible manager].
>
> (Field, 1993, p. 1)

> As [a senior manager] I'm less interested in the detail than the [managers directly responsible] are – they want the detail. What I want to know is how well received the course was. I can ascertain this by comparing ratings with past similar courses and by comparison with other courses in the same year.
>
> (Womphrey, 1993, p. 1)

Timing of the approaches

The level of detail required about a course in the feedback does, to a certain extent also affect the the timing of the feedback. For example, if detailed comments are wanted from students about the content of particular modules on the course, and there are, say, 20 such modules, then it is likely that there would need to be several approaches to the students during the presentation of the course. For example:

> All the students were asked to complete questionnaires at three points in the year. Each one asked questions about the three or four units and allied materials and also more general questions which cumulatively showed how students responded to the content and teaching style of [the course] over the presentation. Response rates to surveys were 65%, 61% and 70% respectively.
>
> (Swift, 1991, p. 1)

The problem in this situation is to get the students to give regular feedback without losing their co-operation. While feedback after every module, unit or session might give detailed feedback with the freshest recall, the danger of losing the co-operation of the students at an early stage and hence ending up with biased results at the middle and later stages of the evaluation would be high. If large numbers of students (say a thousand or more) are involved, then splitting the students into different samples to approach at different times might be one way forward, but with small samples (say less than around 300), there can start to be statistical problems because of sampling error when you're looking for relatively small differences.

The frequency of monitoring

The question about how frequently courses should be monitored is a little like asking how long is a piece of string. Ideally, courses should be monitored after every presentation. Depending on the number of courses you present, however, this can be a costly business, particularly if the data from all your courses are entered into a central database in order to compare results across different courses and different years.

At the UK Open University, all new courses are monitored at the end of their first presentation. However, when courses are presented over a number of years, the student profile may gradually change, and the course materials may start to feel 'dated'. Changes may also be introduced by the course designers in response to the earlier feedback, or in order to update the academic content. A likely compromise is that all courses will in future be monitored on a regular cycle of once every three or four presentations.

Although the routine-monitoring approach focuses on the student, and occasionally the tutors, as the main source of feedback information, the issues covered through the feedback can cover the concerns of a wider range of stakeholders. For example:

- Student ratings of the course materials and components, in particular usefulness, difficulty, helpfulness and interest.
- Student perceptions of the ease of study of course materials.
- The extent to which different components of the course were actually used.
- Reactions to the balance between different components.
- The workload and difficulty levels of the course.

At a deeper level, the usefulness and helpfulness of teaching devices within the materials may also be investigated, together with the identification of those areas which caused problems or difficulties.

Data-collection methods

Even with open and distance learning, the full range of data-collection methods is available for course evaluation. These can include the following:

- *Postal questionnaires* – the most common approach. If posted directly to the student or tutor together with an explanatory letter, response rates of over 60 per cent can be regularly achieved.
- *Self-completion questionnaires* – these can be handed out by tutors at face-to-face sessions and collected at a later stage. Response rates vary considerably depending on how it is handled by the person organizing the distribution and collection.
- *Phone surveys* – these can be effective for getting hold of students who have dropped out or have stopped studying and who are less motivated to complete a questionnaire.
- *Group discussions* – these can provide very useful insights into the 'whys' of problem areas, together with a better understanding of the 'students' eye view'. However they are expensive to run and they do not provide measures of the actual extent of problems experienced, or of satisfied students.

There are other less common methods of collecting data from students such as using diaries, getting them to tape comments (Lockwood, 1991) or using computer networks such as through CMC. The deciding factors are really the amount of resource you are able to commit to the evaluation, the most appropriate research approach for the issues you want to investigate – whether it should be qualitative or quantitative and the time available in which to collect, process and interpret the data.

In addition, the importance of student record statistics in providing a statistical context for both the feedback studies and the in-depth studies should not be forgotten. Student drop-out, completion of assignments, exam pass-rates – all provide comparative background information against which student and tutor feedback can be interpreted.

USING COURSE EVALUATION DATA

'Owning' the data

The criteria which are used will depend to a considerable extent on who determines them. Problems can arise when the people who should be using the data are not involved in the initial process of deciding what the criteria should be. One way you can encourage 'ownership' of the evaluation findings is by involving more closely at an early stage the people who will be involved in actually using and making decisions based on the findings.

For example, the Distance Education Centre of the University of South Australia tries to involve individual teachers in the course feedback because they see it as a necessary part of staff development (Nunan, 1992). They provide templates of questionnaires which individual teachers are encouraged to modify for their own purposes. These cover issues such as the subject-matter, resources for learning, teaching arrangements and interactions, and assessment.

The UK Open University course monitoring uses a two-part feedback questionnaire. Again, one part is developed directly with members of the course team to collect data on the issues of particular interest to them. The other part, which is common to all courses, was developed for programme managers as well as course teams in order to provide a common set of comparative data across courses and over time.

Another method, used more commonly in the evaluation of face-to-face teaching, is where the students themselves determine what criteria they want to use to provide feedback on their evaluation of the course. This approach can be used in open and distance learning through the involvement of the students in the development of the evaluation instruments through specially set-up group sessions.

Mechanisms for quality assurance

The use of the information collected through course evaluation is an essential but frequently neglected phase. Whatever form of course evaluation has been carried out, the time and effort spent in carrying out the evaluation is wasted if the findings are not used. With major in-depth course evaluation studies *ad hoc* arrangements may have to be made. With routine feedback studies, regular mechanisms need to be set up. Whatever the evaluation approach used to collect the data, four steps need to be incorporated into the follow-up actions:

1. The timing of the receipt of the findings and the deadlines for subsequent action needs to be agreed in advance.
2. The people who are to receive the findings for action or for information must be identified and clearly distinguished
3. Those who receive the findings for action need to be clear about the procedures to be followed.
4. A report-back loop on action taken as a result of the findings needs to be present.

Even with these procedures in place, there can be no guarantee that evaluation findings will be acted upon. Decision-making in any organization is based on a range of factors, of which evaluation data is only one part. Nevertheless the demands for greater accountability and for demonstrations that quality-assurance mechanisms are in use do mean that the number and range of stakeholders in course evaluation is greater than ever before.

REFERENCES

Brown, S. (1990) It ain't what you do, it's the way that you do it. Conference paper presented at Teleteaching 90, WCCE/90 Associated Mini-Conference, Sydney, Australia.

Field, J. (1993) Internal memo to author reporting a field interview, 23 August.

Jones, A., Kirkup, G. and Kirkwood, A.(1992) *Personal Computers for Distance Education*. Paul Chapman Publishing, London.

Lockwood, F. (1991) *Data Collection in Distance-Education Research: The Use of Self-Recorded Audiotape*, IDE806 and UDE606, Research in Distance Education, Institute of Distance Education, Deakin University, Geelang and the University of South Australia, Underdale, South Australia.

Nunan, T. (1992) *Student Feedback for the Evaluation of Distance Teaching and Learning.* Distance Education Centre, University of South Australia, Underdale, South Australia.

Parlett, M. and Hamilton, D. (1972) *Evaluation as Illumination: A New Approach to the Study of Innovatory Programmes*, reissued in 1981 as *Introduction to Illuminative Evaluation: Studies in Higher Education*, M. Parlett and G. Dearden, by the SRHE, University of Surrey, Guildford.

Stufflebeam, D. *et al.* (1971) *Educational Evaluation and Decision-Making*, F.E. Peacock Publishers, Itasca, IL.

Swift, B. (1991) *B881, Strategic Management: Main Findings of an Evaluation of the First Presentation*, Student Research Centre, Report no. 47, IET, The Open University, Milton Keynes.

Womphrey, B. (1993) Internal memo to author reporting a field interview, 21 June.

Index